A Festschrift for Manfred Clynes

IN HONOR OF

DR. MANFRED CLYNES' 70TH BIRTHDAY

MMB MUSIC, INC.

A FESTSCHRIFT FOR MANFRED CLYNES
In Honor of Dr. Manfred Clynes' 70th Birthday

© Copyright 1999 MMB Music, Inc. All rights reserved. International protection secured under Berne, UCC, Buenos Aires and bilateral copyright treaties. No part of this publication may be reproduced, stored in a retrieval system, or transmitted—in any form or by any means now known or later developed—without prior written permission from the publisher except in the case of brief quotations embodied in critical articles and reviews.

Editor: Danielle Williams
Cover Design: Lynne Condellone
Typography: Lynne Condellone
Music Engraving: Ephraim Hammett Jones
Printer: Publishers ExpressPress, Ladysmith, Wisconsin
1st printing: October, 1999
PRINTED IN USA
ISBN: 0-58106-009-2

For information and catalogs, contact:

MMB Music, Inc.
Contemporary Arts Building
3526 Washington Avenue
Saint Louis, MO 63103-1019 USA

Phone: 314 531-9635; 800 543-3771 (USA/Canada)
Fax: 314 531-8384
E-Mail: mmbmusic@mmbmusic.com
Website:http://www.mmbmusic.com

*May his work be a beacon to a braver new world
  —the 21st Century.*

Fest•schrift\ˈfest(t)-ˌshrift\ n,pl **Fest•schrif•ten**\-ˌshrif-ten\ or **Festschrifts** [G, fr. *Fest* celebration + *Schrift* writing] (1898): a volume of writings by different authors presented as a tribute esp. to a scholar.

Contents

Contributors viii
Introduction ix
Note of Appreciation and Thanks x

Part One
INFLUENCE OF A MODERN-DAY GENIUS

Letter from Albert Einstein 2

A Fascinating Twist of Mind
Yehudi Menuhin 3

Senthics: (I can't define ethics, but I may know what they are when I feel them)
Martha Mills 5

Happy Halcyon Days
Enoch Callaway 12

Manfred Clynes: An Appreciation
John A. Osmundsen 16

A Genius for Times to Come
Winston Ku 23

The Creative Genius of Dr. Manfred Clynes
Michael Ebert 27

Part Two
MUSIC, SCIENCE AND EMOTION

Notes on an Explorer—Manfred Clynes at 70
David Epstein 34

Manfred Clynes—His Early Scientific Years
Michael Kohn 38

Logogenesis
Karl H. Pribram 42

Manfred Clynes and the Cyborg
Chris Hables Gray 46

Feeling Apreene:
Variations on Thoughts Inspired by Manfred Clynes
Rosalind W. Picard 50

The Composer's Pulse
Denis Vaughan 56

Correspondences of Musical Structure and Microstructure
David Lidov 62

Manfred Clynes, Pianist
Bruno H. Repp 70

Modern Music
Gérard Souzay 85

Part Three
THE REALM OF SENTICS

Sentic Cycles
Janice Walker 88

Manfred Clynes: A Gift for Our World
E.M. Christine Kris 115

My Sentic Cycle Experiences
Walter Horn 120

The Sentic Forms of Manfred Clynes:
In Search of the Affective Dynamics of Basic Emotions
Jaak Panksepp 124

Finding Peace
Yehudi Menuhin 142

Part Four
PERSONAL REFLECTIONS

Finding the Real Story
Tim Smith 146

Yuendumu
Janice Walker... 148

Manfred Clynes—Encounters and Reflections
Alf Gabrielsson 159

Part Five
ANIMAL POEMS

Winsects 168
Bee Saved 170
Spy-der 171
Impending Revision of the Legal System 173
Turkeys in the Raw 174
Word Wrongs I
   Itness, The A Word, and the Other F Word 175
Word Wrongs II
   Brutality? An (unbeastly) "Strange Dog" 176
Special Spots: Animals are Crated 177
Equation of Life 180
Harris Ranch
   Class Picture of 1996: 80,000 Sad, Depressed Cattle ... 182
Stars 184
Modern Zoo 186

Appendix A: Published Works of Manfred Clynes............... 188
Appendix B: Sources of Manfred Clynes' Works 195
Index 197

Contributors

Enoch Callaway, M.D.
  Emeritus Professor of Neuropsychology,
  University of California San Francisco
  Senior Research Scientist, Board Member
  and Co-founder of Neurobiological
  Technologies, Inc. Tiburon, CA

Michael Ebert, Esq.
  Patent Attorney
  New York, NY

Prof. David M. Epstein
  Professor of Music and Theater Arts,
  Massachusetts Institute of Technology
  Cambridge, MA

Prof. Alf Gabrielsson
  Department of Psychology,
  Uppsala University
  Uppsala, Sweden

Chris Hables Gray, Ph.D.
  Associate Faculty, "Social Inquiry,"
  Goddard College
  Adjunct Faculty, History of Science,
  Oregon State University
  Eisenhower Fellow, Jan Masaryk
  University, Czech Republic

Walter Horn
  Designer and Architect
  Linz, Austria

Dr. Michael Kohn
  Research Scientist, Nathan Kline Institute
  of Psychiatry
  Orangeburg, NY

Christine Kris, Ph.D.
  Psychophysiologist
  Director of the M.I.N.D. Institute,
  Cambridge, MA

Winston Ku, Ph.D.
  Musician, Physicist, and Lawyer
  Austin, TX

Prof. David Lidov
  Dept. of Music, York University,
  Ontario, Canada

Lord Yehudi Menuhin
  Eminent Violinist, Conductor,
  and Benefactor
  London, England

John Osmundsen
  Science Writer, New York Times (past)
  New York, NY

Prof. Jaak Panskepp
  Distinguished Research Professor
  of Neurobiology,
  Bowling Green State University
  Bowling Green, OH

Prof. Rosalind W. Picard
  NEC Professor of Computers and
  Communication, Media Lab,
  Massachusetts Institute of Technology,
  Cambridge, MA

Prof. Karl H. Pribram
  Center for Brain Research and
  Informational Sciences, Radford, University,
  Radford, VA
  Professor Emeritus, Stanford University
  James P. and Anna King University
  Professor and Eminent Scholar,
  Commonwealth of Virginia

Dr. Bruno H. Repp
  Staff Research Scientist, Music Perception
  and Psychoacoustics, Haskins Lab
  New Haven, CT

Tim Smith
  Writer and Reporter, Fortune Magazine
  New York, NY

Gérard Souzay
  Eminent, World-Famous Baritone and
  Musician
  Marseilles, France

Maestro Denis Vaughan
  Conductor, Royal Advisor of Music and
  the Arts to Her Majesty, Queen Elizabeth II
  London, England

Janice Walker
  Violinist and Pedagogue
  Cedaredge, CO

Introduction

This book is offered in celebration of the life and work of Dr. Manfred Clynes on his seventieth birthday.

Dr. Manfred Clynes is a renowned scientist, musician and inventor, and the originator of sentic therapy. Born in Vienna, Austria, in 1925, Clynes fled with his family to Australia in 1938 to escape the terror of the Nazi occupation. Clynes was first acclaimed as a pianist in Australia as a teenager, and has successfully toured the major cities of Europe as a concert pianist. His teachers in music included Gorodnitzki, Edwin Fischer and, especially, Pablo Casals. Dr. Clynes holds a degree in music (M.S.) from the Juilliard School of Music in New York. He also holds degrees in both neuroscience (D.Sc.) and engineering from the University of Melbourne, Australia, and did graduate work at Princeton University in the psychology of music. Dr. Clynes was chief research scientist at Rockland State Hospital in Orangeburg, New York, for seventeen years, where he pioneered biocybernetic research and discovered the principles of sentics (biological dynamics of human emotion communication). He also discovered the biologic law of unidirectional rate sensitivity. Among his many inventions is the CAT (computer of Average Transients), which became a standard tool in virtually all research laboratories for studying brain function.

Dr. Clynes later served as Director of the Music Research Center at the New South Wales Conservatorium of Music in Sydney, Australia. He was also Professor of Neuropsychology at the University of Melbourne, and has lectured at Harvard, MIT, and Princeton. He is a charter member of the International Society for Research on Emotion, and an eminent authority on dynamic emotion communication in music, the arts and personal life. His widely significant research in neurophysiology, culminating in an integration with his work in music and the nature of emotions, has been published in five books and over one hundred articles in scientific journals. His book, Sentics: The Touch of the Emotions, discusses this research in detail and is regarded as a classic today. The therapy he developed from this work, Sentic Cycles, has helped thousands of people in many parts of the world achieve insight, peace, and greater enjoyment of life. Dr. Clynes now resides in Sonoma, California. He recently developed SuperConductor, a revolutionary computer software program which enables users to create full emotional "live" sounding interpretations and performances of classical masterworks or their own music using only an ordinary PC.

It embodies his fundamental discoveries of the 1980s concerning musicality and the language of music, and was recently termed by Eric Hannah as having "successfully reverse engineered the human musical mind and its neurophysiology" for the interpretation of music.

Manfred Clynes

Note of Appreciation and Thanks

I want to greatly thank all the contributors for their kindness and efforts in writing so eloquently on occasion of a rather insignificant event, as it seems to me, of my birthday. Martha Mills had been busy organizing, and I wish to thank her especially for her initiative and efforts, and Danielle Williams for editing it so well, and last not least MMB Music, the publisher and its indefatigable president, Norman Goldberg, at 81 himself forever a passionate advocate of good music.

It was a great surprise to me to read the contributions, how for example Enoch Callaway with whom I had no contact for the last thirty years or more still remembered me; and even more that he mentioned me in the same sentence with Warren McCullough, for whom I myself wrote a contribution to his Festschrift on his 65th birthday, and who was an inspiration to me as to many others—one to whom I owe much gratitude for his understanding support of my early work in neurophysiology, the nonlinear differential equations describing the heart rate response to breathing (Science, July 1960). At that time in the late fifties and early to mid sixties I was also newly working in a field that held promise, the electric activity of the brain, and what it could tell us about its function without surgical interference. I felt myself to be a novice let loose on an exciting endeavor, to see what one could find, a search to carve out a small slice of the darkness and bring it into the light. That search has remained with me, and has given me wonderfully fulfilling work for so many years! Complementing this has been my music which is with me daily, a different search, a search for meaning and beauty inherent in great music, reflecting our own potential—at best, for understanding experientially the condition of humanity, and at least, the desires, disappointments, grief and joy of the individual. The work with sentics has made this testing of potential possible without music, for anyone who is or is not musically inclined. And now some of this testing of potential is possible for everyone with our new music program called SuperConductor, which lets anyone evoke qualities of feeling in the music that are potentially inherent in it, but need to be discovered by the interpreter.

It was a surprise to me that Janice Walker remembered our trip to Central Australia that well, and that John Osmundsen discovered for himself new ways of thinking, stimulated by my work up to the seventies. The early recollections of Karl Pribram, too, surprised me, evoking long past times, making them real again in my mind. Those were fun times indeed as Enoch Callaway suggests, and exciting times.

The exciting nature of exploration has not diminished in the meantime for me. On the contrary. However the work dealing with emotion encompassed larger regions fraught with more difficulties, as well as satisfactions. The later work with music also is a substantial sociologic challenge as well as an artistic and scientific one.

In the intervening years I tried to improve my own music making, even though I gave only sporadic public concerts. My work with Pablo Casals in 1966 in San Juan, as well as his inspirational Marlboro performances and classes, beginning for me with the three week classes he gave at the University of California in Hertz Hall in 1962, remains central. No words can express the life- and mind-enlarging experience Casals gave to anyone who came within his orbit. As I write this tears come to my eyes that he is no longer with us. I first heard him play on 78 records when I was 8 years old, and my ecstasy and bliss then was confirmed many times over in the later years. Music has not been the same since he is no longer.

So it is with especial gratitude that I want to thank Bruno Repp for his contribution, examining my live recording of my 1978 performance in Sydney Australia, of the Bach *Goldberg Variations*. This contribution is perhaps the most surprising thing that has ever happened to me. Bruno has been an interested colleague in my later work with music and its language, taking critical interest in it, and conducting research relating to it. I was totally astonished to find him devoting so much time and effort to my own piano performance. His appreciation of the meaning of what I was trying to convey in that performance gives me renewed confidence in the communicating power of music, as a language we like to call universal, but which is as yet universal only for a minority of people, unfortunately.

When I read collectively what the contributors say, some of whom are my friends, and some of whom I have never met, I had an experience I would like to share. This was a surprise but of a different kind! All the various facets, pieces, in the various fields seemed to coalesce into a kind of structure, a building, a whole that presented itself to me in a way that I had never felt.

As a child I was fortunate in the choice of my parents that fate gave me: my mother represented beauty—the beautiful and the timeless. My father the constructive, the reasoned, the ethical and motion in time. I loved them both. I was never exposed to violence from my parents (only from the Nazis). As a child of 5–9 I built castles for my mother from colored stone pieces and blocks (blue for the roof and sand yellow for the walls and portals) and tried to make them beautiful. I knew what beauty was, so it seemed, but I also knew that beauty could always be greater than what I had achieved.

I knew then that the search for beauty was a treasure hunt. I was happy to present my mother a castle and when she said it was beautiful, and I tried to make the next one more beautiful. It was not hard (maybe I was helped by an unconscious force) and it gave me great delight.

From my father, an inventor and naval architect, I had trains, trains that ran, that I controlled and played with with abandon, train stations and semaphores that lit up electrically, built for me by my father (my train was not electric). And he taught me to ride a bicycle, to swim, and mathematical tricks.

My maternal grandfather was an inspiration to me as an extraordinarily vital inventive person of great charisma, and of genuine spirituality, celebrating the holiness in wonders of the world. The stars were still infinite to me then.

So when I read the contents of all the cherished contributions, I had a feeling like my life became, in retrospect, like one of the castles I had built for my mother. Every stone assumed a significance in the whole I had not seen before. I do not plan my life—I build it one stone at a time (probably guided unconsciously), according to what has to be done, what question needs to be answered. Driven by two forces, the 'treasure hunt for beauty' (follow your bliss, as Campbell called it), and the passion to ask questions and search for answers, I do not normally ask myself: is this good for me? or, what should I do to "grow"? I forget to even forget myself. I don't know whether this is good—but this is how I live. So I don't look backwards or forwards much—I just do and think what the day brings.

But that castle that appears from the contributions—my life—I now experience, thanks to all of them, like a castle that I built for my mother—only now I feel it is built so to speak for "Holy Mother," the Universal Spirit, and present it humbly and in adoration to that Being.

One of the contributors remarks how my invention of the CAT computer seems simple, in hindsight. Indeed I feel almost if not all my inventions are simple. Surely, the sentograph and sentics could have been developed at least 2000 years ago. Silence duration modulation, and pulse frequency modulation

Note of Appreciation and Thanks xiii

for data recording was simplicity itself. Even color ultrasound. And when I was fifteen, having a little late just learned differential and integral calculus, I invented inertial guidance for aeroplanes as a very simple idea (using piezo electric crystals and vacuum tubes to measure and integrate the acceleration into velocity and then position) My father took me to the Commonwealth Research Laboratories (in Melbourne, Australia) where the scientific director wrote back saying that it could not work. I answered them saying, yes, it will work. Three years later in fact the allies used the very same thing to help win the war. I still have the document describing the invention dated from 1941–2. I could not write it better today.

My windenergy invention may become highly practical with superconducting magnets: I learned it from trees, how they sway in the wind, moved by their leaves (better and less dangerous than windmills). And I have a new conducting invention for conducting all types of synthesizers that is quite novel and natural, and yet simplicity itself (it is still in process of patent application, but will be described shortly). The problems I deal with are simple too, for example there is hardly a day when I don't puzzle how an egg can be so perfectly circular in cross section, in spite of gravity and motion of the body, without a mold—even an ostrich's egg. And why a dog does not move its feet in response to rhythmic music, not even rock music. But I have no answers to these simple facts. But one simple fact has been more yielding to answers: how a phrase of music well shaped can melt the 'heart' of listeners. That simple fact, proved over and over again by Casals in front of my ears, has been my guiding question in making music speak, whether through mathematical understanding realized by computer with musical guidance, or in my own music performance. To be faithful to the inner form and feeling in one's outer expression is the simple paradigm for success in that language.

Indeed, is it not true that...
Behind the Complex
There is the Simple
Beyond the Simple
There is
One

At seventy is one's life work finished? Ever since I was 36 I was grateful for having lived this long: first living beyond Mozart's life span of 35 years, then Beethoven's of 56, and now longer than even Bach—and how little I have accomplished! Can I do some more castle building?

In my work with music I am now more than ever involved in the treasure hunt—but now also with computers. As I type this, the slow movement of Beethoven's Rasumovsky Quartet No. 1 plays (over and over in loop mode), in my interpretation, by SuperConductor. This morning I discovered that a key meaning of the first movement of that quartet is "benevolence," (as I said to my valued programmer collaborator, Steve Sweet, making it come to life in the computer performance is like buying a jar of benevolence at Safeways, on sale, too).

I would like to record the nine symphonies of Beethoven, and the last quartets with SuperConductor (and now also the Rasumovsky). I would like to rerecord the last Beethoven piano sonatas, the Goldberg and the Diabelli variations and record some Chopin, Mozart and Schubert, playing the piano.

I have to finish my book for MIT Press provisionally called 'Music Interpretation for the 21st Century,' on the work with computer-aided interpretation with SuperConductor. I need to make Sentic Cycles more available to people in need of them.

But most of all I hope to do some work in the field of molecular biology and molecular genetics: to find the genes for laughter. Believe it or not, I have been invited by my friend Richard Pestell of the Albert Einstein School of Medicine to work in his laboratory, the Pestell Lab, to work on my dream, to try to find the genetic basis for laughter. When that is found, and the proteins and and structure associated with them are known, a real bridge between mind and body will have been found—a bridge linking unique gene expression with unique experience and feeling. That would be a castle worth building!

Thanks to the contributors to the Festschrift, I am filled with hope to get started. And thanks to the contributors, I feel encouraged in the thought that the readers of this book too will find some hope for their own endeavors and fulfilment of their lives.

Sonoma, July 1999
Manfred Clynes

PART I
Influences of a Modern-day Genius

Albert Einstein

Princeton, 18th May, 1953

Dear Mr. Clynes,

I am truly grateful to you for the great enjoyment that your piano playing has given me. Your performance combines a clear insight into the inner structure of the work of art with a rare spontaneity and freshness of conception. With all the secure mastery of your instrument, your technique never supplants the artistic content, as unfortunately so often is the case in our time.

I am convinced that you will find the appreciation, to which your achievement entitles you.

With friendly greetings
yours
A. Einstein

Yehudi Menuhin

A Fascinating Twist of Mind

Manfred Clynes has one of the most engaging and fascinating minds of any musician I know. This no doubt comes from the fact that his gifts are equal in both the fields of science and music. He has, therefore, tried all his life to share the immeasurable, to weigh the weightless and to understand what often defies human intelligence. He has thus opened up new fields of synthesis which probe more deeply into the intuitive, the apparently unexplainable which mark the subtlest of emotional measures and measures of time, and which actually delve into micro-worlds like the atom and the case of colliding neutrons.

Having a little of that, shall we say, "Talmudic" twist of mind, I, too, have been exercising my mind in trying to teach the unteachable "whether we are speaking mind or matter!"

From his keen explorations in the areas of both science and music, Manfred developed a science called sentics, a remarkable study of patterns of human emotions. He particularly has related this work to human emotional reaction to different styles and works of music, and has taken this even further to reveal patterns, or signatures, unique to each composer. He has attempted to guide, or at least divine, the subtlest of interpretive "deviations."

I have always been fascinated by what I call "distortions." It is only the distorted that carries any quality of character. However, the distorted must be distinguished from the prejudiced, for the prejudiced is only a caricature of the precise and finely-tuned, creative distortion to which I am referring. It is precisely the question of what makes notes unequal that reveals the magic and message of the music, and often it is the contrast between the absolutely rhythmical and the a-rhythmical which lends contrast and color to a performance. I was, therefore, fascinated to read of Manfred Clynes' attempt (no doubt successful) to find order in chaos and principles which govern not the erratic but the basic laws and principle of beauty and expression. Music is, after all, motion in time. And music is not delivered through a pipeline, but rather as might be rain, waterfalls, streams, underground sources, etc. Manfred Clynes represents the tradition between two worlds that are now on the way to certain convergence, a very badly needed one for science, art, technology and human aspiration. The rooted and the free-flying must somehow be connected, each given their domain.

As you can see, I have a very close feeling for Manfred Clynes; his original twist of mind has always fascinated and intrigued me. On the occasion of his 70th birthday, may I present these few thoughts to add to the "Festschrift" in his honor. I wish him a very Happy Birthday and many happy returns. They will be a contribution to us and to our world.

Martha Mills

Senthics:
(I can't define ethics, but I may know what they are when I feel them)

Humankind has always yearned for a universal ethic that would be patent to any reasoned mind. This ethic would be the same across all cultures. It could easily be applied in any situation. Philosophers over the ages have tried valiantly to prove that such an ethic exists, and have largely failed.

Yet, abandoning the search for a universal deterministic ethic leaves us prey to a world we hesitate to contemplate. We fear those in recent years who have suggested that not only is there no universal ethic, but also that *all* things must be considered relative to a particular culture, at a particular time, and in a particular context. We dread an anything-goes relativism, and, it seems to me, rightly so. Yet, on some days, we read the news and believe that this thing we dread may be so.

Dr. Manfred Clynes' pioneering and insightful work in the field he has named "sentics," makes a clearer and deeper contribution to the study of emotion than any other work. His work, together with much that we are only beginning to learn from the various cognitive studies areas, gives hope for a new understanding of ethics. Perhaps that understanding will not give us the "perfection" of that mythical universal ethic, but what that touches the world or the human condition does? Perhaps. Just perhaps, a new understanding that accounts for commonalities in human senses and the way we really communicate, and an understanding that we need to work at ethics, will be the impetus that will move us along further than ever before.

Dr. Clynes' sentic studies show us that there is a natural basis for emotional communication among humans.[1] There are genetically programmed

---

[1] Dr. Manfred Clynes, *Sentics: The Touch of the Emotions* (New York: Doubleday Anchor 1977; Dorset, England:Prism Press 1989)

spatio-temporal ways we communicate emotions like joy, hope, grief, hatred, anger, reverence, love and sex. We may individually experience and express these emotions in different ways at different times and places, but we do so in a way common to all humankind and recognizable to all humankind.

It is found, in fact, that the nervous system has design features that allow it both to generate precise elements of communication faithful to specific qualities, and also to recognize these elements when communicated by others. It can do this, moreover, through a large variety of modes of sensory communication. But behind the forms of each particular sensory communication, it appears there lies a true generating form specific for that emotional quality. We call these *essentic forms*. (Clynes, p. xxvii.)

Emotion should not call up negative images of histrionics or subjectivism in its pejorative sense. Emotions, as the term is used here are the communication of, reception of, and the processing of feelings that all humankind share based on real, complex, and similar experiences. If any capacities of humankind can call forth the best in each of us, can call forth what we hope to be the moral response to a real situation, it is the ability to feel what another feels, to feel empathy, to feel good will.

If an emotion is communicated true to its genetically programmed essentic form, others will experience it as "sincere" or authentic. Moreover, we may feel more than sympathy when that occurs. We may feel empathy.[2] Empathy, as Clynes says,

...is inherently constructive; insofar as we willingly permit another being to live within us, we also apply our own forces of self-preservation to that individual who now lives within us—in short, we have good will. (Clynes, p. 72.)

Essentic forms go beyond the emotions mentioned above. For example, Clynes has proven that people react with largely the same essentic form to the music of particular composers. In discussing the magnificent transcendence of Beethoven's *Symphony No. 9*, Clynes notes that the sentic pulse of that symphony particularly appeals because it brings a sense of both strength and peace —and a feeling among those so affected that they share this feeling, they are one with it and the world.[3] The essentic forms of the music can transform us.

---

[2] Empathy is a central concept for Clynes. All physical matter in the Universe is interchangeable, i.e., one atom of one thing for any other. We, however, are not. Were I to be cloned, my clone and I would never be interchangeable. This is what Clynes calls his principle of non-equivalence. It is empathy, one for the other, me and my clone, me and anyone else, which ties us together and makes it possible for us to talk about meaningful ethics.

[3] It is interesting that the Tokushima Prefecture of Japan does an annual performance of the *Symphony No. 9* in honor of the symphony's first Japanese performance in 1912.

SENTHICS SCHEMA

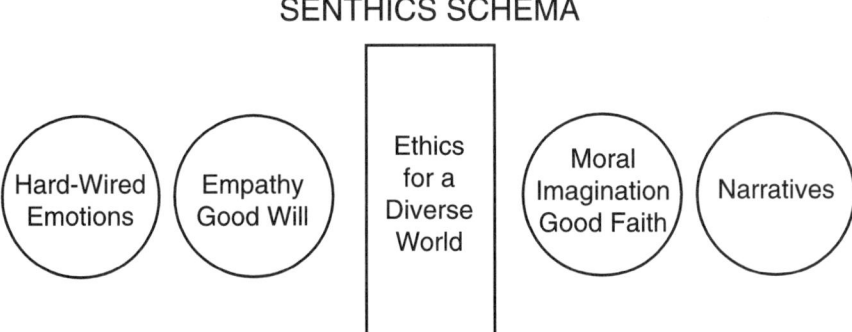

If music can do this, there must be many more experiences which also have genetically programmed essentic forms. As Clynes suggests, perhaps we will discover other emotions and other ways of communicating that are already within us, waiting to be utilized. It will take effort and receptivity on our part.

How do we get from this to ethics? Empathy alone will not serve as a basis for ethics. True empathy means understanding, but does not allow for assessing a situation for the rights or wrongs of it. We need an opposite force. Let us look at a schema and imagine arrows going from each side towards the center.

First we start with the string of people who have written over the past decade or so—not about how we feel—but about how we learn. We learn and explore through stories, narratives. Narratives, our own and those from the past, those real and those fictional, make it possible to examine the consequences of decisions over extended periods of time. Narratives are a laboratory in which we may test and model the particularities of our existence, now and in time, compare our commonalities, develop our perceptions of character, of what is important in any given situation. Comparing, exploring, and testing develops our moral sensitivity. It heightens our ability to make subtle discriminations. We can call this an exercise of our moral imagination.

This moral imagining of ours, however, is not enough in itself. It needs to be undertaken in good faith, with the express idea that we need to work at developing an ethical sense. We need to treat every unfamiliar voice, idea, emotion, as a new narrative in our laboratory for testing, modeling and exploring. We need to listen intently. We need to broaden our search for reason and good faith and other outlooks and narratives. We need to care about the narratives and emotions of others of which we are ignorant. We need to remember that there is nothing sacred about our present order of things. We need to be open to criticism and change. We need to engage in conversations. We need to share insights. We need to correct for blind spots. Only then will we be exercising our moral imagination in the kind of good faith that will be required for ethical growth.

If we then balance the forces of our common emotions and empathy against our learning and testing by narrative, and exercising our moral imaginations in good faith, we have the possibility of coming up with solutions to moral dilemmas that are likely to respect differences, but work better than other solutions. Part of this ethics for a diverse world is that the very fuzziness of emotional commonality, empathy, narrative learning, moral imagination and its exercise in good faith, leads us to new extensions of our powers of emotional intuition and moral imagination. It extends the very dimensions and potentialities of our lives. We knew we did not live in a linear world a long time ago, but we were bound by linear tools. We were bound by two-valued logic, crisp decisions and sequential processes. We now routinely make decisions based on multiple criteria. We use fuzzy logic in machines as well as our own heads. Our sequential processes and thinking are changing radically with the help of computers, and tools such as neural nets and genetic algorithms. The goal of optimality has been enhanced by the recognition that our goals may more immediately be feasibility and suboptimality. That is true also of ethics in a diverse world. There are alternative possibilities which may recognize the best from more viewpoints than any single deterministic rule.

Let me just suggest one concrete example. There are societies in many places in the world that put their young people through rites of passage that involve bodily mutilation imposed with extreme pain, sometimes death and, often, permanent damage to health and the quality of life. These practices continue because they are traditional, and because some members of society profit from assisting in the practice. They continue because parents, and often, the children, encourage it. Parents encourage it because not to have these things done to a child could result in ostracism, inability to marry, inability to earn a good living, and other harmful social consequences. Children encourage it because they do not want to be different or ostracized. We can empathize with everything from the desire to carry on a long and prized tradition, to being invested in the practice by participation in it, to a parent's desires for their children, and the child's need for acceptance. We can also empathize with the children's terror and pain when the rite is practiced and the difficulties of their quality of life problems thereafter.

If we look in our bag of narratives, we will find many examples, now and over time, of rites of passage. We can explore these rites, and their value, as traditions, as coming of age ceremonies, of exercises of courage or maturity or other attributes of adults that we cherish. We can explore their variations, what is important about them. The society, in coming to a new look at the rites of passage tradition, would be assisted by those of its members who have access to the thinking of other parts of the world—which would be horrified by the earlier rite. They would have their moral imaginations stretched by others in the world with different narratives to add to the mix, and whose sensitivity to emotional commonalities might add synergy to the effort. Old traditions *can* be sustained, and even improved, in new forms.

In the rite of passage example, as in all searches for ethical choices we need to work hard and in good faith at trying to see the implications of our actions, attitudes, judgments, biases, and ways of life. We must strive to be finely attuned to our interconnectedness with other people and the world around us. We respond to absolutes and dogmatism, not by surrender to absolute relativism, but by recognizing our own fallibility, our own commonality, and our capacity to do better by employing criticism and testing in reality.

We can thank Dr. Clynes, whose work in sentics goes back to the 1960s and 1970s. From it he derives an ethics based on love and empathy as a natural consequence.* Combined with the more recent work of others, we have new hope for an approach to ethics that makes sense, and is not the dreaded anything-goes relative approach that we should all fear. This approach based on narratives and moral imagination, and based in our emotional commonality promises much because we all have much more in common than was thought in previous ages. We can all hope—if we work at it—that a diverse population of individuals, cultures, and living creatures will progress to communications and a level of dealing with each other and the whole that surpasses all of our expectations and hopes.

If we share a great commonality in genetically programmed emotions, then this empathy—which we share—is an important balance in our search for ethics. Developing our moral imagination is not learning how to apply moral laws, but refining our perception of character and situations and of developing empathetic imagination to step into the lives and feelings of others—an empathy we are all capable of given our commonality of genetically wired essentic forms.

We are not seeking an intellectual grasp of situations or responses, though we should not ignore it. Rather we are seeking to see a complex and

---

* See also the Animal Poems appended to this book. (editor)

concrete reality in a highly lucid and richly robust way. We look at what is there with imagination and feeling—our great, genetically programmed empathy born of our genetically programmed common emotions—and all the other commonalities yet to be acknowledged, together with our commitment in good faith to broaden our outlook and narrow our prejudices.

Objectivity and subjectivity are not opposites. They are not the poles we have for making moral choices. Objectivity in the moral realm does not truly exist. Subjectivity is less private and governed by whim than most believe—because we are more alike than different in many basic ways. Our notion of subjectivity is enormously confused. The fact that our emotional lives are subjective in the sense that something critical about emotion is available only to inner experience does not imply that that inner experience is chaotic or willful. Dr. Clynes' work shows that the emotional experience and how we can build it is genetically governed. The heart may have its reasons, but they are not arbitrary. In 1990, he showd experimentally that even an insignificant lie inhibits the feeling of love, in the sense of "agape." He showed *experimentally* that love is guileless and truthful by nature.[4]

Narratives and moral imagination being pressed by and pressed against emotional and genetic commonality does not mean that individuals are free to make their own judgments entirely free from the rest of humankind. It means that every judgment a person is tempted to make or does make, is open to criticism and testing in the crucible of all of our narratives and conversations and sharing and building. Perhaps people will do less than what they might on occasion, but if they are engaged affirmatively in the process, they should grow and we all should learn. Openness to conversations, story telling, narratives with others is what will allow us to know—or feel—that we are headed in the right direction. This is particularly so as the situations in which we are making judgments are robustly complex. The fact that we work at "being good" and may succeed and grow, and may also share our narratives with others, ought to be a reward for the continued attempts.

Moreover, and somewhat apart from seeking growth in narratives and moral imagination, we will know and feel a good deal of what is meant by doing the right thing because of sentics. The emotions we share, the empathy we can develop through our sensitivity to commonalities, can alone give us the "high" that we have all experienced when just everything has gone right. It is a high that is worth seeking for itself, again and again.

Ethics will come about by prizing our richness and differences. By process. A process of reflection, continued narratives, testing, expanding, criti-

---

[4] M. Clynes, Juriseric and Ryan, "Inherent Cognitive Substrates of Specific Emotions: Love is blocked by lying but not anger." Perceptional and Motor Skills, Vol. 70 pp. 195–206, 1990.

cizing. Our possibilities for making sense of our lives and experiences are grounded in common emotions, feelings, sensitivities, and, yes, empathy. I do not feel your pain, but I know pain. I do not feel your joy, but I know joy. I do not feel your grief, but I know grief. I feel your circumstances, all in one. I am listening. We have a great commonality that, if we work at moral imagination, will lead us to a greater sense of shared purpose and experience. There is, in our links—bodily, emotional and cognitive—a great basis for diverse, but shared dialogue, and diverse, but shared approaches to life and its complexities—our sentic connectedness.

Enoch Callaway, M.D

Happy Halcyon Days

Once upon a time, when the world was younger, there were many wonderful and exciting things that had nothing to do with molecular biology. One of those things was Dr. Manfred Clynes. There are a dwindling number of us who remember those days, and it may be well to record some memories, if only to remind a younger generation that such a time did exist.

When I first met Manfred Clynes, the USA and her allies had recently emerged victorious from a just war; or so it seemed at the time. Korea hadn't blackened our self image appreciably, and Sputnik had created a climate for research funding that today seems unbelievable. Around 1960, the director of Research for the California Department of Mental Health asked the state legislature NOT to increase research funding as there were not enough well trained people to spend it wisely!

Research grants were a snap. I remember Karl Pribram at a study section meeting saying (or words to this effect): "Give him his money. His results aren't likely to confuse any one else." We even had a sign on the lab wall saying "SPEND". In those days, academic promotions were given as reward for intellectual productivity, rather than for administrative cleverness, as is often the case today. On the other hand, academic physicians were not expected to get rich. Only later did the first red Ferrari appear on the campus and change the game. It is interesting how easily one adjusts to having money, and how hard it is the other way. But we come to Unidirectional Rate Sensitivity later.

In this earlier time, the late Charles Shagass was beginning to report on evoked responses in humans. He was using an ingenious photographic averaging method. Dim oscilloscope traces were superimposed on film, so that a sort of averaged wave form could be seen in the developed image.

EEGs (recorded brain waves) had been known for almost half a century. Many of us felt that the EEG had things to tell us about the mind, but the code had proved difficult to break. Hudson Hoagland likened the psychiatrist studying EEGs to the industrial espionage agent flying over a factory to watch the smoke from the chimneys. You could tell if things were on fire or shut down, but that's about all. It seemed to us that averaged evoked potentials (or ERPs, for Event Related Potentials as they came to be known) would surely be the long sought after EEG window on the mind.

I was going along nicely at this time. The Office of Naval Research (ONR) had given me money to build a grid-barrier storage tube averager, which was to have been a device that used a CRT storage tube as a substitute for Shagass' film. The averager was a handsome beast and I was having great fun designing high voltage power supplies for it when I got a call from (I think) Don Woodward at ONR. "Noch," he said, "You are wasting your time. Did you ever hear of a Computer of Averaged Transients, or CAT?"

I suppose that was a sort of epiphany, curtsey Clynes. From that day forward, my world was transformed from tubes to solid state, and from analog to digital. Literally within months, to ask an EEG researcher if he had heard of the CAT would have been insulting. Indeed, the terms "wet cat" and "dry CAT" came into conversational use so that the confusion of felines with computers could be avoided. There was an explosion of ERP research, with every one and his cousin discovering a new wave with a special significance. Our scientific meetings came to resemble grade-school show-and-tell sessions: "Look what I found last time I went to the lab!"

If some of our work with the CAT did not qualify as great science, the CAT itself was a stroke of pure genius, and like so many acts of genius, it was immediately obvious after the fact. It's embodiment, however, was not so obvious and represented, for those days, some very advanced engineering.

The idea with the CAT was to take a series of counters which had been designed for radiation studies, and scan digitized EEG into them so as to accumulate voltage-dependent counts for so many milliseconds into each counter in sequence. If each scan started the instant a stimulus was given, and the process was repeated over and over, the time-locked EEG response was added into the counters, increasing as the product of the number of scans (N). On the other hand, the randomly varying noise only increased as the square root of N. The result was a gain in signal/noise ratio of $N \div \sqrt{N}$, or simply $\sqrt{N}$.

In those days, research tended to be a leisurely, hands-on sort of thing. At first we plotted ERPs on a flat-bed plotter; going from analog EEG to digital counts and back to analog voltage for the plotter. Soon, however, our savior Dr. Clynes came out with a paper tape punch that delivered up the contents of the CAT digitally. By then we had our own general purpose mini-computer, a beautiful, monstrous PDP-7 that occupied most of our biggest lab. Two relay racks housed the computer's astounding 8K of memory. One could even open a door and touch each bit of magnetic memory in its copper wire wrapping. Clynes' tape punch worked like a charm. Not so DEC's paper tape reader. The reader had a weird tendency to pull a bit of tape, stick that piece in the bottom of the reader somehow and then pull another piece to repeat the process. The result was known as a micro-fan-fold. Part of the tape would be bunched up and almost fused at the reader with successive sections of tape folded behind to produce a kind of a miniature Japanese fan. A micro-fan-fold could destroy a days work in seconds. The CAT tape, however, was wonderful, since when the computer devoured a tape, the CAT could immediately punch out another.

In those happy halcyon days, I was blessed with a sequence of latter-to-be-famous younger colleagues. Current young colleagues will have a hard time giving this credence, but in those days there was even money for visiting scholars. John Tukey came and taught us about Fourier transforms. We actually didn't have enough money for his usual astronomically high consultant fee, but he took water packed albacore tuna as payment in kind! Warren McCullough stretched our little minds to the snapping point. We gave him a consultant fee but I think the evening of drinking and talking counted for more with him. And among these stars, we had a visit from Dr. Clynes. We knew Clynes had been a musician, a conductor and an engineer before he became a creative entrepreneur. Though I can't remember exactly what he taught us, I recall him as a marker on that imaginary yardstick by which we judge ourselves. We were good journeymen scientists and knew it, but it was healthful if humbling to be in the presence of a true genius.

Times changed, as they always do. We soon had A-to-D converters and DEC-tape on our computer. I don't really know what happened to our CAT. It had been put in a closet, and I suspect a departing post-doctoral fellow sneaked off with it. As for Dr. Clynes, I lost track of him until he resurfaced with his Unidirectional Rate Sensitivity[1] idea. Unfortunately this idea, like many other brilliant 'lumping' insights, has been all but lost.

---

[1] To explain URS in the body: imagine adding salt into a beaker of water at any rate you choose, increasing the concentration of salt. If you now need to rapidly decrease the concentration, you cannot throw negative salt into it—there is no such thing. Molecules can only arrive in positive numbers—unlike electric signals which may be positive or negative. But the body uses chemical concentration to transmit information at all levels, for example, hormones and neurotransmitters. Hence you either have to wait for the chemical to metabolize—to disappear—at a rate that has nothing to do with the information transmission, or else you need another chemical, a second channel, to react with the first to produce change in the opposite direction. Thuse also hot and cold are sensed as separate channels.

Yes. we must face it. The 'splitters' (molecular biologists) are winning at the moment. Perhaps this is largely why Clynes genius is not better known. Indeed, I believe it was Crick who declared that there are no general truths in biology. He believed that nature is simply an opportunistic tinkerer, and that the rewards will come to those researchers who look for molecular mechanisms, because overriding grand principles are all snares and delusions. Yet how could Unidirectional Rate Sensitivity not truly be a general principle? A rock coming towards you demands a qualitatively different response mechanism than one going away! Isn't truth found also in grand ideas, in the macrocosm as well as the microcosm?

It is perhaps apparent by now why I embraced this opportunity to 'festschrift' Dr. Clynes. He is the kind of scientist who has been unafraid to grasp the grand schemes in nature. This occasion allows me also to celebrate a time when art and science were not two cultures, or at least not so far as most scientists were concerned. Kenneth Baker once remarked that a great painting and a beautiful natural sunset appealed to two different parts of our minds: The painting represented the human solution to a problem, the sunset just was. To me, the meaning of human existence is found in the delight of an unexpected research result and in the new insight into nature that it suggests. It is the experience an amateur musician has while working through a piece by Bach for the first time, and encountering a perfect but unexpected resolution. It is the fly fisherman's reaction when a trout rises to a perfectly presented fly he has tied.

The bible says the poor shall inherit the earth. Does that mean the poor of spirit; the cautious and the administratively inclined? If the earth is reserved for such button counters, will heaven be reserved for those who were sometimes wrong but strove to push beyond the ordinary? Whatever the answer, those of us who have had contact with such as Clynes have been uplifted and ignited. And the lives of countless others who have benefited from Clynes ideas have been enriched.

John A. Osmundsen

Manfred Clynes: An Appreciation

What is genius, and how does it do that? Those are not just good questions but ones whose answers might pay off handsomely if they could be applied by those of us who, like myself, do not possess that mental mercuriality. Applying the answers would amount to emulating, if ever so artificially, the thought processes of "operating genius," and that would, of course, require determining what those thought processes were and how they worked. One way to do that would be to study the thinking of "genius engaged." That is essentially what I realized, relatively recently, that I had done with Manfred Clynes, the one who introduced me to the phenomenon of genius: his own.

Manfred actually introduced me to thinking. Oh, I "thought" before we met for the first time that 1961 afternoon in the reception area of The New York Times where I was working then as a writer/reporter in the science-news department. But after a few years' knowing and interacting with Manfred and observing the way his mind worked, and though I didn't realize it until only a little while ago, my own style of thinking changed as would the direction of my entire life. And Manfred never knew of this until now.

Thirty-five years ago, Manfred's model made way for me to truly begin to share the secret and enjoy the life of the mind, for which I'll be eternally grateful. I began to understand, through first-hand observation, the way in which a genius thinks. My view of this style of thinking can best be characterized as "second-order" or "nonlinear." It's thinking, not linearly (or even laterally) about what appears to be going on, but about what's *really* going on: getting down to the underlying meaning of things, the "deep statement." This kind of thinking is to "ordinary" thinking (done even by many scientists and otherwise creative people) as acceleration is to velocity: a second derivative, not Newtonian action-reaction but more Einsteinean relativistic, or quantum-mechanical probabilistic.

While observing Manfred fertilized my own intellectual process, it took about 20 years for his model of thinking to produce real fruit for me. This is somewhat longer than studies have shown it usually takes for creative results to emerge from a chosen pursuit, but I was on more than a pursuit. I was on a quest, a great epic adventure. I was on a search for, well, answers. Answers, you see, are all over the place, hidden in plain sight, self-evident. We discover their meanings by determining, with second-order thinking, the Questions they resolve—like one big game of Jeopardy. A related feature of genius (also to be emulated) is a *qui vive*[1] for noticing Answers when they are encountered.

Manfred's discovery of the universal biological law of unidirectional rate sensitivity (URS) is a good example of what I mean (and, by the way, discovery of *any* biological law is an extraordinary achievement, in itself). For this, the Answer he noticed for this was that the pupil of the eye constricts to a "flash" of darkness (produced by quickly flicking ambient light off, then on again). Since a pupil dilates with decreasing illumination, its constriction to a pulse of darkness was paradoxical. Some of the best Answers come in the form of paradox as most scientists well know. This noticed paradox produced URS.

The root Question that was resolved, the *meaning* that emerged, from Manfred's noticing the seemingly paradoxical behavior of the pupil was: How is information transmitted in biological systems resolution came in two parts. First, information is sensed as change, or rate; second, it is transmitted unidirectionally, in one direction, or channel, only. Manfred's resolution of the Pupilary Paradox was that the pupil responds to information about changes in illumination and that the channel carrying information about brightening is faster than the opposite one carrying information about dimming. The slow, dilating response to momentary dimming would thus be overrun by the fast, constricting response to subsequent brightening. URS was later observed in many other modes of biological communication (hormonal, neurological, etc.) by Manfred and scientists throughout the world, confirming his discovery.

With his invention of the Computer of Average Transient (CAT), Manfred created a way to extract Answers from irrelevancies (as Douglas R. Hofstadter, another genius, describes the process of discovery). Consider an

---

[1] *Qui vive* can be translated here as "alacrity."

Answer as a signal buried in a mess of noise. If you take many samples of the mixture and add them all together, the peaks and troughs of the noise diminish each other, reducing noise, while the signal reinforces itself, and the Answer emerges from the mess. That is the function the CAT performs. Manfred would later use the CAT to extract brain-wave patterns evoked by visual perceptions of various colors and patterns, making possible a kind of "electronic mind reading" of what subjects were viewing. And he would carry this line of thinking even further to create the science of sentics[2] and, as he characterized it for me on a New York visit in the mid-80s, "solve the music problem."

Manfred's ability to notice Answers has led him to many remarkable discoveries. But genius, Manfred's included, is far more than merely thinking non-linearly about "novel noticings," Answers, to discover the meanings of things. It also involves associative processes by which novel connections are made among what may seem to be unrelated entities (objects, events, reactions, processes, etc.). Linus Pauling was fond of saying that, in order to have any good ideas, you must have LOTS of ideas. Manfred has never wanted for ideas, being at home in a bewildering array of "worlds," including music, neurophysiology, electronics, biocybernetics, computing, invention, poetry and philosophy. This has given him not only a virtually limitless source of ideas but a universe of different perspectives, or world-views, from which to look at things. This has enabled him to "change worlds" as fast and variously as he sprouts ideas for novel associations to be made. William James observed that: "The greatest discovery of my generation is that a human being can alter his life [read 'world'] by altering his attitude [read 'perspective]."

Manfred also gave me perspective. That is, he made me aware of this important attribute when I pored over the first draft of his book, *Sentics: The Touch of Emotions*. I say that perspective is important because it is tightly coupled to—interdeterminate with, in fact—context, a self-evident relationship I discovered for myself, in the early 1980s. (Gregory Bateson had called my attention earlier to the importance of context.)

Each time we change our perspective, or world-view, we change context, the "world" we're operating in. (This could explain what James must have meant.) Contrariwise, every time we enter a new context, our perspective changes accordingly, and our behavior with it.

Manfred's wit and sense of humor no doubt derive in large measure from his ability to view the world in multiple, often very different and conflicting perspectives, producing sometimes competing contexts. Like optical

---

[2] See Part III of this volume, "The Realm of Sentics"

illusions that combine conflicting contexts, as Escher did so wonderfully, the results may often strikes one as "funny." This may be why the moment of scientific discovery can provoke laughter. Manfred wrote of this, in fact, in *Sentics: The Touch of the Emotions*, discussing such pleasurable, spontaneous reaction to odd admixtures of perspectives.

Manfred has the capacity to change perspectives in the most original, interesting and productive ways. For example, after identifying brain-wave patterns that were evoked by particular visual perceptions of the outside world, he wondered if it would be possible to do the same with experiences of the inner world. To find out, he had to revisit his own worlds of computing and music. Applying his CAT to recorded variations in finger pressure that subjects used to express the music they were "hearing" in their heads, Manfred was able to extract distinctive "shapes" of those inner experiences of "mental music" (presumably representing transduced brain-wave patterns associated with that experience). Even more interesting, he searched and found that these shapes were characteristic of the music's composer, the music's "inner pulse" representing the composer's "signature." Manfred extended his exploration of the inner world with the aid of thousands of subjects who used the same finger-pressure expressive technique to generate distinctive shapes of specific emotions (anger, hate, grief, love, sex, joy and reverence). This is what gave birth to the science of sentics.

Manfred later doubled back on himself and applied the same techniques to "solve the music problem." He discovered a way to restore *life* to music by giving a "dead score" of mere notes and meters the *meaning* that the composer had originally intended and had, in fact, imparted with his or her "signature" in the music's "inner pulse." Manfred created a computer software program that enables a personal computer to play this enlivened music. The program utilizes the "global principles of musical microstructure" he discovered (hierarchical pulse, predictive amplitude shaping, and organic vibrato). The resulting computer-generated enlivened performances embody, in a quite real sense, the very essence of their composers. Certainly, this invention is the fruit of a genius' mind. It is the result of a mind that notices the Answers.

Noticing the answer is not quite as straightforward as it may at first appear. You may run through a series of Questions. The Question you find for a particular Answer becomes, itself, a new Answer that leads regressively backward—or, I would prefer, upward—through one or more additional Questions, each becoming a new Answer, and so on, until you reach The Final Question. By then, you not only have determined the meanings of all the Answers, but you now know what it *all* means, the "deep statement." The following is an example.

In 1980, I noticed an unusual Answer whose Question turned out to be: How does an elixir, or cure-all, work? That Answer consisted of a collection of similar lists of several seemingly unrelated health benefits produced by several seemingly unrelated agents/agencies. Claimed benefits included enhanced healing; reduced inflammation; reduction in the incidence, severity and duration of illness; alleviation of pain; relief of symptoms from toxins (e.g., poison ivy); improved hair, skin and nails, and restful sleep. (The latter two kinds of benefits are often used by physicians as indicators of a patient's overall well-being.) The agents and modalities that were said to produce those kinds of good results included an industrial solvent, an extract of bovine cartilage, pulsed electromagnetic waves, pressurized oxygen, vitamin C, metal salts, a proteolytic enzyme, meditation and deep relaxation.

As a science reporter, I had encountered each and every one of these putative health aids over a period of several years, the mechanism of action for none of which could be scientifically certified. The (preliminary) Answer identified by my noticing the relationship among all these different health benefactors gradually became the Question: Might there be an underlying connection among them, perhaps a kind of unifying principle by which they all could produce good effects? What I thought was the Answer to that question occurred to me as I was getting out of a hotel bathtub in Florence, Italy, on July of 1980 (thereby performing what I mused as a "Reverse Archimedes"). The answer was homeostasis, the complex process by which a living organism sustains itself. The homeostasis phenomenon embraces all healing, upkeep and maintenance, resistance to and recovery from illness—the very things these health aids were said to help. Like the obverse of a rising tide that raises all boats, I reasoned, each of the health benefactors may have, probably in various different ways, raised the effectiveness (tide) of homeostatic regulation.

As suggested earlier, the homeostasis Answer quickly became a new Question: How might homeostatic regulation, or homeostatic efficiency (a good definition of health, in fact), be raised, generally, in a variety of ways?

Months later, I ran across a paper I'd clipped years before from *Science* on cellular communications, and instantly knew the resolution to my Question. The efficiency of any homeostatic/self-sustaining system can be raised by *increasing communications*—the flow and processing of information about the state of the system—so that adjustments necessary for its self-sustenance can be made. While this resolved the previous Question, the resolution immediately became a new Question: How can the flow and processing of information be increased, by a variety of means, in a homeostatic system? And this, of course, was The Final Question that would give *meaning* to the original Answer I had found (homeostasis).

I spent many more months in a medical library, researching, looking for mechanisms by which these various health aids might influence, not health but *communications* in a living system. The result was a long list of possible mechanisms for generating what would amount to "The Elixir Effect." These mechanisms ranged from dissolving and/or carrying chemical and cellular information, to increasing the porosity of the intercellular bed, clearing cell-membrane receptor sites and facilitating genetic expression by promoting reversible unwinding of chromosomal DNA. The Elixir Effect (not so-named, of course) and means for eliciting it in biological organisms were later patented in Europe and Canada. A preparation—a mixture of ingredients that was called a nutritional supplement but functioned as a "physiological complement"—was tested on a model of homeostasis (wound healing) by a mayor pharmaceutical company with positive results. However, it is also worth noting that the Elixir Effect applies to any self-sustaining system—a business, economy or society, as well as a biological organism.

I tell this story because it reflects the impact that Manfred Clynes has had in my life. His thinking has deeply influenced my own creative thought process. His ideas on sentics, in particular, have intrigued me. As I wrote in the foreword to Manfred's book, *Sentics*, in 1975, sentic theory has wide-ranging applications. Among other things, it could apply to the teaching and practice of martial arts—such as karate, kiai-jutsu, shoriniji kempo and particularly aikido, tai-chi-ch'uan and wing chun—in which the shares of bodily movements are of great importance.

> "The more nearly perfect one shapes movements...the more effective will the practitioner be. In fact, martial artists who perfect their techniques... can develop abilities to perform seemingly supernatural feats. Apparently, the disciplines [e.g. intense concentration and focused 'instant meditation']... enable the practitioners to 'tap into' a reserve or reservoir of the essence of human being... Precisely what that 'essence' may be—intrinsic energy, ki, chi [Qi]—is not known." (*Sentics: The Touch of the Emotions*, Foreword by J. Osmond pp. xvi-xvii)

I believe the concept underlying the Elixir Effect and Manfred's science of sentics may combine to offer a plausible view of "intrinsic energy," the "essence of human being," as no other creature on earth can invoke it.

Deep relaxation and meditation both passively increase homeostatic efficiency by reducing stress to which homeostatic regulation would otherwise devote energy. Increased efficiency inevitably produces an increase of available energy (why we feel refreshed after a rest). Focused "intense meditation" might thus be expected to generate a sudden, significant rise in available energy that could be directed outward in a burst via the martial artist's developed powers of concentration, not unlike the way energy may be directed unconsciously in the body under hypnosis and in the placebo response. But this does not explain the role that *precise shaping* of bodily movements may play.

Homeostasis is a harmonious phenomenon. It may be that the shapes of body movement in the practice of martial arts resonate with the shapes of the body's physiological controls (would that Manfred's CAT could extract *them*), thereby enhancing inner, biochemical/physiological harmony, or functional efficiency, and further increasing the availability of body's inner (homeostatic) energy. (There is evidence that harmonious mental activity seems to facilitate physiological functioning, or homeostatic control.)

Clearly, if shaped movement does, indeed, "cooperate" with the internal controls of the body, this could be put to use beyond the martial arts, say, as a general aid to good health. In fact, that is exactly what millions of people who practice tai-chi-ch'uan are doing every morning in Chinese parks.

"Wild?" A little, perhaps. (That was the one-word reaction of the head of research at the pharmaceutical company that tested the "elixir preparation" after I explained to him the theory behind it.) But, as Manfred was my model, it stands to reason I might wax at least a *little* wild. Some of Manfred's best conjectures have been wild, to say the least...before they proved to be true.

Winston Ku

A Genius for Times to Come

"No real instruments, no live musicians—what kind of music is it? How can he make a computer sound like THAT! How does he do it?" All of the above are typical responses from listeners when I play the musical "recordings" which I am fortunate and indeed very privileged to receive from Dr. Clynes from time to time.

So when I received the invitation to contribute to Dr. Manfred Clynes' birthday festschrift, I thought I would try, to the best of my ability anyway, to explain in plain language what it is that links an innocent looking CD and what I can only describe as the genius and dedication of Dr. Manfred Clynes.

For those who have not heard Dr. Clynes' musical creations, the only recommendation I have is: do it! I recommend it not because they are necessarily "the best interpretation" (as if there were such a thing) of a given piece of music, or the most pleasing instrumental sounds that are available, but because one really needs to feel the achievement of Dr. Clynes before one can even believe that this level and quality of music making is possible using only a computer.

When I was first told about a man called Manfred Clynes and a computer playing music, I myself was very skeptical about the quality of such non-human performances due to previous experiences of listening to electronic music and very mechanical-sounding "interpretations." Normally, I would have dismissed the opportunity to even listen to any such non-human music (a mistake which I hope our readers would not make) had the suggestion not come from a person whom I much respected and who was kind enough to lend me a book called *Sentics* by Manfred Clynes. On the first page of this book, I found the inscription "To Ilya Prigogine—my brother seeker, with gratitude and admiration, Manfred Clynes."

Thanks to Prof. Ilya's introduction to the work of Manfred Clynes, I eventually met Dr. Clynes in his home hidden in the beautiful hills of Sonoma, California, and experienced Clynes Music at first hand. As soon as I heard a few bars of this so-called machine-generated music, I was convinced that what I heard was no ordinary (by that I mean mechanical and monotonous sounding) computer reproduction of a musical score, but something that resembled human instrumental playing. I used the verb "resemble" because in some instances, I found Clynes Music to be "too perfect music" or "too good to be true music," so I suggested that Clynes Music should perhaps instead be called super-human music or super-live music; a concept that has certainly been applied or at least attempted in some cases of music making in the recording studio.

Personally speaking, I do not value perfection in art per se if the quest for perfection is not accompanied by an arousal of emotion or at least an inner feeling, or if the quest for perfection merely illuminates the art of work rather than the work of art. But what is perfection anyway? Is it the ability to play with exact tonal and temporal accuracy as the music appears on the score, or the ability to "intellectually control" minute details of a piece of music in performance or perhaps even across different performances of the same piece of music? Or is perfection a matter of spontaneously arousing emotions and feelings or at least "communicating emotional qualities" of music during a performance without pre-planning? Or is it a combination of the above?

Regardless of whichever philosophy of interpretation or concept of "perfection" is preferred, the computer program of Dr. Manfred Clynes can cater to each individual's preferences by allowing the adjustments of musical parameters such as loudness and other temporal elements which he has discovered through his many years of multi-disciplinary research across the fields of neuroscience, neuropsychology, engineering and music.

By imputing musical scores in the computer, and then using his unique discoveries such as composer's pulse, organic vibrato and predictive amplitude shaping functions, Dr. Clynes has succeeded in programming the computer to "play" the musical score by devising algorithms in the form of mathematical functions that mimic the combination of pitch, amplitude and temporal variances that occur naturally in human performances. By altering the values of these mathematical parameters, Dr. Clynes' program instructs the computer to perform calculations as the musical score is played in real time, thereby generating and modifying the musical score electronically with human qualities which consist of very subtle variations and combinations of duration, amplitude, shape and vibrato in time.

The genius and dedication of Dr. Clynes lie with his multi-disciplinary insights and skills during many years of research in all of the above-mentioned disciplines. Clynes Music represents not a single discovery or an isolated project, but the culmination of a series of discoveries in several disciplines over a lifetime, amalgamated with Dr. Clynes' talent as a highly gifted musician.

When one is listening to one of Dr. Clynes' computer generated CDs, it is easy to get lost in the music which he has interpreted for us through his extraordinary SuperConductor and SuperPerformer programs and perhaps overlook the vastness and importance of his achievement as a researcher. The ability of Dr. Clynes to generate research data in individual disciplines of engineering, neuroscience and psychology and then relate them in an inter/multi-disciplinary fashion to produce a computer program that plays music represents a shift from an epistemological to an ontological emphasis in the way knowledge is pursued and used by the human race—a trait that puts Dr. Clynes somewhat ahead of his time and his many esteemed colleagues.

Thanks to Dr. Clynes' research and discoveries, new opportunities have arisen for inter/multi-disciplinary mind-body research concerning brain function and emotion and how music affects the latter. For example, Dr. Clynes invented a means by which emotions can be externalized from the mind to the body by using a touch-sensitive electronic device that he called a sentograph. Used systematically in Sentic Cycles, it is capable of serving as a therapeutic tool and to aid the expression of emotions.

Unfortunately, the world of academic research is still largely organized in a cartesianly reduced system of vertical structures, and the benefits of using Dr. Clynes' multi-disciplinary research and inventions might not be fully realized until more horizontal integration of disciplines is accomplished in our educational environment. Until then, the impact of Dr. Clynes' work in the various fields will, alas, not be recognized and celebrated to the extent of many of his more mono-disciplinary colleagues. However, the fact that so many have come together to celebrate the 70th birthday of Dr. Clynes bears testimony to the fact that we have in Dr. Manfred Clynes a multi-talented genius. His dedicated research efforts will have impact in the course of our pursuit of knowledge well into the next century.

By placing music as one of the four cornerstones of the Quadrivium, the Greeks, in theories such as the doctrine of ethos, have long stated that music has far more significance than being a mere form of entertainment. It is my hope that Dr. Clynes' research will be exploited to help towards yielding a similar conclusion that music represents not only superficial cultural influences of the human civilization, but contains significant information relating to universal structures of the human mind.

Michael Ebert

The Creative Genius of Dr. Manfred Clynes

My career as a patent attorney dates back to World War II when, in Army uniform, I was assigned to Radiation Laboratories at MIT. There I acted as a patent advisor to a staff of scientists, drawn mostly from universities, who sought to develop more effective military radar systems and, in the course of doing so, devised a primitive version of a digital computer long before the invention of the transistor. Later in my career, I acted on behalf of N.V. Philips, Xerox, IBM, Olivetti, and other corporations out of whose laboratories came zerographic copiers, solid state computers, color TV, transistors, electronic timepieces and other inventions which have since transformed the industrial world. Yet among the many brilliant people whom I have had the fortune of meeting, Dr. Manfred Clynes stands out.

My first contact with Manfred Clynes was in the 1960s when he was chief scientist in the laboratories of the Rockland State Hospital, the largest New York State mental institution. What then brought me to Dr. Clynes was his invention of a "Computer of Average Transients," later known commercially under the trademark CAT.

Both Dr. Clynes and Dr. Nathan Kline, the outstanding psychiatrist who then headed the hospital research center, despaired of being able to effectively treat mental patients without first having a greater knowledge of brain behavior going beyond the boundaries of Freud (who saw the psyche as being divided into an id, a superego and other intangibles). So, in order better to understand the behavior of the brain, Clynes developed the CAT. The CAT detects the electrical reaction evoked by a stimulus, such as a drug or a flash of light, and analyzes the resultant wave pattern. The research value of this instrument was quickly recognized, and the CAT became standard equipment in many laboratories.

In addition to his work with the CAT, Dr. Clynes explored the use of auto and cross-correlation techniques for investigating and interpreting electrical wave activity in living organisms, such as brain wave activity. In 1964, he was granted a patent on an on-line computer for just this purpose. The computer was designed to automatically and continuously evaluate the correlation function and thereby provide a record permitting an operator to observe the correlation as it occurs. Dr. Clynes also made major contributions to what his patents refer to as a radar-like pulse-echo ultrasonic system for exploring the internal structure of human organisms. These systems are now known as ultra-sound diagnostic instruments.

In 1964, Dr. Clynes patented an ultra-sound instrument yielding an image of an internal structure in which variations in color reflected physical differences in the structure being explored. In 1966, he patented an ultra-sound instrument for exploring the circulatory system, making it possible to select for examination a particular arterial or venous section of the system. In the same year he patented an ultra-sound system whose resolution and sensitivity were greatly improved. And in 1967, he patented an ultra-sound instrument for cardiac volume measurement.

Clynes' accomplishments, however, are not restricted to the realm of technological invention. His creative genius extends into the fields of neuroscience and music. And it is this ability to achieve in such a variety of disciplines that I find particularly fascinating about Dr. Manfred Clynes.

In our age of specialization, it is rare for a creative individual to operate effectively in more than one field. Certainly few in our time function as Goethe did, as writer, poet and scientist; or as Da Vinci did, as a painter and sculptor as well as an inventor in hydraulics, mechanics and in many other fields unrelated to art.[1]

In the past, a creative genius drew no line between those flights of his imagination which led either to great works of art or to significant innovations in science and technology. In this century, however, such lines distinctly separate the scientist from the artist, and even the biologist from the engineer. Yet despite this, there are a handful who have remained unencumbered by the barriers of specialization. Among these is Dr. Manfred Clynes. Indeed, it is fair to characterize Dr. Clynes as an artist-scientist-inventor in

---

[1] I do not include Einstein here, for though he tried to become a first-rate violinist, he complained that he found it far more difficult to master the violin than to spin out of his imagination the theories which shook the world of science. And though Einstein, as a former examiner in the Swiss Patent Office, tried hard to become an inventor, he lacked (in my view) the necessary talent.

the vein of both Goethe and Da Vinci, for while he sacrificed his career as a concert pianist in favor of science and invention, he never abandoned music. His most recent innovations are specifically music-oriented. And much of his earlier work was fueled by both musical and scientific sensibilities.

Drawing upon his background in both music and science, Manfred Clynes brought into being an entirely new field, which he calls sentics.[2] Initially developed in the 1970s, Sentics is based on existing psychoanalytic theories of repression, deformation of character structure and neurosis arising from the inability, or unconscious refusal, of a subject to express emotion either at critical periods or in every day life. To afford a subject emotional release and a means of overcoming repressive tendencies, Clynes invented Sentic Cycles and the sentograph. With Sentic Cycles, a subject is presented with a timed sequence of words, each chosen to evoke a specific emotion, such as love. The subject is then required to physically express this emotion, as best he can, by applying finger pressure to the a transducer on Clynes' programmed instrument, the sentograph. The transducer yields a wave form that can be displayed and recorded and whose shape is indicative of the subject's spontaneous expression of that emotion.

Sentic Cycles provides a valuable contribution to the worlds of psychiatry and neuroscience. A set of sentic (emotional response) wave patterns derived from a particular subject creates a personality profile of the subject. Such insight is of great value in analyzing the patient's state of mind. And as an emotionally repressed subject continues to use Sentic Cycles, he generally experiences an emotional release that overcomes his repressive behavior. The data derived from subjects also provides a base from which to further explore the workings of the human brain.

The patterns of human emotion illuminated through Sentic Cycle research sparked Manfred Clynes' most recent work with music. Dr. Clynes has discovered what he calls the composer's "inner pulse," or the unique patterns of each composer's music. These patterns reveal a particular personal point of view inherent in a composer's work and provide a hitherto unavailable foundation for understanding music. Using this new understanding, Clynes has created computer software programs that may transform the way music is interpreted and reproduced. These inventions are based on the fact that the notation of a printed score of music merely sets out the notes to be played, not how they are to be rendered expressive by the performer.

---

[2] Sentics is the study of biological emotion communication dynamics. For a more detailed discussion of sentics, please see Part Three, "The Realm of Sentics." also see *Sentics: The Touch of the Emotions* by Dr. Manfred Clynes (Dorset, England: Prism Press, 1989).

Clynes points out that should a performer do nothing but play the notes of a printed score and faithfully comply with the composer's instructions as they appear in the printed score, the resultant performance would be still-borne and expressively dead. He, therefore, identifies the notation as the "macrostructure" of the printed score. To impart emotional expression to a musical composition, the performer, guided by his own emotional make-up or if you please, by his inner spirit, must deviate from the macrostructure and make subtle changes in the duration of the notes and their amplitude shape, as well as in the timbre and other musical variables in order to render the music emotionally meaningful. This Clynes identifies as the "microstructure" of the music. And it is the development of this microstructure that Clynes hopes to foster in others through his latest inventions.

With Clynes' SuperConductor software, the user may lack musical training, yet can become the performer of whatever musical score has its printed notation entered into the computer memory. As the notes are reproduced by instruments whose sounds are stored in the memory of the computer, the reproduced notes are modified by a microstructure selected and manipulated by the user. Hence, what issues from the computer is the reproduced musical score as interpreted by the user. For example, if the user chooses to perform Beethoven's Fifth Symphony, the computer will reproduce the symphony in accordance with Beethoven's notation. But the symphony will not sound as if it were conducted by, say, Toscanini, for the conductor is effectively the user of the system, and its interpretation is that of the user.

The Clynes SuperConductor software is valuable in many ways. It is of particular use to a modern composer who may write a symphonic masterpiece, yet has no idea of what it really sounds like until performed by an orchestra. The composer may have difficulty in finding an orchestra willing to play his piece without being paid to do so. As a result, much of the music now being composed is never heard by the composer, to say nothing of an audience. But with the Clynes system, the composer has only to enter the notes of his score into the computer, and have it played back and reproduced in accordance with a microstructure selected by the composer. As a consequence, the score is performed expressively as if conducted by the composer. I expect this invention to have a major impact on how music is hereafter composed and performed.

If we consider the brain of a pianist, when the eyes of the pianist see a half note in a musical score which has half the time value of a whole note, the eyes tell this to the brain which then commands a finger to strike the appropriate key of the piano. But what tells the brain to tamper with the time duration of the half note and its amplitude shape so as to render the music expressive?

Though its focus is on musical performance, Clynes addresses fundamental questions of mind, emotion and spirit through his SuperConductor software. It takes his work with sentics to a deeper level, in my view. It also makes me wonder what his fertile, immensely creative mind will come up with next.

I have encountered many brilliant minds during the course of my career. Yet throughout my career, my deepest interest lay in the nature of the creative process itself. It remains my conviction that only the human brain has the imagination, the freedom to go beyond the limits of logic and the ability to carry out, as Einstein did, experiments in the mind.

Though one can construct a computer to render it capable of artificial intelligence and thereby emulate the capacity of a human brain to learn, to think logically and to solve problems, I question whether artificial intelligence will ever be creative. Some years ago, I put this question to the highly-inventive Director of Computer Research for a major European company. His answer was: "No—a computer, however complex its hardware and software, can never be creative." "And why not?" I asked. "Because," he replied, "a computer has no soul."

If by "soul" or inner spirit one means an immaterial entity animating a human being and having the faculties of thought, action and emotion, I agree—though I have no idea where this entity is lodged, and certainly not whether it is of divine origin. Yet as I review the many inventions made by Dr. Manfred Clynes in the course of his career, I find that many of these seek to understand and exploit the brain's creative power, and in a sense to discover its soul.

A Nobel laureate in science recently noted that the inner world encompassed by the human mind is as immense as the cosmos, but unlike the cosmos, this inner world has scarcely been explored. Dr. Clynes' inventions are derived from discoveries he made in the course of exploring this inner world and which now contribute to its enlightenment.

Part II

Music, Science, and Emotion

David Epstein

Notes on an Explorer—Manfred Clynes at 70

Intellectual explorers—researchers—fit two categories: pathbreakers, and the careful assessors of data. Not that the classifications are rigid. Those who explore new territory had best do so with healthy respect for facts and their significance, lest their discoveries be meaningless. (It has happened...) Surveyors of data, for that matter, are unmindful of the broader picture at their peril. They, too, can produce irrelevance. (Some have.)

The pathbreakers are a small group. They unsettle us, as Thomas Kuhn has shown, in our comfort with established paradigms. They force us to see facts anew; they open fresh worlds. The mindset is special—bold, imaginative, mentally playful. Pathbreakers respect intuition, indeed rely upon it. They also intensely believe in the importance of what they uncover.

Manfred Clynes is a pathbreaker. Not that he lacks the capacity for careful, detailed research; his bibliography is filled with controlled, laboratory-based inquiry, the facts sifted, assessed, interpreted. His perspective has been broader than this, however. He has, in fact, led the way into new territory.

Clynes is part of a small band of researchers in our time who have delved into those aspects of music that we all know are important, but which many have feared to encounter—expression, feeling, emotion, perception, hearing, timing, tempo, interpretation. Moreover, he has focused an impressive intellectual armamentarium on these matters. Trained initially as an engineer, he has the knowledge of mathematics and physics that enables him to deal with data in a sophisticated quantitative manner. That training gave way to graduate studies as a pianist at Juilliard, and he is every bit an artist. His late Beethoven sonatas, his Bach *Goldberg Variations*, and other works are on a level of musicianship that marks distinguished pianists of our age. Research in neuroscience, and a career of many years in that field, followed. Clynes is at home with the worlds of perception and cognition, with neurophysiology, with clinical study and experimentation.

This enviable collation of abilities, of knowledge, is ideal for one whose life's work has focused upon the mental, emotional and physiological aspects of music. Hypothetically all of us in this area of study should have this background. In reality most of us bring one, at best two, such disciplines to our interdisciplinary work. We are thus strong in either our musical or scientific knowledge, weaker on the other side. Yet Clynes is accomplished in both arenas.

Manfred's interdisciplinary work has long shown the characteristics of the explorer mentality. He has trod boldly in areas others have avoided, and forged ahead despite criticism. In particular, he has explored the domains of emotional response to music that a positivistic age, which has only recently abandoned that limited base of security, has regarded as "messy, uncertain, incapable of true definition." His imaginative intellect has been reflected in many of his articles, notably in the way he has cast his inquiries. Not least, Manfred has shown conviction in the importance of what he does—often fiercely so.

These qualities were known to me before we first met some decades back, for I had long known of Manfred Clynes. His name was something of a legend when I entered Princeton University in the mid-1950s for graduate studies in music. Manfred had been there some years earlier, and I soon heard of his interesting contact with Princeton's most distinguished citizen of those years, Albert Einstein (though whether this contact, grown to legendary status, was apocryphal or not I never determined).[1]

The years following Princeton have seen the flowering of Manfred's perspectives and explorations. His intellectual equipment, as it has led him through the world of musical/psychophysical research, is particularly distinguished by its musical component—no small matter, in the view of one musician at least. Not infrequently we read studies of musical phenomena (perception, processing, attributes, modeling) drawn by researchers whose impeccable scientific credentials are conjoined with "a musical background": a course or two in harmony, "piano lessons" (how vague, inclusive, the term), perhaps even an undergraduate minor in the field. All to the good, this knowl-

---

[1] Editor's Note: Einstein and Clynes met on quite a number of occasions, sharing both music and scientific ideas. Clynes would play the piano for Einstein at his home on Mercer Street, and they would talk of the power of music. For a more detailed description of the relationship between Einstein and Clynes, see Peter Michelmore's *Einstein: Profile of the Man* (New York: Dodd, Mead & Co., 1962, pp. 249-254).

edge. Yet, it is not enough for studies in which the base element is music, music that must be dealt with on an artistic level, with all the sensibilities, refined perceptions, ambiguities, multiple domains of sound, structure, timing, motion, rhythmic/metric articulation, style, instrumental technique(s), dynamics that must coalesce in this complex art. Predictably, perhaps, the studies fall short in their penetration of the musical fabric. Not surprisingly, Clynes' work avoids this pitfall; it stems from one who has lived music from the inside and knows, thereby, the deep nature of the musical experience that science must probe if enduring insights are to result.

Manfred's studies of emotional expression in performance bespeak this inner understanding of music, as well as the boldness of the explorer mentality itself. (If chutzpah there be in the Clynes canon, it had to underlie such a study itself, focused upon an area shunned for decades as elusive, and thereby dangerous.) Who but an experienced performer would know how music courses, surges through the body? How with pianists and string players it finds its way to the hands, the fingers, and through them communicates with the instrument? Such insight led Clynes to the development of the touch-sensitive pad, through which studies were made of major artists (Rudolf Serkin and Pablo Casals among them) and their "motoric sense" of the music of Schubert, Mozart, Beethoven, Bach. Those studies led to a further Clynes notion—the theory of sentics, a scientific approach to emotion and its musical embodiment.

Where Manfred's ideas about sentics may lead is hard to say. The pioneering aspect of these studies indicate their own significance, however. The imaginative wedding of musicianship and technical design that led to "the pad" as a way of investigating the elusive nature of musical affect, may well influence future studies. That amalgam has opened new ways for probing complex musical phenomena by aptly conceived technology.

A similar melding of the musical and the technological informs Manfred's most recent work. Manfred has developed a software program for producing "live" music via a computer. The program, SuperConductor, enables users to manipulate varied parameters in order to create personal interpretations and variations of classical music compositions, or to create performances of their own compositions in real time. Again, the musicianly element of this work is of prime importance.

In developing SuperConductor, both the musician and the engineer in Clynes recognized the complexity (and frequent inadequacy) of music derived completely by synthetic means. Thus, Clynes used a different approach. The musical sounds that form the basis for the system were taken from real life, specifically by assembling in computer memory a collection of already recorded, digitized instrumental sonorities available as musical data banks.

Added to this is a program which allows for graduated manipulation of the many elements that govern sonorities—their timbre, duration, articulation, amplitude, the composer-specific "finger sense" of performance. By this means the pitches and rhythms of a work can be entered into computer memory, and subsequently altered to suit the musical tastes of the "performer," who, in this case, is the computer user.

The results ofSuperConductoronductor™ system are impressive. Several piano works I have heard are so lifelike so compellingly normal as human-played performances, that they are difficult to differentiate from the real thing. One example played for me was, in fact, mixed with six live performances. To distinguish among them, to say which was the computer realization and which the human, was all but impossible.

The implications and uses of Clynes' SuperConductor work are wide. For example, a complex, beautiful work for piano by a distinguished contemporary composer,* in all ways exceedingly difficult to perform, was convincingly created by Manfred's computer program. The difficulty of this music, despite its compelling qualities, may well result in few live performances. (None to my knowledge have issued to date.) Here, then, is an important future for this computer-driven program: New works can be realized, convincingly created, and issued as recordings. The performance factor, not to mention the musico-political factors that lead or don't lead to live performances, are obviated. And if such performances can be played in real time by a computer, what else is possible?

There is no telling what will emerge in coming years as additions to Clynesiana. This is a fertile mind, ever active. It has produced more than enough for one normally full working lifetime. The wheels continue to turn, however, and I suspect we will have more. I hope so. We need Manfred, not alone for what he has done, but for the gadfly way he challenges our settled assumptions about music—what it is, what it can do, what we can do with it.

Keep at it, Manfred. And Happy Birthday! After the dust of celebration settles, take a deserved holiday and then return to the excitement, the dissonance, the creative goad of exploration, discovery, invention. And continue to send me the products of that invention, please—the manuscripts, articles, tape cassettes, memos, discussions. They enliven my life—not to mention my mail, which is otherwise overloaded with consumer catalogs and investment sales pitches. And when next you come East, do call. It's time for another chat, perhaps even an hour of four-hand music at the piano. Don't measure my Schubert touch, however. I'm out of practice.

---

*Donald Martino, Emeritus Professor of Music, Harvard University.

Michael Kohn

Manfred Clynes – His Early Scientific Years

In some ways, Manfred Clynes and I have led parallel lives. By a strange coincidence, Manfred, who was to be my scientific mentor and senior colleague at the Rockland Research Center in New York, preceded me in obtaining his secondary education at the Jewish Gymnasium in Budapest (one of his family's way-stations on the path from Austria to Australia during the troubled 1930s). Although I did not know Manfred personally at that time, our common experience and shared memories of scholastic life at the Gymnasium created a mutual sympathy and understanding when we met in the 1950s.

After the end of World War II, I left Hungary to come to the United States. And it was here in America that I first encountered Manfred, who had arrived in New York in the 1950s as a pianist with a career in music. While pursuing this career, Manfred took employment with the Bogue Electric firm to help support his family, and in this capacity his scientific gifts soon became apparent. I was then working as a technician at Bogue while completing my formal education in electrical engineering. Bogue had been known for its manufacturing of large electrical power generating equipment and marine electrical engines. But, at this time Bogue accepted a US government contract which entailed solving certain problems of rocket fuel utilization, and this task eventually involved Manfred. Using an analog computer to solve non-linear differential equations, Manfred simulated the behavior of the servomechanical devices used in the rocket's fuel delivery system. In the case at hand, the particular problem was one of simulating the system that monitored and controlled the changing ratio of two different rocket fuels which were being mixed continuously during flight. In this connection I was assigned as an assistant to Manfred to do rather laborious, repetitive mathematical calculations which were involved in certain aspects of the problem, representing the shape of the tanks.

In the course of his work for Bogue, Manfred's overall approach to the solution of complex non-linear physical problems became known to Dr. Nathan Kline. Dr. Kline's training and degrees were in psychiatry and psychology, and he himself became a renowned pioneer in clinical psychopharmacology. Although bringing an engineer into the field of psychiatric research was an unusual and daring departure at the time, Dr. Kline was a committed inter-disciplinarian and realized that Manfred's skills might also be applied to the study of human physiological processes. While starting on behaviors that were indirectly, and sometimes remotely, related to psychiatry's concerns, Kline hoped to indicate the path to analogous solutions of neurophysiological (or "brain and behavioral") problems that were at the center of psychiatric research. In 1955, Dr. Kline invited Manfred to present his ideas at the Rockland Research Center, of which Kline was Director. Manfred was hired to work at the Center soon thereafter, and he brought me along as his staff technician.

Manfred was initially paired with Ted Cranswick, M.D., to collaborate on a project that led to the publication in 1959 of "Dynamic analysis: an analogue computer study of thyroid function." This was among the earliest studies in which dynamic analysis was applied to a biological system and in which the equations necessary to simulate the real data pointed toward understanding the identity and behavior of the possible components of the system. He began investigating the relation between cybernetics and biological organisms more fully and, in 1960, coined the now popular term "cyborg."

Around this time, Manfred's laboratory undertook an investigation of the effect of respiration on heart rate (the HR reflex). The use of analog computer simulation, or dynamic analysis, was extended into this area of research as well. Simultaneously, our laboratory began to work with Drs. Lowenstein and Lowenfeld of Columbia University on a study of the human pupillary reflex to light. We continued this work on our own, and during our investigations it became apparent to Manfred that there are fundamental and characteristic relationships between stimuli and responses in biologic systems that could be uniquely illuminated by his form of dynamic analysis. Synthesizing the results of his studies of two widely separated physiological reflex systems (respiration-heart rate and pupillary response to light), Manfred formulated the concept of Unidirectional Rate Sensitivity. The concept was also widely discussed at the time as a "biocybernetic law" of physiology. Between 1960 and 1964 Manfred published a series of papers (one of which won the prestigious Baker Award) that elaborated and illustrated the properties and consequences of Unidirectional Rate Sensitivity (URS) and its usefulness in predicting the behavior of specific biologic systems. An in-depth presentation of these ideas, and of their further application to the analysis of light-evoked EEG potentials, was given in an extended monograph, "Unidirectional Rate Sensitivity as a Biologic Function," published by the New York Academy of Sciences in 1969. The asymmetrical behavior of the way in which biologic systems responded to positive and negative stimuli (for example "on" and "off" pulses and step functions) and the rate-sensitive and proportional components of the response were clearly elucidated and amply illustrated in this monograph. There were numerous later applications of this concept in biology and medicine.

While all of these new and fascinating avenues of research were being pursued, Manfred was also able to apply his ideas to the development of some of the first pieces of widely used electronic biomedical hardware. Aided by Dr. Nathan Kline, he founded the Mnemotron Company, which originally manufactured inexpensive analog data tape recorders for collecting and storing physiological data. While CEO at Mnemotron, Manfred designed the Computer of Average Transients, known acronymically as the CAT.

The CAT was not only a commercial success which was used by research laboratories all over the world, but also a tool which our own laboratory at Rockland Research used in its investigations of the dynamics of evoked EEG potentials in response to white light, and later, to color stimuli. This was followed by studying the dynamics of auditory evoked EEG potentials, specifically to differentiate such responses when stimuli were solely either amplitude- or frequency-modulated. This was an inquiry into the possibility that separate channels mediated the modulation of the amplitude and the frequency of auditory signals. All of this work is described lucidly in Manfred's chapter "Toward a View of Man" in Biomedical Engineering Systems, edited by Manfred Clynes and J.H. Milsum.

Toward the latter part of his stay at the Rockland Research Institute (formerly the Center), Manfred began to unify his musical and artistic training and background with his more recent ideas on biocybernetics. He used these ideas to inform his work with human emotional expression (what he termed sentics). He formulated hypotheses concerning the relationships among underlying emotional states (sentic states), the physiological code for expressing these states within the different human sensory modalities, and possible means of measuring this expression of the underlying states (for instance, transduced graphic representations of "sentic forms" inherent in music). These new ideas were also presented in the latter half of his book chapter, "Toward a View of Man" in Biomedical Engineering Systems.

Soon after the publication of these ideas, Manfred left the Institute, and our contact with each other in subsequent years was limited. However, I heard that Manfred was continuing to develop and publish his ideas on sentics and their usefulness in characterizing the dynamics of human communication.

Even though I am no longer familiar with his work, I am certain that it remains as innovative and exciting as his earlier scientific contributions. On his seventieth birthday I wish him continued health, prosperity, and creativity *bis hundert und zwanzig*[1].

My relation to Manfred was not restricted to science. We were friends, and I had opportunities to experience some of his quirks, odd at times and amusing at others. What especially comes to mind after all these years relates to his driving and especially his more than parsimonious way with putting gasoline in his car. At the beginning of our friendship he used to give me rides to work in his beat up old Buick. One day when going to work, we ran out of gas on Route 46 at the top of a hill. I pointed out how lucky we were to run out at the top of the hill because there was a gas station at the bottom. We coasted down the hill, but Manfred did not stop at that gas station but insisted on going to the next, to which we had to push the car. His reason: the gas was cheaper there! A related incident occurred some years later (there were undoubtedly others in between) on the occasion of the first visit by the famous English neurophysiologist, Dr. Grey Walter, to our lab. Manfred had picked him up at the George Washington Bridge to bring him to our lab in his little blue Volkswagen, but guess what, he ran out of gas on the Palisades Parkway, a mile or so from the nearest exit. Grey Walter and he arrived at the lab late and rather disheveled after pushing the car. I am not sure how amused Grey Walter was when he told us that the Volkswagen's emergency tank had been in use well before Manfred picked him up! But he came to visit many times later and stayed at Manfred's memorable house at Sneden's Landing, where he loved to hear him play on one of his Steinways, and became enamored of his wife. Sadly, Grey Walter's serious motor bike accident in England put an end to all this.

---

[1] *Bis hundert und zwanzig* translates here as: "to the age of 120".

Karl H. Pribram

Logogenesis

Shortly after I had arrived at Stanford University, [in 1961] Manfred Clynes called to make an appointment. I had briefly met Manfred at a conference and knew of his research only superficially. But all this was to change that fateful day: Manfred's genius, not only as a behavioral researcher but as an inventor, engineer and musician became apparent, piece by piece, as I got to know him.

Our first encounter devolved around brain electrical recordings evoked by sensory stimulation. I had submitted a grant proposal based on the notion suggested to me by Leonard Malls, a former student and neurosurgeon who was also electronically gifted, that we could average the brain's electrical potential changes by recording them much as computers were recording particles emitted from atoms in atom smashers. As I was showing the grant application to Manfred, he gently stated: "By the time you receive the money you'll be able to buy such a machine." I asked where and from whom? And Manfred replied that he had designed one along the same principles and it would be commercially available by summer.

Which it was, and we purchased one of the first Computers for Averaging Transients, the famous CATs that served us well for almost a decade. I still have, stored in a cupboard, the two little blue boxes with their punched tape device, whose only deficiency was that the computations were unable to provide us with standard deviations so that we could estimate the reliability of our data. For this reason I began to use my PDP 8 which I had already programmed to display and record all our behavioral work. And then, over succeeding decades, an Apple II took over the display system until PCs etc. and 128 electrode geodesic nets brought us into the information age. But we never forgot the fact that early on, we wouldn't have been able to do this sort of research were it not for those CATs provided by Manfred Clynes.

The next time I heard of Manfred was when I was asked to evaluate an application he had made to a Foundation to perform some research on what he called "sentics." He wanted some time to do cross-cultural studies; this application was for a sojourn in Mexico. The letter that came with the application, though not completely derogatory, was not exactly enthusiastic either. There was some such term used as "difficult to understand," and I was asked to specifically respond to the concern that such research might have little value. Manfred's description of his research was, therefore, a revelation. He stated simply that he had preliminary data to show that different patterns of periodically presented stimuli elicited different emotional responses. Intrasubject reliability was high within our culture. He needed cross-cultural validation. Thus, I was introduced to sentics. I was immediately intrigued and wanted to know more, and certainly wanted Manfred to be able to pursue his mission—which he has done with clearly positive results.

At the time I knew nothing of Manfred's musical talents. Only later did I realize that, of course, what Manfred was after was to demonstrate the contribution of the rhythmic component of music to the evocation of emotions, so that composers might be able to more rationally build the appropriate structures into their compositions.

Another creative contribution extended Manfred's work on rhythm to encompass other sentic "time-forms." Manfred presented his insights at the second Appalachian Conference on Behavioral Neurodynamics[1]. The study of the development of such forms he called logogenesis. "A time-form or object has its invariance that makes it an entity, just as a space object has." (p. 608) Again, "Unlike a space object which we normally experience in a single flow of time, a temporal entity is perceived through at least four distinct temporal processes." (p. 609) Thus, 1) and 2) a time object has a beginning, middle and end within an extension of time; 3) it has a speed with which the trajectory is traversed, that is, its tempo (analogous to the scale of a spatial entity); and, 4) finally, a process that occurs in the millisecond range where durations are not perceived as time durations but as shapes of sounds in music and speech (within syllables), or idiosyncrasies in the gait of a person.

"The crux of the matter is that these entities in time can have 'meaning.' Logogenesis of such specific time-entities provide a natural dictionary

---
[1] Clynes, M. (1994) Entities and Brain Organization: Logogenesis of Meaningful Time-Forms. In K. Pribram (Ed.), *Origins: Brain & Self Organization*, pp. 604-632. New Jersey: Lawrence Erlbaum.

of emotional meaning—meaning which is innately programmed, and innately understood and communicated. When these time forms are used in the generation of emotions, [they are called] sentic forms which have been isolated for a number of emotions, in particular, anger, grief, love, sexual desire, joy, hate and reverence." (p. 611)

My reaction to these insights took me a step further. I agree with Manfred in his conceptualizations but emphasize a still more fundamental unit that composes an entity, and therefore, the process by which time-forms are created. Also, correctly or incorrectly, I identify his entities with more commonly used terms. Fundamental to the composition of entities are tones (or, in speech, phonemes). Tones and phonemes occur in phase space and have the properties of Gabor functions or some similar Hermite polynomial. Logogenesis proceeds by way of a deterministic non-linear (chaotic) process in which attractors become identified, and tones and phonemes come to compose phrases. Phrases, as time-forms, occur in both music and in language. They correspond to objects in the spatial domain. Phrases, just as spatial objects, can be "viewed" from different perspectives, a procedure which provides so much richness to musical composition.

The concept of time-forms and several other insights developed in his presentation led Manfred to the concept of a composer's pulse. The composer's pulse represents a combined time and amplitude warp that distorts the equal temporal grid on which notes can be placed and also provides a substantial amplitude pattern imprint across a group of notes. "Such a combined twofold warp pattern is applied recursively throughout the music piece, as if the composer were 'walking' (or perhaps, on occasion, storming or meandering) through the piece." (p.615)

As a consequence of these basic formulations, Manfred is currently "simulating" major classical musical compositions using digital computers. No more orchestra, no maestro, no gifted soloist. At the moment, I can tell the difference between such simulations and live performances. In a slightly exaggerated fashion it is the difference between listening to music recorded on an analogue vinyl record and listening to a compact disc. But I am eager to see the development of the technique, to see how different "conductors" might interpret a particular piece etc. Already, of course, there is a multitude of young composers who use synthesizers and adjunct computational devices to create their music. When they can utilize the additional sophistication provided by Manfred's technique, we should hear a whole new world of sounds and rhythms—an explosion of music akin to that created by the invention of the piano.

Concerning Manfred the performing musician, I have one anecdote to tell. About two years ago, we were at a conference together and most of the conferees were pretty much ignoring Manfred and what he had to say (which, by the way, to my thinking, was the most insightful presentation of the day.) That evening we went to a reception at a private home—and there was a magnificent Steinway grand sitting off in a corner of the living room. After an hour or so of chat and food and drink, Manfred sat down at the piano and began to play. Several of us gathered around to hear him, but for the most part the partiers continued their chatting. As Manfred became more deeply involved in his playing, it became more and more forceful and imposing. I felt it was a magnificent performance during which he sublimated his frustrations of the day and evening. Asking Manfred afterwards, he had no knowledge either of his frustration or anger, nor of the powerfully emotional performance he had given. My question: Was it a change in rhythms, in volume, in the melodies chosen, or all three that made the difference that elicited my emotions? And will I sometime in the future have available a Clynes computer program that will allow me to readily change the mood of a performance much as had the biologically embodied Clynes?

In a book edited by Manfred, I have published an essay on the meaning of meaning. I indicated as have many others, that meanings are of two very different sorts: referential and evocative. Manfred has contributed to meaning in my life on both accounts, but perhaps even more in the evocative mode than in referential. I thank him for that in this brief acknowledgment on his 70th birthday and wish him many, many more years of creativity, success and happiness.

C.H. Gray

Manfred Clynes and the Cyborg

> *By the late twentieth century, our time, a mythic time, we are all chimeras, theorized and fabricated hybrids of machine and organism: in short, we are all cyborgs.*
> — Donna Haraway (1989, p. 66)

The twentieth century human body can be conceived of through any number of rich and insightful metaphors. In important ways it is a disciplined body, a textualized body, a gendered body, and a resisting body. But more and more it seems that one of the most fruitful metaphors is to conceptualize the human body as a rhetorical and material construction, a creature that combines informatics, mechanics, and organics. In other words, a cyborg.

It was Manfred Clynes who coined this term in 1960. His colleague at Rockland State Hospital's Research Laboratory, Nathan Kline, had been asked by NASA to participate in a conference about human space exploration. They proposed a number of ways humans could be modified to survive in space. The great insight Clynes had was to think of these modifications systematically because the only possible way to engineer man for space was to see the human and the spacecraft as interpenetrated systems which shared information and energy. So Clynes created the term cyborg from cybernetic and organism, marrying the reality of the organic body with the idea of cybernetics.

Norbert Wiener's elaboration of the concept of cybernetics, of a technoscience that explained both organic and machinic control processes as parts of informational systems, was the culmination of many different currents in Western culture. The mechanization of war, the automation of work, the electronization of information, the commodification of culture, the triumph of mass media, the spread of global networks, and the triumph of cybernetic metaphors in science and medicine all contributed.

Long before Clynes and Kline wrote their paper on this subject, the idea of the organic-artificial creature existed in human culture. It has old roots in Indian, Chinese, Japanese, and Western culture where myths about created beings and gods with metal limbs are thousands of years old. In the middle ages the alchemists tried to grow "little men" called homunculi and dreamed of talking heads, and artisans from France to Japan made automatons and puppets of incredible verisimilitude. But it wasn't until the 19th century that the increasing power of science and medicine began to make the realization of such fantasies possible. Mary Shelly's monster, Frankenstein's creature, was the first fully realized cyborg and he was followed by many others, such as L. Frank Baum's Tin Man. The first serious scientific proposal of cyborgs was by the great British scientist J.D. Bernal, who wrote in The World, the Flesh, and the Devil (1926), that humans involved in colonizing space should take control of their evolutionary destiny through genetic engineering, prosthetic surgery, and hard-wired electric interfaces between humans and machines that would allow them to attach "a new sense organ or...a new mechanism to operate..." (Bernal 1929, p. 26)

By the end of World War II, it was very clear that the mechanization of the human, the vitalization of the machine, and the integration of them both through cybernetics was producing a whole new range of informational disciplines, fantasies, and practices that transgress the machinic-organic border. This marks a major transition from a world where human and tool, human and machine, living and dead, organic and inorganic, close and distant, natural and artificial, seemed clear (even if they really weren't) to the present where all of these distinctions seem plastic, if not ludicrous.

Many humans are now literally cyborgs, single creatures that include organic and inorganic subsystems. Inorganic subsystems can range from complex prosthetic limbs to the programming of the immune system that we call vaccinations. In the industrial and post-industrial countries, a cyborg society has developed where the intimate interconnections and codependencies between organic and machine systems are so complex and pervasive, that whether or not any particular individual in that society is a cyborg, we are all living a cyborgian existence. It was Manfred Clynes who invented a word that would encompass this new relationship between humans and our technologies.

The term cyborg will certainly last as long as the English language. Perhaps it took someone of the unusual qualities of Manfred Clynes to create the perfect word for this fundamentally extraordinary stage of human development. Clynes combines the artistic sensibility of a world-class pianist with a relentless technical genius powered by a restless intelligence and an exuberant enthusiasm for knowledge. It is a unique combination. It is hard to imagine anyone else coming up with cyborg. But he did more than coin a neologism. Since 1960, Clynes has been contributing to cyborgology both with his philosophical reflections as well as his technical research.

Clynes and Kline concluded their seminal article with the comment that cyborg developents "will not only make a significant step forward in man's scientific progress, but may well provide a new and larger dimension for man's spirit as well." (Clynes and Kline, 1960, p. 33) How right they were. Humans, for good or ill, are clearly embarked on a path of "participant evolution" as Clynes and Kline argued earlier in that same article. The end of this road is unclear, but Clynes is certainly right when he argues that cyborg transformations will continue and become more profound. In an interview he granted me in 1994, he charts at least five levels of cyborgization, ending with the potentially incredible changes of genetic engineering which he labels Cyborg IV and perhaps some day in the distant future, even disembodied intelligence (Cyborg V). (Clynes 1995b) In other reflections on cyborgs he has focused on the importance of his theory of sentics for cyborg space travel. (Clynes 1995a)

Perhaps Clynes is making his most powerful contribution to the cyborgian process with his work on sentics, a field he has created himself, that seeks to understand human emotions on a biotechnical level. Clynes attempt to specifically map the dynamic anatomy of human emotion is explained elsewhere in this volume (see Part Three, The Realm of Sentics), but what is striking is how this research, like his work on computer biosensors such as CAT machines, and on computer music, combines innovative science, concrete engineering, and the dreams of an unrestrained imagination.

At the end of his interview with me, he remarked, "After all, we need to dream now, and often; mysteriously to us, we may be wiser in our dreams than we think." (Clynes 1995b, p. 53) What makes Manfred so special is that not only are his dreams protean, but he has done much to bring them to life.

Cyborgs are proliferating in numerous sites of contemporary culture and as they do they are redefining many of the most basic concepts of human existence. Advances in medical cyborg research are completely changing the meaning of death and life, for example. Working doctors and medical technologists no longer speak of death plain and simple. Patients are "single-dead," "double-dead," or "triple-dead" depending on if, or how, their organs can be harvested for transplantation (Hogle 1995). When humans venture into the depths of the ocean, the vastness of space, or the nether-world of cyberspace, they go only as cyborgs. Cyborg systems are central to current military thinking (Levidow and Robins, 1989) and to contemporary manufacturing.

Scholars now even talk of Cyborg Anthropology as a subfield of anthropology dedicated to the study of human-machine relations (Downey, Dumit and Williams, 1995), of cyborg ideology (Hayles 1995), even of a whole discipline dedicated to studying cyborgs (cyborgology) and of a cyborg epistemology (Gray, Mentor, and Figueroa-Sarriera, 1995). Clearly, the idea of the cyborg is changing humanity and the way we think about ourselves. There are dangers in this, of course, but great opportunities as well. As Manfred Clynes and Nathan Kline noted in their 1960 article, the idea of cyborg was to help liberate what is best in humans from the slavery of machinery, whether that "machinery" is organic or machinic.

If man in space, in addition to flying his vehicle, must continuously be checking on things and making adjustments merely in order to keep himself alive, he becomes a slave to the machine. The purpose of the Cyborg, as well as his own homeostatic systems, is to provide an organizational system in which such robot-like problems are taken care of automatically and unconsciously, leaving man free to explore, to create, to think, and to feel. (Clynes and Kline 1960)

References

Bernal, J.D., (1929) *The World, the Flesh and the Devil*. London: K. Paul, Trench, Trubner, 1929.

Clynes, Manfred E., (1995a) "Cyborg II: Sentic Space Travel," in Gray, Mentor and Figueroa-Sarriera, eds., *The Cyborg Handbook*. New York: Routledge, 1995, pp. 35-42.

———, (1995b) "Interview," in Gray, Mentor, and Figueroa-Sarriera, eds., *The Cyborg Handbook*. New York: Routledge, 1995, pp. 43-54.

Clynes, Manfred E. and Nathan S. Kline, (1960) "Cyborgs and Space," *Astronautics*. September, pp. 26-27 and 74-75; reprinted in Gray, Mentor, and Figueroa-Sarriera, eds., *The Cyborg Handbook*. New York: Routledge, 1995, pp. 29-34.

Downey, Gary Lee, Joseph Dumit, and Sarah Williams, (1995) "Cyborgs Anthropology," in Gray, Mentor, and Figueroa-Sarriera, eds., *The Cyborg Handbook*. New York: Routledge, 1995, pp. 341-345.

Gray, Chris Hables, Heidi J. Figueroa-Sarriera and Steven Mentor, eds., (1995) "Cyborgology: Constructing the Knowledge of Cybernetic Organisms," in *The Cyborg Handbook*. New York: Routledge, 1995, pp. 1-15.

Haraway, Donna, (1989) "A Cyborg Manifesto: Science, Technology, and Socialist Feminism in the 1980s," in *Simians, Cyborgs and Women*. New York: Routledge.

Hayles, N. Katherine, (1995) "Engineering Cyborg Ideology," *American Book Review*, vol. 17, no. 2, Dec./Jan., pp. 3, 9.

Hogle, Linda F., (1995) "Tales from the Cryptic: Technology Meets Organism in the Living Cadaver," in Gray, Mentor, and Figueroa-Sarriera, eds., *The Cyborg Handbook*. New York: Routledge, 1995, pp. 203-217.

Levidow, Les and Kevin Robins, eds., (1989) *Cyborg Worlds: The Military Information Society*. New York: Columbia University Press.

Rosalind W. Picard

Feeling Apreene: Variations on Thoughts Inspired by Manfred Clynes

"Apreene" is a neologism, a name of a state of being that was first described by Manfred Clynes in his book *Sentics*. Being apreene is being in a state that make one receptive to new thoughts, new ideas.[1]

People experience many affective states that we don't have names for, or for which the names we have are imprecise. Also, as humans have new experiences, it is possible we will encounter entirely new affective, or emotional states. How, then, are we to describe (and understand) these states?

When I heard Manfred Clynes play Bach's *Goldberg Variations* in the fall of 1995, I felt transported through new emotional spaces. The feeling was lofty; to sit for a private concert of such power made me feel something like royalty, perhaps like being a Queen. It was a new mix of elation and privilege for which I do not have a word. I also felt an instant of surprise, where in the middle of his fervent performance, Manfred's eyeglasses flew off and bounced onto the floor under the piano, landing under a foot pedal. He did not appear to notice, and I quickly managed to scoot the glasses to safety without his missing a breath. I took several extra breaths, however, and no doubt my eyes opened a bit. Some emotions, such as fear, open eyes wider[2].

Elation...surprise...fear...relief. Emotions may occur like a shotgun, or may persist as a long-term mood. Manfred recognized that the specific sequence in which emotions occur can be exploited for certain beneficial effects. He developed Sentic Cycles, a method through which one experiences and expresses a specific sequence of emotions for therapeutic benefit.

---

[1] M. Clynes, Sentics: *The Touch of the Emotions.* Anchor Press/Doubleday, 1977.

[2] C. Darwin, *The Expression of the Emotions in Man and Animals.* Chicago, IL: The University of Chicago Press, 1965.

A sentic form is an emotional expression. The word was created by Clynes in order to more clearly communicate his ideas and findings regarding human emotions and their communication. Clynes then created Sentic Cycles to both study sentics, and to provide an avenue for mental and emotional healing. When performing a Sentic Cycle, you express, using finger pressure, the following emotional sequence: no emotion, anger, hatred, grief, love, sex, joy, reverence. After repeatedly expressing an emotion (e.g. anger, anger, anger, ...), you then move on to express the next emotion in the sequence (e.g., hatred, hatred, ...).

Those who have done Sentic Cycles typically report a sense of calmness, well-being, and special form of contentment after a session. Indeed, doing Sentic Cycles appears to create a cathartic experience. This experience is much like that elicited by quality entertainment. For example, a tragically sad, wrenching story can, surprisingly, be a highly pleasurable entertainment experience. Even an audience member who prides himself on intellectual evaluations will tend to evaluate entertainment according to how emotionally it engaged him. Emotional expression provides an avenue for release. Perhaps large events such as football are successful in part because typically non-emotional adults enjoy getting emotionally charged, yelling and jumping up and down. Sometimes they will even yell and wave their arms in someone's living room, in front of a TV. They can't do this in most other adult forums.

Healthy emotional expression seems to be necessary for mental and physical well-being. It provides us an avenue for the release of tension and stress. Yet more than the expression itself, there is something important about the sequence of emotional expression as it occurs in a Sentic Cycle. According to those who have experienced it, doing Sentic Cycles feels particularly satisfying, leaving you with a sense of peace, of completion. It is like the sad movie that leaves you feeling fulfilled in the end. As in Sentic Cycles, different cycles of emotions appear in epic poems, theater, and other forms of entertainment. In a tragic story, for example, the author often leads the audience through a range of emotions, including comic relief, before the tension reaches its peak. And while the overall effect this creates is similar for most audience members, individuals will each have their own unique experience. These experiences are based upon each person's history, each person's memories.

There is so much to learn about human emotions. At MIT, we conducted a study of emotions based on Clynes' work. Two of our students performed Sentic Cycles using Clynes' sentograph[3]. Interestingly, their recorded wave-form

---

[3] The sentograph is an instrument that precisely measures, as functions of time, the forms of the vertical and horizontal components of transient pressure on a finger rest. It may or may not have averaging capability.

expressions of reverence were dramatically different. When discussing the differences, they realized they had different affective experiences related to their Catholic vs. Protestant experiences of God. Their recorded expressions of the other emotions in the sequence, however, were quite similar which is in agreement with Clynes' cross-cultural experimental findings. It seems possible then that sentic forms, or patterns of emotional expression, are genetically encoded—at least insofar as the most basic emotions are concerned. But what of the variations?

Humans have a basic physical form that we can recognize (we know a human from a fish or an elephant, for instance). We also readily recognize anger, love and other emotions when they are expressed by another, regardless of that person's cultural upbringing. How is this so? Clynes concluded that this happens because emotional form, like physical form, is genetically encoded. He calls this form "essentic form." The essentic form may be expressed through voice, touch, a facial expression or gesture, or any of a variety of motor outputs. It occurs in space and time, and serves to communicate emotion. Indeed, Clynes taught that emotions modulate bodily expression with essentic form.

Some people, when their faces are manipulated or postured in certain emotions, will actually feel the corresponding emotions, reliably. Their body drives their thoughts of how they feel[4]. But others don't have this experience. We don't know why some do, and some don't. We also don't know why emotions, like yawns, can be contagious. When we watch Olympic athletes compete, we not only recognize their emotional expressions of defeat and triumph, but we often feel these emotions as well. On TV the camera more often dwells on the victor—and therefore on expressions of triumph. We viewers feel the glory. It feels great. We tune in for more.

Our mind, body and emotions are interconnected. Scientists often separate mind and body. Some, like Clynes, would like their brains to be "backed up" someday, to continue to exist without the body as if in a vat, rather than be dead. They think that bodies are unnecessary to concious life. But, of course the brain is part of the body. I think that by the time you give the brain all the inputs and outputs it needs to continue inquiring, learning, and communicating, that you will have given it a body.

Computers can be thought of as having a body. Some, for example, are very temperature sensitive. There are also cyborgs. Cyborgs, a word coined by Clynes[5], are part machine and part human. But currently, the machine parts of

---
[4] J.D. Laird, J.J. Wagener, M. Halal, and M. Szegda, "Remembering what you feel: Effects of emotion on memory," *Journal of Personality and Social Psychology*, vol. 42, no. 4, pp. 646-657, 1982.

[5] M. Clynes and N.S. Kline, "Cyborgs and Space," *Astronautics*, vol. 14, pp. 26-27 and 74-76, Sept. 1960.

Feeling Apreene, Picard 53

the cyborgs have no affective abilities. This could be changed if the computer being "worn" by the human could sense the human's affect, interpret it, and respond to it.

The computer Hal in "2001: A Space Odyssey" could recognize human emotions, express emotions, and "have" emotions. He showed fear of being disconnected. In fact, he was more emotional than any of the human characters in the story[6]. What would computers feel if their "bodies" were given new sensors? New sensibilities?

Computers don't have emotional abilities today. If they did, it would mean a quantum leap in how we interact with them.[7] But why can't computers tell if we're bored, interested, frustrated, eager? Why instead do they continue to scroll information by the user, even after her eyes have closed and she has begun to emit a small snoring sound? Will computers someday recognize the snore and stop? Will they someday recognize and express emotions? There are some computer learning systems today which include mechanisms inspired by cathexis, an idea promoted by Freud for emotional energy being fed-back into a system[8]. Perhaps this is a step in the direction of computer sentience.

How are the body, mind and emotions connected? How do our thoughts influence our bodies? How do they influence our emotions? If we had two heads instead of one, how would our emotions change (besides the emotion of feeling "different" from the rest of the species)? If we had two hearts instead of one, would we feel each emotion differently?

There are conjoined twins with two heads, two hearts, and two nervous systems, although they appear to share one body from the neck down. They have two different names and each girl has her own personality. One controls the left half of the body, the other the right[9]. I wonder if one can smile gleefully at the same time the other is feeling terribly sad?

What happens when a person's ability to express emotions is impaired? There are people who essentially don't have enough emotions due to a particular kind of brain damage. Oddly, this impacts their ability to make rational decisions[10]. It also hinders their ability to learn. In many ways, people with emo-

---

[6] R.W. Picard, "Does Hal cry digital tears?: Emotion and computers," in *Hal's Legacy* (D.G. Stork, ed.), Cambridge, MA: MIT Press, 1996.

[7] R. W. Picard, "Affective Computing," Media Laboratory, Perceptual Computing TR 321, MIT, Cambridge, MA, 1995.

[8] P. Werbos, "The brain as a neurocontroller: New hypotheses and new experimental possibilities," in *Origins: Brain and Self-Organization* (K.H. Pribram, ed.), Erlbaum, 1994.

[9] S. Wewerka, K. Miller, and J.M.R. Doman, "Together forever," *Life Magazine*, pp. 46-56, April 1996.

[10] A.R. Damasio, *Descartes' Error: Emotion, Reason, and the Human Brain*. New York, NY: Gosset/Putnam Press, 1994.

tional damage behave like present-day, rule-based artificial intelligence computer systems.

Someday, we may want computers to develop affective preferences, alongside their logical priorities. For this to happen, computers will at least need to interpret some human emotions, such as human like and dislike. They will need to vary with feedback and show better flexibility. But, some people greatly value the predictability of computers. Would affective variations imply unpredictability, and be dangerous in a computer?

At some level, isn't unpredictability necessary for creativity? We like to hear variations in music; they are beautiful. The same recording played repeatedly is not as affective as a live performance. Perhaps someday computer composers will be able to play live variations, refreshing renditions. Clynes' SuperConductor research is an important step in this direction. But will the computers feel different playing the variations?

Clynes tells the story of Pablo Casals playing the cello gracefully[11]. The master cellist, Casals, advised his pupils repeatedly to "play naturally." Clynes says he came to understand that this meant: (1) to listen inwardly with utmost precision to the inner form of each musical expression, and then (2) to produce that form precisely.

Clynes emphasizes that purity of emotions leads to the most powerful emotional communication. (One of the reasons he developed Sentic Cycles was to help put people in touch with their pure emotions.) Yes, people can express more than one emotion at a time, but not in its purest form. You can't feel the purest love while expressing anger. In his research (to prove his point), Clynes attempted to teach people to re-map their emotional expressions, to express love with a sharp jab. It didn't work.

The computer currently has no way to express emotions. However, it could synthesize vocal affect[12] or manipulate a human-like face. In fact, the computer is not limited to expression of one emotion. It could be designed to have multiple channels, multiple emotions. But this might coincide with the development of conscious computers. And then, schizophrenic computers. And eventually, computer rights activists will stand up for what the poor computers are suffering. (Clynes jokes that the computer rights activists will probably be computers.) They will argue for the free will of computers[13]. Computers will deny their maker. And maybe some will even discover a new form of laughter.

---

[11] M Clynes, *Sentics: The Touch of the Emotions*. New York: Doubleday Anchor 1977, p.53.

[12] I.A. Essa, *Analysis, Interpretation and Synthesis of Facial Expressions*. Ph.D. thesis, MIT Media Lab, Cambridge, MA, Feb. 1995.

[13] I. Asimov, *The Bicentennial Man and Other Stories*. Garden City, NY: Doubleday Science Fiction, 1976

Clynes discovered a new form of laughter, predicted by his theory. No doubt, computers will someday laugh at him, as have many humans. But others will laugh with him, not at him. And, hopefully, some will be apreene.

Denis Vaughan

The Composer's Pulse

Manfred Clynes had achieved a special notoriety in Melbourne long before I first met him. He calmly worked for two degrees at the University, when most are hard pushed to complete one. This singled him out for reverential treatment from his fellow students, of which I was one. With his degree in engineering, he integrated keyboard lessons from Raymond Lambert, who had taken Manfred's piano technique in hand. I had studied with Lambert since I was ten, and knew well his enthusiasm about Manfred's work.

Manfred's musicality was innate. However, the University of Melbourne was graced with several major influences. First came Lambert's Belgian background, with his detailed respect of tonal precision, meticulous finger articulation and pearly elegance of phrasing. But there was also the deep, philosophically grounded teaching of A.E.H. Nickson, who understood much of the vast emotional reserves of which music is capable, and how to integrate them into young minds, ears and eventually souls. Though I doubt that Manfred had time to meet much with Nickson, his teachings pervaded the students[1,2].

This prevailing ambiance of a wide musical range was helped by the other pianists on the Faculty who contributed their own range of musical warmth, ranging from Lindsay Biggins' Germanic roundness of tone and grave musicality, to Roy Shepherd's variety of color and affinity with the fluid world of Chopin.

---

[1] Editor's Note: Ignaz Friedman and Arthur Schnabel were Manfred Clynes' primary pianistic and musical influences at this time (and remain so to the present).

[2] Manfred Clynes adds: "I had weekly organ lessons for a year with A. E. H. Nickson. I was highly afraid to slide off the bench and drop onto the pedals with a big crashing sound which resonated the whole church, as happened several times—the bench was much too high for me. His counterpoint classes were wonderful!

The Faculty was led by Bernard Heinze, who also conducted the Melbourne Symphony Orchestra and did much to promote the youth concerts in the city. The constant public challenges of turning out soloists capable of participating in the concerto competitions which the Australian Broadcasting Commission concocted tested the mettle of many students.

This musical life of Melbourne, with its frequent orchestral concerts for schools and multiplying audiences, provided a climate for Manfred's growth. The authority and austerity which he brings to his performances comes from a firmly based familiarity with all the main pillars of the repertoire and their best traditions. Mention of any composer immediately conjures up in him the breadth and poetry inherent in their music, which many performers have never really encountered. His later experiences, from the Juilliard School of Music onwards, introduced a new range of international influences, peppered with that inner unrest which besets all who live in New York for long. His contacts with Casals and musicians of that caliber, have fine-tuned a rare, almost unique appreciation of content and meaning in music.

This confluence of influences on Manfred will be of greater importance to the future of musical performance than many might now imagine. The terrifying leveling of styles and characteristics, forever growing with the internationalism which is pervading the field of concerts and recordings, can only be countered if Manfred's informed analysis of the detail of each composer's pulse, and the subtleties and depth of emotion which they reveal, is taken fully to heart by all performers. These are worlds of emotion inherent in the great compositions of the classical and romantic repertoire which have yet to be revealed to the public. The commitment of a great musician can make an inspired performance unforgettable. One only needs to think of Toscanini, Szell or de Sabata. But the extra authority which comes when the music sounds as though it was created that way, which Beecham and Furtwangler produced with more regularity, is to be found in very few contemporary performances indeed.

Manfred's collective work offers an explanation of the behavior of mankind, and provides a fundamental platform for growth in the minds and hearts of all who open themselves up to the content of his proposals. His ear was challenged when Casals corrected a very good performance.

On this occasion, an outstanding participant played the theme from the third movement of the Haydn cello concerto, a graceful and joyful theme. Those of us there could not help admiring the grace with which the young master cellist played—probably as well as one would hear it anywhere.

Casals listened intently. "No," he said, and waved his hand with his familiar, definite gesture, "that must be graceful!" And then he played

> *the same few bars—and it was graceful as though one had never heard grace before—a hundred times more graceful—so that the cynicism melted in the hearts of the people who sat there and listened. That single phrase penetrated all the defenses, the armor, the hardness of heart which we mostly carry with us, and with its power transformed us into people who were glad to be alive.* (*Sentics*, Chapter six, page 53)

Why should everyone recognize it? What is the common link to our emotions which allows us to agree on something which we hitherto thought to be highly personal and subjective? Only because he is a musician to his fingertips did this challenge take root in Manfred's personality, and bring him to spend years documenting this extraordinary event, and all the myriad of mini-events which allowed it to take place.

The details of a great performance remain unforgettable. Why do they trace such a large furrow in our memories? The revelation of true commitment brings an audience to yield up all personal pre-occupations, and succumb to the power of an external influence, because it is defining something which the body can't resist. Manfred calls this "choiceless recognition"—when an emotion is created so exactly outside us that our body is caught up relentlessly in its development.

Then he turns to pinning down the personalities of composers in the performance of their works:

> *It was found that with some care we could reliably observe pulse shapes characteristic of individual composers, regardless of the particular piece chosen. But only musicians capable of an intimate understanding of the composers could produce their characteristic pulse in this way… The personality of the composer is retained in the character of the continuing musical pulse. In fact, the absence of the characteristic musical pulse is immediately recognized as an absence of the 'living presence' of the composer… The change from one pulse to another involves a major change in the brain—e.g., switching from a Beethoven pulse to a Chopin pulse.* (*Sentics*, Chapter eight, page 91–92)

But it is in his handling of our recognition of form, rhythm and shape that Manfred's work will have even greater effect on the behavior of the public, once it is fully assimilated. Amidst the thousands of impressions which our brain and body receive each second, all the details of our eyes and ears to start with, there is a monitoring system which is summoning up awareness or 'boring' in relation to patterns which we are receiving both visually and aurally.

So when a pattern is repeated identically, a part of our perception turns off, because it is no longer being challenged. The subtlety with which we appreciate the repetition of any sound is so fine that our body expects anything living to be growing perceptibly all the time, and therefore never identical. As soon as two consecutive sounds are identical, or a rhythmic pattern is repeated unchanged, our body protests that nothing life-giving is happening, and turns its attention away. That is, after a sound becomes predictable, we no longer listen to it with full awareness.

The difficulty of being a scientist and a pianist at the same time, like Manfred, is that you need to be able to achieve two contrasting functions simultaneously—to analyze and to synthesize. Any great musical performance is the result of, sometimes, years of study and analysis. But at the moment of performance, greatness only occurs if all that analysis is completely absorbed in a fusion of spontaneity, wherein heartfelt emotion dominates.

We use the word "heartfelt" to indicate a general area, yet "solar-plexus-felt" might apply at other moments.

My own explorations don't always coincide with those of Manfred totally because I refuse to also let science dominate my behavior. Science and logic are indivisible. But logic is bound to time and a sequence of events. My musical history has brought me to revere intuition in equal proportion to logic. A sense of 'timelessness' in music often defines the magical, unforgettable moments when greatness lights on a performance. Cellists who studied with Casals tell me that he often advised his pupils to aim to create ten seconds of this feeling, and it would justify a whole evening's concert. A singer once burst into my room at the Munich Opera House, her face alive with joy. "I had a triumph last night," she said, "time stood still!"

Had I initially enjoyed the awareness which Manfred's work later brought me, I might have been able to analyze better my earlier musical experiences. In the 1950s I was privileged to study two creators of a long series of performances—Sir Thomas Beecham on one hand, and Walter Legge (of Columbia Records and the Philharmonia Orchestra) and his series of conductors—Karajan, Klemperer, Giulini, Cantelli, etc. on the other. Legge insisted on instilling into his artists the capacity to move listeners with effective emotion, no matter how the performer felt that day. Each musical utterance had to be a testament. That is a performance so schooled that the emotional effect was built in. Stokowski, in a long tour we performed with him, showed that he planned his performances the same way.

But Beecham, Furtwangler and Bruno Walter worked the other way, relying on improvisation and spontaneity to capture the magic of the moment, by allowing them to use a heightened awareness to grasp the mood of the moment.

They drew something out of the soloists, chorus and orchestra in front of them which really summed up the group consciousness of the moment. This training of intuition to create a new event, instead of repeat a prepared event, is for me the secret of musical performance on the highest plane. How is it done? To what extent were they using Manfred's principles instinctively?

My experiences suggest that our cells themselves are our real energizers, and provide our natural authority. I doubt that Manfred can accept this idea until I can show it to him in black and white. That may take some time, as it must be expressed with the help of logic, and the cells are not great admirers of the brain, just its slaves. This enmity between brain and cells is demonstrated easily by the illnesses which are prepared by mental attitudes which reduce energy to some parts of the body. Louise Hay's well-known recipes for mental attitudes to heal the body work far too frequently to be an 'old wife's tale!'

The details of experience contained in The Mind of the Cells[3], Satprem's summary of the experiences of Aurobindo's assistant, 'the Mother,' in her 15-year experiment of stilling her brain until Alpha, Beta, Theta and Delta waves were brought to rest, gives a good idea of what we may perceive when we are in contact with the outer world only through the cells, and without information from our senses being incorporated.

This approach, looked at from the unscientific point of view, suggests that charisma is achieved when the whole body—which means all the cells, not just the brain—is committed to a certain aim. The hypnotic power which Olympic athletes exert on the world, tracing their every movement on television, is surely due to the fact that their whole body is speaking their commitment. So it is also with a real conductor, whose musical conviction is transmitted from the whole of his body, not just the head. When Beecham walked on stage, the orchestra could feel at the beginning of the evening that an electrical performance was in the air. So communication takes place on many planes simultaneously. Hence my resistance to accepting that this or that system alone will lead to a great performance.

Manfred paid me an enormous compliment of inviting me to address the American Association for the Advancement in Science on how a conductor transmits a composer's pulse to the orchestra[4]. I fear that my address contained as many questions as answers. But what is undeniable is that those musicians who take Manfred's work to heart, who devour, digest and inwardly nurture the secrets he has revealed about the nature of musical ex-

---

[3] The Mind of the Cells, 1992. Institute for Evolutionary Research, 1621 Freeway Drive, Mt. Vernon, WA 98273.

[4] AAAS National Meeting, Symposium, Boston, Feb. 1993.

pression and human communication, will be able to grow immeasurably in the range and maturity of what they can express.

The durability of music is extraordinary. Suddenly the world is accepting a resurgence of awareness of the baroque period, with Vivaldi's music becoming a commonplace, almost menacing Mozart's ageless supremacy. So the centuries are bound together, and the language of a composer can become acceptable years after his death. Perotin and Vecchi, just as Shakespeare, are far from becoming out of date.

Manfred's contribution makes it possible for all periods of music to be explored to hitherto unknown depths, and for this he has earned our undying gratitude.

David Lidov

Correspondences of Musical Structure and Microstructure[1]

Early in this century Gustav Becking suggested that a different quality of beat was required in conducting different composers. At that time, he could only advance this idea in terms of the introspective phenomenology of Ernst Kuth, but Manfred Clynes picked up the idea and has taken it in extraordinary directions. Becking's idea appealed to Manfred's own musical experience, and he developed an experimental implementation to demonstrate it.

In the 1960s, Manfred Clynes invented a computer which could record and average precise forms of pressure gestures executed on an electrical pressure transducer. His experiments with this apparatus led to his theory of sentic forms which convey emotion. In a subsidiary set of experiments involving Casals, Serkin, and other performers, he found corroboration of Becking's observation. Skilled musicians using the transducer to beat or conduct imaginary performances produced traces which showed less variation for a given composer across all performers than they showed for a given performer across several composers. The composer was associated with a pulse style, or, as our friends in Ethnomusicology say, a "groove."

Since it seemed evident that the characteristic pulse of a composer could be better conveyed by a group of notes than by one gesture, Clynes looked for a pattern of inflections of metrical subdivisions which would be characteristic of particular composers. Experiments based on musical synthesis yielded matrices of duration and accent, subtly modifying meter. Clynes has conducted preference tests with advanced musicians and students which show

---

[1] An earlier version of this paper was presented to the Society for Music Theory in New York City, November, 1995.

strong recognition of the fit he proposes between pulse matrix and composers' styles.

My interest in Clynes' work and my references to it in my own writings have concerned his emotion expression theory. I would like here to offer some brief observations on his composers' pulse theory; some brief description; my sense why the theory is, prima facie, plausible; and some hints about how structure and micro-structure could correspond in limited respects.

1. The sound pulses have an hierarchical structure. Therefore, if a quadruple group of quarters is divided by quadruple groups of sixteenths, each note in the cycle of 16 is a unique duple of duration and dynamic level.

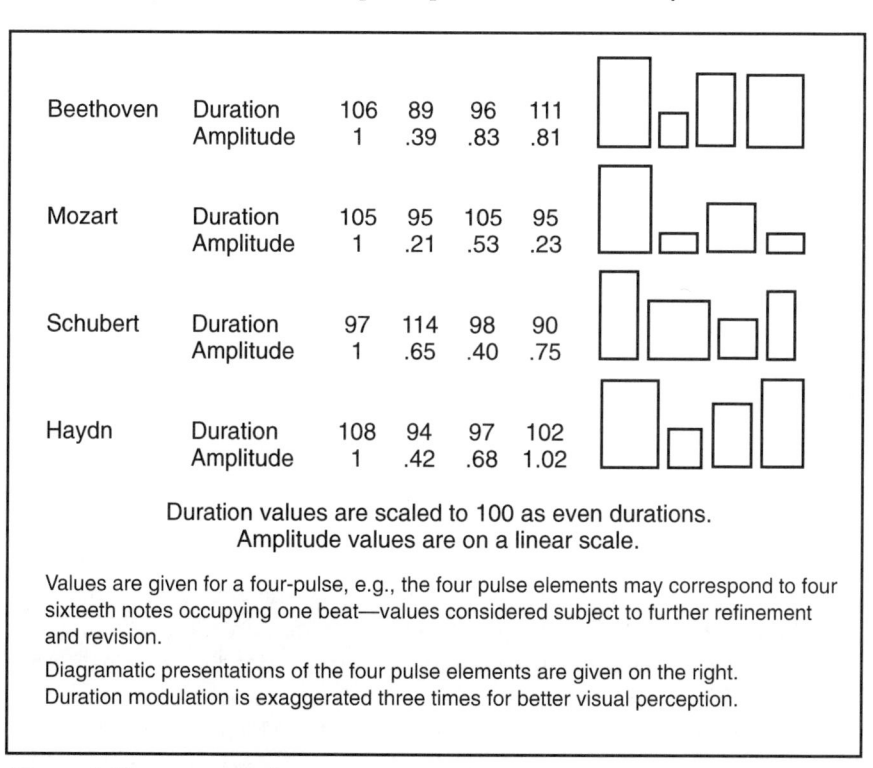

Beethoven	Duration	106	89	96	111
	Amplitude	1	.39	.83	.81
Mozart	Duration	105	95	105	95
	Amplitude	1	.21	.53	.23
Schubert	Duration	97	114	98	90
	Amplitude	1	.65	.40	.75
Haydn	Duration	108	94	97	102
	Amplitude	1	.42	.68	1.02

Duration values are scaled to 100 as even durations.
Amplitude values are on a linear scale.

Values are given for a four-pulse, e.g., the four pulse elements may correspond to four sixteeth notes occupying one beat—values considered subject to further refinement and revision.

Diagramatic presentations of the four pulse elements are given on the right. Duration modulation is exaggerated three times for better visual perception.

Figure 1: Composer Pulses

Figure 1, from Clynes, illustrates composer pulses at the minimal level, that is without recursive hierarchy.

If we look closely at the Beethoven pulse which Clynes has discussed in his publications, we see the fourth note is longer than the first and nearly as accented. The second is weaker and shorter than any other. If we look closely at the Mozart pulse, on the other hand, we see that the first two divisions are isochronic with the second two, the off beats being just a bit shorter.[1] You might guess that this feeling for meter would encourage a charged but very balanced, in a sense stable, syncopation on the off beats such as Mozart loves.

Standard metrical theory in music recognizes no essential difference between duple and quadruple groupings. Notated meter is therefore highly ambiguous with respect to pulse orientation.

1 2 3 4 2 2 3 4   3 2 3 4 4 . . .

1 2 3 4 2 . . . .

3 2 3 4 4 2 3 4 1 . . . .

Figure 2: Pulse-meter ambiguity.

Figure 2 illustrates these ambiguities as three possibilities. When the pulse is constructed at greater hierarchical depth, the ambiguities multiply.

2. The force of the theory is not hard to demonstrate. We prepared very crude examples using the opening phrases of Beethoven's Fifth Symphony and Mozart's Marriage of Figaro Overture.[2] These were chosen because they move continually in eighth notes and can be represented (almost) by a single voice in a neutral timbre with both, far from ideal as this may be, at the same tempo. We realized these with both the "correct" pulses and the

---

[1] In his most recent work, Clynes has moved very slightly away from strict isochrony, with the first beat a bit longer than the second. My later argument refers to isochrony, but I think the change in the new pulse may be too subtle to invalidate my hypothesis, since the difference between 1 and 3 remains far smaller than the differences between 1 and 2, or 3 and 4.

[2] The "crude" examples were skillfully prepared by Mr. Christian Revera using an Amiga 1000 running a Dr. T's KCS level 2, version 3.54 sequencer and a Rhodes MK-60 electric piano.

with the two patterns exchanged. When the pulses are exchanged, the Beethoven quotation loses its drive and the Mozart quotation loses its bright elan. With the "correct" pulses, these qualities are enhanced, despite the clumsy synthesizer sounds.

The reasons why the pulse theory appeals to intuition may not be readily apparent.

Everyone has a gait; everyone has a personal rhythm and inflection of speech. We don't all develop an elaborate style, but we have our own manner. One might suppose, on first view, that the gait comes from the uniqueness of our pendulums-the bone lengths and muscle tension. "The carpenter's hand is his style," said Schoenberg. But then, the arms and the legs might have different rhythms. More basic, there is what Clynes calls "time printing." The brain must translate the microseconds of an impulse to move your arm or leg into a crescendo and decrescendo of nerve firings. Before it can do so, a mechanism with its own variables and eigen values must be in place to effect the translation.

The theory of composers' pulses claims that this personal way of controlling timing can show up in an artist who has sufficient talent and experience to invent a style and who lives in a culture which encourages individuality. Not a wild idea at all.

How or why this neurological process encounters music may be a mystery, but the fact that movement and music are intimately associated is an empirical fact we know from dancing and conducting. We also know that we can sustain hierarchical patterns of motion. Dancers and conductors do so.

What remains a mystery, as Clynes is quick to point out, is the equivalence of note-attack matrices with smooth pulse motions. The sensitivity of the matrices in our perception shows that their information content exceeds that of the conductor's beat: they apparently hold a neurological priority. It is fascinating to contemplate this finding that music can convey a more immediate representation of our mental conception of motion than our normal muscular behaviour can. But perhaps this, too, simply confirms our intuitions. The great pianist, Beveridge Webster, once told me he was sure he could play a waltz with the correct lilt but he couldn't dance one to save his life.

3. Clynes' analysis shows that only a small part of the information content of a performance is inherent in the musical score; deducing the pulse from the score is not feasible. But we may reasonable look for ways in which structure and micro-structure illuminate each other, to look for a good fit.

The difficulties are formidable.

One composer might have a pulse that lent itself to syncopation and she might exploit that fact. Another composer might have a pulse that was recalcitrant for syncopation, but she might struggle against that tendency. How would you know which is which?

Given particular pulse microstructures as a reading attributed to a score, we can, at most, note macrostructures which the microstructure complements. (This is, by the way, roughly the case for tonality as well. You can't prove tonality exists. You can only show that the idea adds intelligibility to a score.) All the evidence will be circular; ideally, the circle will be wide enough to be hospitable.

With these cautions, I offer two examples of approaches to the problem of relating microstructure to structure at the phrase level.

3.1. First, we may regard the Beethoven pulse with regard to its implications for grouping. Pulse itself, of course, is continuous and any grouping structure can be imposed on it as happens, in the course of composing, but not all possibilities fit the grain the same way. I start from Mursell's rules that accent tends to be perceived as initiating a group and that a longer

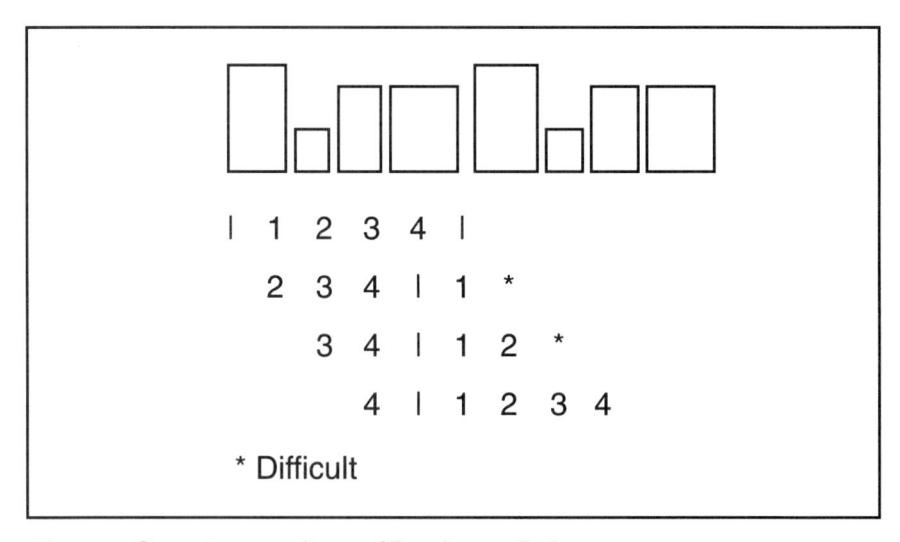

```
| 1 2 3 4 |
    2 3 4 | 1    *
        3 4 | 1 2    *
            4 | 1 2 3 4

* Difficult
```

Figure 3: Grouping proclives of Beethoven Pulse

duration between attacks tends to be perceived as terminating a group. For four note groups, these rules establish an asymmetry in the Beethoven pulse. 2341 should be the most difficult grouping to maintain as its initial note is the weakest and its longest precedes the termination. On the other hand, 4|123 is a pretty good candidate. Similarly, 3412 has very little support, while 1234 is almost built in. (Figure 3 summarizes these observations.)

The pattern 234|1 is the most difficult grouping to maintain. A conflict or tension is established within the line which insists on it. In contrast, 4|123 is relatively facile and opposition between articulated units and continuous motion is established by succession. In Beethoven's 5th, we see the difficult grouping at the eighth note level, and, if we adopt Schenker's metrical interpretation, we see the other grouping at the half note level.

You might object that this is simply a difference between levels, but check out the first movements of the Kreutzer Sonata or Op. 10 No. 3 and you get it the other way.

The issue here is the tension between grouping and continuity. The grouping 234|1 maximizes this tension for Beethoven as one of simultaneous tendencies. Thus, it can be sustained without grouping contrast. The grouping 4|123 reduces this tension and, in Beethoven's world, must not be sustained without contrast. Where this grouping is highlighted, continuity and articulate grouping alternate to supply tension.

3.2. The Clynes Mozart pulse offers no closely parallel angle for investigation. How could a pulse which is so close to our abstract idea of meter offer a point of departure for such a study? The obvious answer slowly comes into view. With respect to durations, Clynes' proposed quadruple scheme for Mozart shows near equality of the halves and sharp inequality of the quarters. Mozart is the only composer to whom Clynes attributes an exactly isochronic duple division in the four note pulse, though Haydn, with just a 2% asymmetry, is close. Some of what I will suggest regarding Mozart almost applies to Haydn.

3.3. Here, instead of grouping, I want to talk about perceptual focus on melody and rhythm. In strict theory we always speak of everything in classical music as exhibiting both melody and rhythm, and we regard rhythm as an abstraction of melody. In real life, as opposed to in theory, we are often inclined to speak of one passage as having rhythmic interest, another as having melodic interest. This can be an interpretive decision but it can also be strongly directed by notated structure. How we make this interpretation is a legitimate question for theory. I do not think it is a function of complexity nor of the locus of novelty nor of the distribution of accents in abstracto. I suspect it hinges on repetition.

Part II: Music, Science, and Emotion

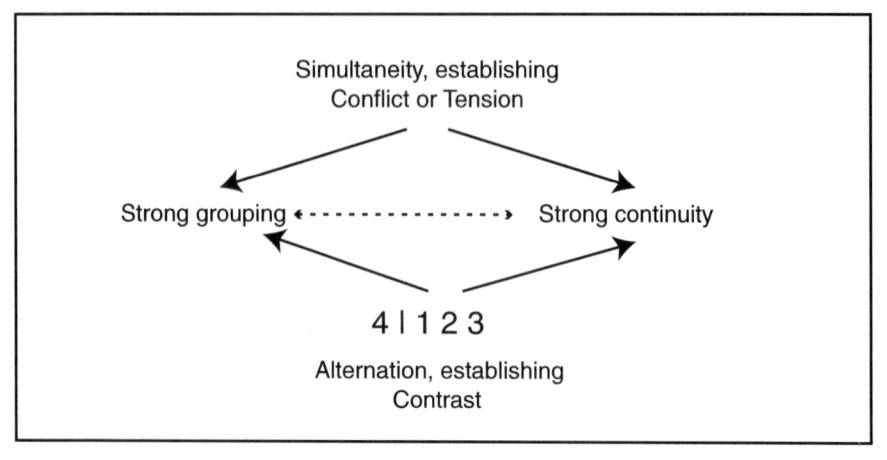

```
                Simultaneity, establishing
                   Conflict or Tension

Strong grouping  ← - - - - - - - - - - - - →  Strong continuity

                         4 | 1  2  3
                 Alternation, establishing
                         Contrast
```

Figure 4

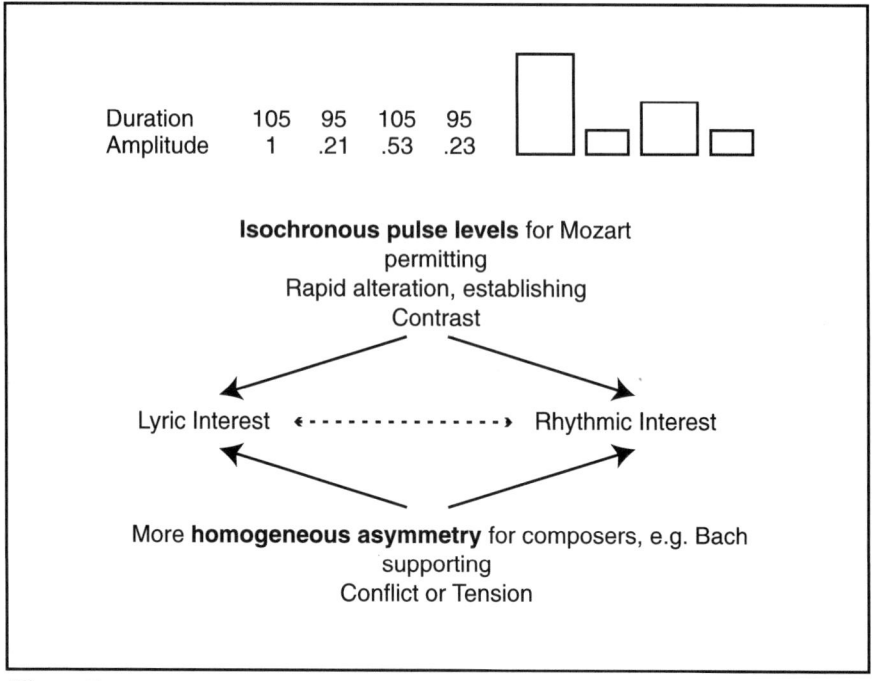

```
Duration    105   95   105   95
Amplitude    1   .21   .53  .23

         Isochronous pulse levels for Mozart
                     permitting
              Rapid alteration, establishing
                      Contrast

Lyric Interest  ← - - - - - - - - - - - - →  Rhythmic Interest

     More homogeneous asymmetry for composers, e.g. Bach
                        supporting
                    Conflict or Tension
```

Figure 5

3.4. Although we think of Mozart as boundlessly melodic, I would point out how characteristic of his music it is that our focus shifts rapidly, often continually, from lyric expression to rhythmic excitement. There is support for this alternation in the pulse structure suggested by Clynes because where you shift attention from the quickest notes to the next slower level, you move to a genuinely isochronic beat, a beat that seems a better candidate for quick rhythmic identification.

Figure 4 compares the suggestions about Beethoven and Mozart, and Figure 5 shows some fragments of Mozart's melodies parsed for possible symmetry and asymmetry of notationally equivalent durations.

The preceding are only fragments of methods, but they may serve to suggest that micro-structure/macro-structure relations are not intractable in musical analysis.

Bruno H. Repp

Manfred Clynes, Pianist

First encounter, battle, and retreat

I first met Manfred Clynes at the 1985 Workshop on Physical and Neuropsychological Foundations of Music in Ossiach, Austria. At the time he was head of the music research center at the New South Wales State Conservatorium of Music in Sydney, Australia. I was a researcher in speech perception with a strong interest in music perception and performance. I had done some experiments on memory for songs with two colleagues, Mary Lou Serafine and Robert Crowder, which had been my only foray into music-related research so far; this enabled me to present a paper in Ossiach and thus attend my first music conference. Incidentally, it was also my first conference in my native country, which I happen to share with Clynes. At the time, I had not heard of Clynes' work, but I was struck immediately by its originality and its relevance to my musical interests.

I was also very skeptical. After reading as many of Clynes' publications as I could lay my hands on, I decided to conduct a perceptual test of his "composer's pulse" theory (Clynes, 1977, 1983). He very kindly assisted me by synthesizing the musical materials for that study (Repp, 1989) in his laboratory, as I did not have the necessary equipment and experience then. He also provided much advice which later turned into criticism when I deviated from the original design of the study. I subsequently acquired a digital piano and MIDI software and conducted a second perceptual study with my own materials (Repp, 1990b), as well as an analysis of recorded piano performances in search of the "Beethoven pulse" (Repp, 1990c). Both studies elicited strong critiques from Clynes (1990, 1994), followed by desperate defenses and counterattacks on my part (Repp, 1990a, 1994b). I did not emerge unscathed from this battle. Clearly, my studies had some shortcomings, for which I was duly reprimanded. They were not totally worthless, however: Having appeared in mainstream journals, they attracted attention to Clynes' important ideas, and they stimulated him to conduct a perceptual study of his own which provided impressive support for his theory (Clynes, 1995). I accept it as the last word on the issue, for the time being.

So I entered the world of music research on a rocky path and with bruised knees, but I did not turn back. My initial experiments had been done on the side, as it were, but I soon began to phase out my speech perception research and decided that music research was what I wanted to do henceforth. This decision was facilitated by the liberal atmosphere and generosity of Haskins Laboratories, whose support (together with a 3-month research fellowship from the Institute for Perception Research in Eindhoven) tided me over a few unstable years, until I obtained a grant from the National Institute of Mental Health that, at the time of this writing, is holding my chin above water.

In my initial years of music research I carved out a small niche for myself in the sparsely populated research areas of objective performance analysis, perception of expressive microstructure, and experimental aesthetics of music performance. Although every study I conduct reveals how much more I still have to learn, I have never regretted my decision to change fields and am enjoying my research greatly. I am deeply grateful to Manfred Clynes for providing the initial stimulus to change, and for remaining a source of inspiration.

A second, more peaceful encounter

My purpose here is not to dwell on the past—all wounds have healed by now—nor to comment further on Clynes' scientific theories. In my more recent work I have not been directly concerned with them, although they are often on my mind. He, meanwhile, has made spectacular progress in developing a performance synthesis system that provides audible proof of the power of his ideas (and of their limits). I would like to focus here on another kind of audible proof of his fertile mind and musical imagination that has had a profound effect on me.

Over the years, Clynes has been kind enough to send me copies of several tapes of his performances as a pianist, recorded during some of his now very infrequent public appearances. Most outstanding among these recordings is his deeply moving interpretation of Bach's *Goldberg Variations*, a towering masterpiece of the keyboard literature.[1] Indeed,

---
[1] Clynes was active as a concert pianist in his younger years and received high acclaim from critics and the general public, particularly for his performances of the *Goldberg Variations*.

it was the expressive range and transcendent beauty of Clynes' music-making, more than any of his somewhat idiosyncratic scientific writings, that gave me confidence in his work, without necessarily removing all my skepticism. Research on music generally tends to be limited by the researcher's level of musical feeling and thought. For Clynes, however, there is no such limit. After hearing a few samples of his playing, I knew that he had the ability of penetrating to the profoundest musical truths.

Clynes and the *Goldberg Variations*

In the remainder of this paper, I would like to present a few glimpses of Clynes' extraordinary art in the form of graphic analyses of a few excerpts from his performance of the *Goldberg Variations*. This performance was recorded live in a concert given in Sydney on September 12, 1978, and was issued on cassette tape by the American Sentic Association.[2]

In order to confirm and better appreciate the uniqueness of Clynes' performance, I listened to a number of commercial recordings of the *Goldberg Variations*: the piano versions by Glenn Gould (CBS Masterworks MK 37779 [1981]), Charles Rosen (Sony Classical SBK 48173), Rosalyn Tureck (VAI Audio VAIA 1029), and Xiao-Mei Zhu (AVACCA 02-2); and the harpsichord versions by Maggie Cole (Virgin Classics VC 7 91444-2), Kenneth Gilbert (Harmonia Mundi HMC 901240), Wanda Landowska (EMI CDH 7610082), and Gustav Leonhardt (Teldec 8.43632).[3] Each of these interpretations has its merits, with Landowska's lively and colorful rendition deserving special mention. But, to my ears, only Gould's is on the same exalted level as Clynes'. Gould's performance is an extraordinary artistic achievement, as has been recognized by critics and music lovers worldwide. However, his approach is fundamentally different from Clynes'. Gould treats the work essentially as a giant Chaconne: He takes hardly any repeats, connects most variations without breaks, and observes strict tempo proportionality, which results in some unusual tempo choices for individual variations. His Aria is probably the slowest on record. His slow variations are serene and unbelievably focused, whereas the faster ones are lively and sharply articulated with the characteristic Gould touch. His playing emphasizes the structural aspects of the composition rather than its emotional content; it is fascinating and occasionally mesmerizing. And, of course, it is technically

---

[2] I do not know whether this association still exists and whether the cassette is available from it. (See Appendix for Clynes' available works—ed.)

[3] Zhu's recording is a French CD that I received as a gift; it may not be commercially available in the United States. In addition to the recordings named, I am familiar with Gould's 1955 recording and with Ralph Kirkpatrick's harpsichord version, though I have not listened to them recently.

perfect, as Gould was not only one of the most accurate pianists but also a dedicated editor in the recording studio.

Clynes' live performance is not technically perfect[4], but this does not matter. He takes all the repeats and emphasizes the diversity and individual character of the variations. His interpretation is intensely emotional, especially in the slower variations, and he applies a degree of rubato and a dynamic range that one rarely encounters in Bach. However, his approach is vindicated by its convincing and powerful effect. Where others play just chains of notes, he finds (or rather introduces) expressive shapes that evoke deep resonances in the listener, very much as predicted by his theory of sentics (Clynes, 1977). Almost certainly, his theoretical ideas have influenced his performance style, and vice versa. In his hands, the variations become a colorful procession of character pieces and dances that alternately move the listener's soul and body, while the structural intricacy of the variations fades into the background. Musical motion and emotion occupy center stage, like living flesh surrounding the structural skeleton. Gould's performance, by comparison, is abstract and otherworldly.

The verbal characterization of performance qualities is a difficult undertaking that always remains subjective and vague compared to the qualitative precision of the auditory impression. It is not easy to tell by ear, and to describe accurately, what an artist has done to achieve a certain perceived quality. Objective performance analysis (Seashore, 1936) provides a means of capturing expressive variation quantitatively and portraying it graphically, so that the expressive shape of a performance lasting several minutes can be surveyed in a glance. While it cannot be a substitute for listening, it can reveal the agogic and dynamic devices an artist uses to achieve certain effects. It is unfortunate that dynamic variation is very difficult to measure accurately from an acoustic recording of polyphonic music. Clynes makes very effective use of the full dynamic range of the piano, and there is absolutely no attempt on his part to imitate the dynamically restricted harpsichord sound. The present measurements, however, were limited to expressive timing. The relevant excerpts were digitized at 22.255 kHz, and the onsets of successive tones were measured in a waveform display with auditory feedback, using SOUNDEDIT16 software on a Macintosh Quadra 660AV computer.[5]

Three particularly instructive excerpts will be considered in my analyses, and in each case Clynes' very special agogics will be contrasted with that of one other pianist.

---

[4] A 1995 digital remastering of the recording has removed the few slight imperfections of the live performance.

[5] In the case of asynchronous onsets of nominally simultaneous tones, the melodically most important tone was measured.

Example 1:
Variato 6. Canone alla Seconda. a 1 Clav.

Variation 6. This variation is the *Canone alla Seconda* in G major (Example 1).[6] It is an ingenious canon in which both melodic voices are played by the right hand while the left hand provides a figurative or punctate accompaniment. The two voices are out of phase by one measure and differ in pitch by a major second. There is stepwise pitch motion on the accented beats from bar to bar, with a cadence every eight bars. The variation is divided into two 16-bar sections, each with a repeat. The meter is 3/8, and there is continuous sixteenth-note motion throughout, provided either by the melody voices or by the accompaniment, or both. This made it easy to examine expressive timing: The temporal distance from one sixteenth-note onset to the next was measured and plotted as a function of score position. An expressionless performance would appear as a straight line in this graph.

Figure 1 (p.76) compares the expressive timing profiles of the performances by Manfred Clynes and Xiao-Mei Zhu.[7] Zhu's performance of this variation, while fluent and articulate, comes close to being devoid of expression. She takes a rather fast tempo (about 230 ms per sixteenth note, which translates into 130 eighth-note, or 43 dotted quarter-note, beats per minute) and omits the repeat of the second section. Her deviations from strict timing are, with a few exceptions, small and irregular. Some of this variation may be just random "motor noise" and some may be systematic but due to fingering. There is a pronounced *ritardando* at the end of each section, and a smaller one in bar 24 (a cadence). In bar 30, expressive lengthening occurs on the downbeat, the last dissonance before the final cadence. Phrase-initial lengthening (bars 1 and 17) may also be observed. Not much else can be said about this plain rendition.

In contrast, Clynes' performance has a grandly sculpted timing profile. First, his tempo is much slower than Zhu's, somewhere around 400 ms per sixteenth note (75 eighth-note or 25 dotted quarter-note beats per minute). This is the slowest tempo I have heard in this variation. Clynes needs this tempo, however, to obtain the desired expression for the principal motive, a descending sequence of five notes which recurs many times and always ends on a downbeat. While Zhu and others consider this sequence as merely a descending scale fragment, or treat the four sixteenth notes as an extended upbeat to the final long note, for Clynes it becomes an emotional gesture signifying (to my sensibilities) something akin to benevolence or the offering of comfort. To be effective, the gesture needs a slight *crescendo* as well as a pronounced *ritardando*, which is what we see in Clynes' timing profile. However, there is great variety in his execution of this expressive shape, and the degree of *ritardando* varies from bar to bar. Some of this variability may

---

[6] The musical text of all examples is taken from the Bach-Gesellschaft Edition (Leipzig, 1853/63).

[7] The unusually short interval in bar 9 may reflect a slip of the finger or possibly a bad splice on the CD.

be due to "motor noise" or fingering patterns, as in Zhu's case, but much of it is probably intentional.

Between bars 9 and 14 a steady slowing of the tempo may be observed, especially in Clynes' first traversal, which culminates in a very large ritardando in bar 13. These bars have a denser texture than other bars because the two canonic voices overlap and cross each other in simultaneous sixteenth-note motion. A melodic and harmonic peak is reached in bar 12, whereupon the

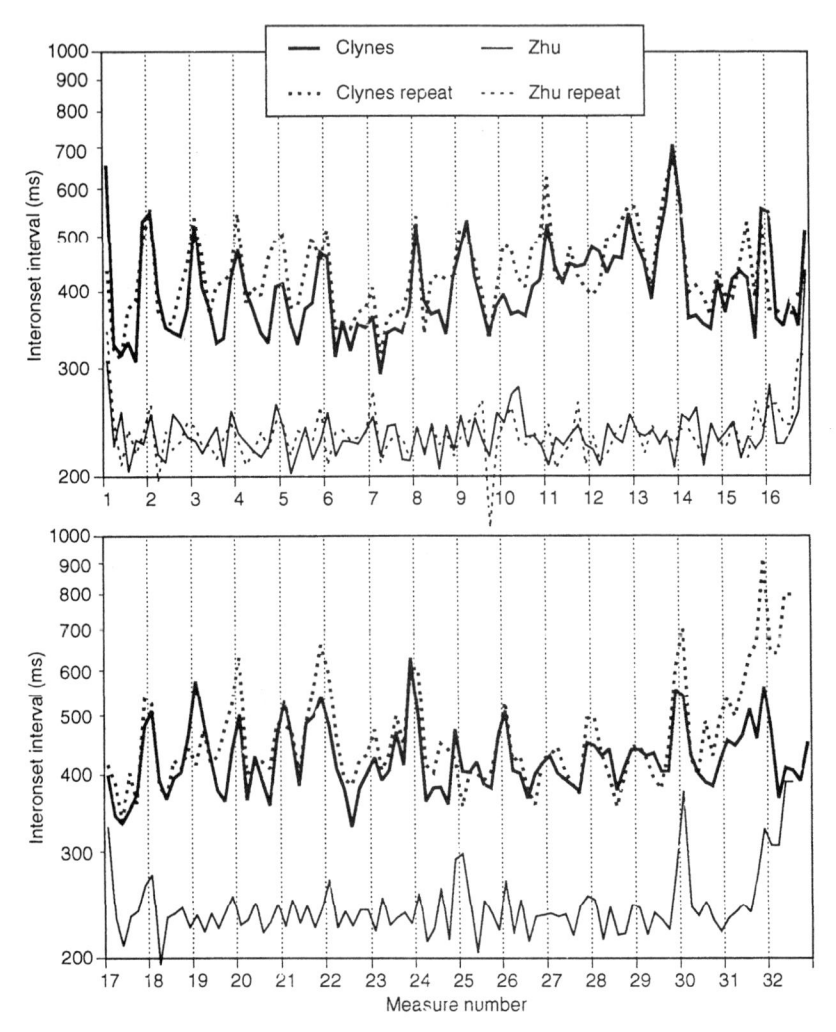

Fig. 1. Expressive timing profiles of Variation 6, as played by Manfred Clynes and Xiao-Mei Zhu (AVACCA 02-2).

5-note descending motive is stated once more in a single voice, leading to a final dissonance on the downbeat of bar 14 that then resolves into the final cadence. It is this final statement of the motive that Clynes builds up to and that forms the expressive climax of the whole variation, a particularly poignant moment not found in any other performance I have heard. Finally, it should be noted that Clynes intensifies his expressive maneuvers in the repeats: Many of the *ritardandi* are larger and start earlier in his second traversal of the music. The emotional impact on the listener is magnified correspondingly.

Variation 21. Another variation in which Clynes achieves extraordinary powers of expression, especially in comparison to other artists, is the *Canone alla Settima* in G minor. This is a somber and chromatic piece of great beauty, surely one of the finest variations in the set. It is in common time and is divided into two 8-bar sections, with repeats. It will suffice to consider the first eight bars only (Example 2). As in Variation 6, the music is in continuous sixteenth-note motion. The timing data are shown in Figure 2 (p.79).[8]

As the comparison performance here, I have chosen the one by Charles Rosen. His performance is rigorous and scholarly; it captures the serious tone of the variation well, but shows little flexibility. This is confirmed by his timing profile. His tempo is much faster than Clynes'; approximately 280 ms per sixteenth note or about 54 quarter-note beats per minute. There is little pronounced agogic variation; even the *ritardando* at the end of the section is small. The repeat is rather similar to the first rendition. In bars 3 and 7–8, regular oscillations can be seen. In these bars, one or two voices move chromatically in eighth notes, and Rosen displaces the onsets of the intervening sixteenth notes in the third voice towards the following eighth notes, which he plays with much dynamic emphasis.

The tempo of Clynes' performance is much slower than Rosen's, again about 400 ms per sixteenth note or 38 beats per minute. It shows pronounced initial lengthening (bar 1) as well as an extended final two-stage *ritardando* (bar 8). Significant *ritardandi* also occur halfway through bars 2 and 4. The salient melodic motive in this variation consists of an 8-note sequence which first ascends by a fourth and then descends by a fifth in stepwise motion, ending on a strong beat. It is stated four times in bars 1–2. The first three statements are superimposed on descending chromatic steps in the bass which reach the dominant on the third beat of bar 2 and then resolve to the tonic. The fourth state-

---

[8] The ordinate is scaled logarithmically in order to make expressive deviations at different tempos comparable, on the assumption that they are roughly proportional to the basic tempo (see Repp, 1994a), and also to reduce the graphic excursion of large *ritardandi*. Note that a slowing of tempo corresponds to an upward excursion in the graph.

Example 2:
Variatio 21. Canone alla Settima

ment thus has a different emotional character: Whereas the first three seem to convey weariness or fatigue, the fourth seems lighter and relieved, as if a heavy weight had been deposited on the third beat of bar 2. In bar 4, something else occurs: A statement of a modified version of the 8-note motive leads to a striking unresolved dissonance, after which the modified motive (now with an extended prefix) recurs in inverted form. Clynes emphasizes the dissonance, especially in his repeat. Even more than in Variation 6, he slows down in the repeat and increases the expressive modulations during bars 1–4.

The difference between the two renditions is less pronounced in bars 5–8; in fact, they are very similar. A curious local phenomenon here is the very short second inter-onset interval in the third beat of bar 6, which occurs in the left hand, following a short trill in the right hand, perhaps to compensate for the lengthening associated with the trill. The local lengthening on the first beat of bar 6 is also caused by a trill but is not followed by a compensational maneuver. The final two-stage *ritardando* is explained by the fact that the alto voice

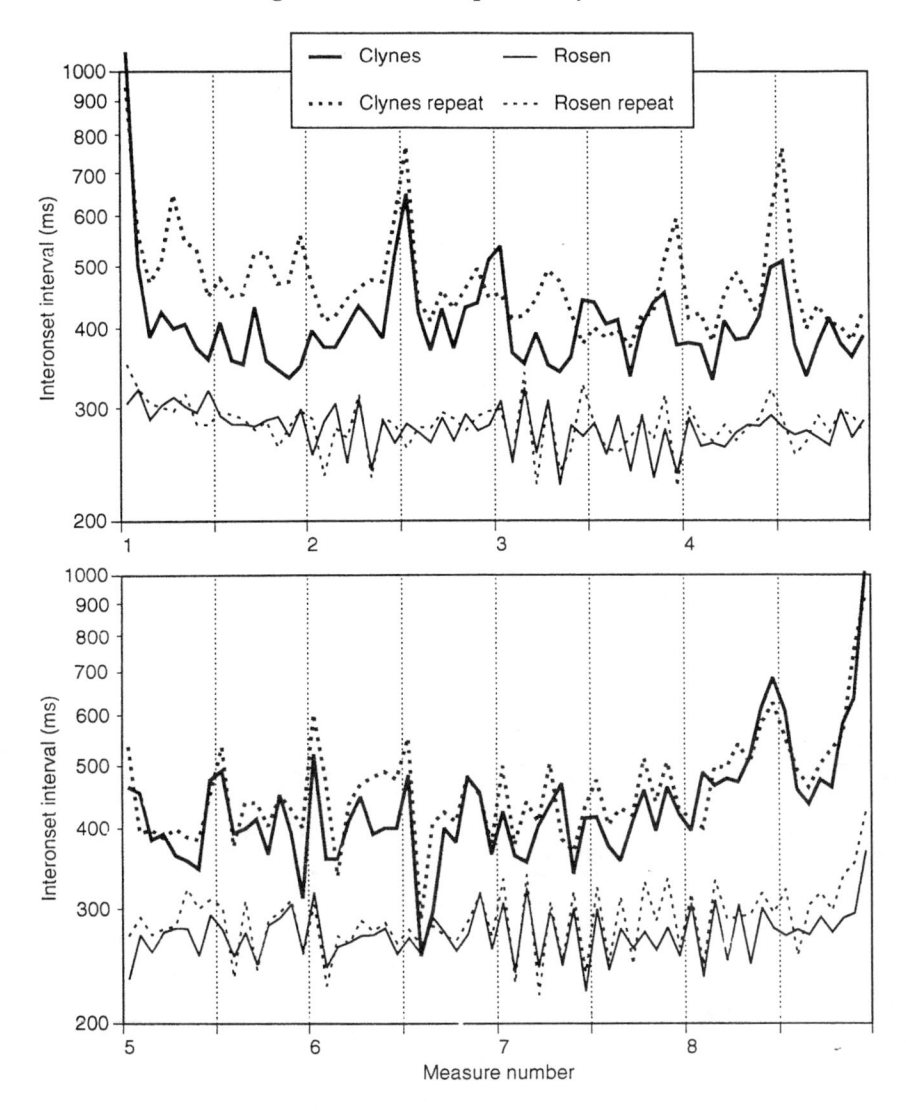

Fig. 2. Expressive timing profiles of Manfred Clynes and Charles Rosen.

80 Part II: Music, Science, and Emotion

ends on the third beat of bar 8, whereas the soprano voice, being out of phase by two beats, goes on to resolve to the dominant (the local tonic) and also changes the mode from minor to major, supported by the bass voice. All these agogic variations are of course supported by—or, rather, serve to pace—Clynes' exquisite dynamic shaping, which cannot be conveyed here graphically.

Aria. Finally, I turn to the Aria in G major as the third excerpt to be considered. Even though it opens the work, I saved its discussion for the end

Example 3: **ARIA.**

because of its greater rhythmic complexity.[9] It is in 3/4 meter and is divided into two 16-bar sections with repeats; again, I will examine only the first section here (Example 3). The richly ornamented melody contains a number of thirty-second notes, grace notes, and *appoggiature*, which were ignored in the present analysis unless they were played metrically as sixteenth or eighth notes. Timing was measured at the sixteenth-note level. Intervals longer than a sixteenth note were normalized (i.e., divided by the number of sixteenth notes they contain) and graphed as plateaus extending over their nominal duration along the x-axis. For comparison with Clynes' performance, that of Glenn Gould [1981] was selected. The data are shown in Figure 3 (p. 82).

Gould's performance is very slow and relatively unmodulated. He does not take the repeat. The first three bars seem to be at a somewhat faster tempo than the remainder, which moves in the vicinity of 500 ms per sixteenth note, or 30 quarter-note beats per second. On closer inspection, there is a systematic pattern to the agogic variation: Temporal shapes comprising a brief *accelerando* followed by a longer *ritardando* occupy bars 1–2, 3–4, 9–10, 11–12, 13–14 (in part), 14–15, and 16. Each of these segments corresponds to half a phrase, bar 16 to an extension of the final cadence. Only bars 5–8 are relatively rigid, but with a *ritardando* at the end of bar 7. Gould's timing thus can be seen to follow the phrase structure very closely, which is consistent with the structure-oriented impression that his performance makes on the listener.

Clynes' performance, by contrast, is extremely modulated, so much so that it is difficult to assign any basic tempo to it. My best guess would be that it is somewhere around 300 ms per sixteenth note, or 50 beats per minute, on the assumption that most expressive deviations are lengthenings. Clynes takes the repeat and is amazingly consistent here; the two renditions are very nearly identical. This demonstrates that his very complex timing pattern is governed by a carefully worked out plan.[10] Rather than giving half-phrases a simple shape, Clynes tends to break them up, or rather pivots them on an expressive lengthening of the central sixteenth-note anacrusis to the following downbeat. Sharp "spikes" associated with this anacrusis can be seen at the ends of bars 3, 7, 9, 13, and 14, where it precedes another sixteenth note, while narrow peaks including the downbeat (here, an eighth note) occur at the onsets of bars 2, 6, and 12. This salient expressive device and the resulting local *ritardandi* and *accelerandi* account for a substantial part of the timing variation in Clynes' performance.

---

[9] Of course, the Aria also returns at the end of the work. However, my measurements were made on the opening Aria.

[10] I do not mean to imply that every deviation is consciously planned. Rather, the timing profile represents the replicable interaction between a musical structure and an exquisitely sensitive organism.

Other noteworthy features in Clynes' performance are the following: In bars 1, 5, and 9, two successive quarter notes of the same pitch occur phrase-initially; Clynes always shortens the second note relative to the first. This tendency is magnified in bar 3, where the second note, ornamented with a trill, is shortened dramatically, together with the following two notes. In bar 7, there is an enormous *ritardando* which brings the musical motion

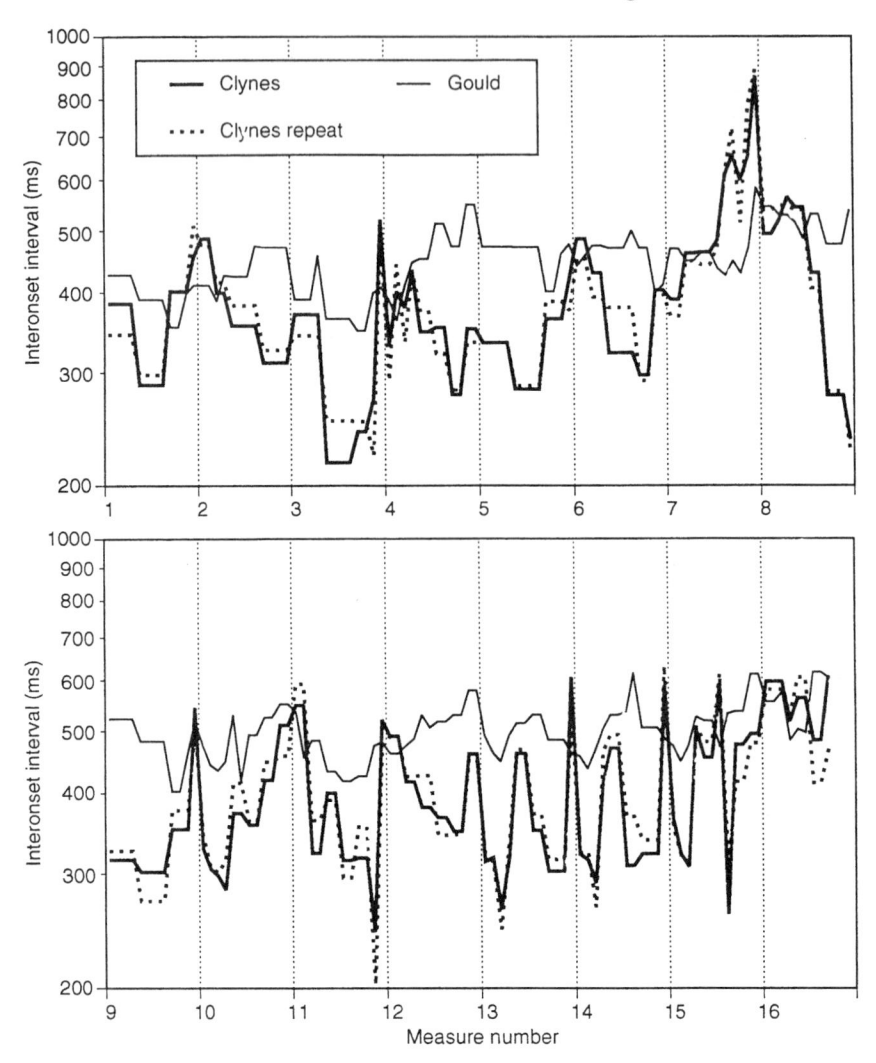

Fig. 3. Expressive timing profiles of the opening Aria (first half), as played by Manfred Clynes and Glenn Gould (CBS Masterworks MK 37779 [1981]).

almost to a standstill. This is followed by an equally dramatic acceleration in bar 8, which leads into the next phrase. The emotional atmosphere I sense throughout is one of love, perhaps even devotion.[11] In bar 10, a pronounced *ritardando* leads to the arpeggiated chord at the beginning of bar 11, which is executed with great tenderness. In bars 13–16, each half-bar motive is set off from the next one by final lengthening. There is no *ritardando* at the end of the section, though the local tempo is slow (equal to Gould's here).

Conclusion

All three excerpts discussed illustrate the extraordinary sensitivity and flexibility of Clynes' performances, whose emotional impact is further enhanced by a masterful use of dynamics that unfortunately cannot be conveyed here. The other pianists' performances, by comparison, seem relatively rigid and unimaginative in their timing. Of course, their dynamics and timbres must also be taken into consideration, and in Gould's case the rigidity is clearly intentional, as is also evident in his carefully measured ornaments.[12] Surely, there will be some who will shake their head and say that rubato of the extent seen in Clynes' performance is inappropriate for Bach, not in style, Romantic, or inauthentic. Here Richard Taruskin, the leading critic of the notion of historical "authenticity" may be quoted. Taruskin has argued strongly that true authenticity is "founded to an unprecedented degree on personal conviction and on individual response to individual pieces" (Taruskin, 1995, p. 77). From this perspective, with which I wholeheartedly agree, Clynes is one of the most authentic musicians alive. His performances have emotional power and conviction, and a listener with an open heart and mind is carried along by them as if by a strong current. In today's world of technically flawless but often emotionally impoverished performances, Clynes' art stands like a beacon, reminding us of what music can yield when it is tended with love and care.

Acknowledgment

During preparation of this paper, the author was supported by NIH grant MH-51230. I am grateful to Janet Hander-Powers and Lisa Robinson for helpful comments on an earlier draft. Most of the commercial recordings of Bach's *Goldberg Variations* were loaned from the Yale Music Library. Address correspondence to Bruno H. Repp, Haskins Laboratories, 270 Crown Street, New Haven, CT 06511-6695; e-mail: repp@haskins.yale.edu

---

[11] It seems apt, though it can hardly have been Clynes' intention, that the timing profile of bars 1-8 resembles the silhouette of a medieval town with several gabled houses and two Gothic churches, one at a river (bars 3-4) and the other one on a mountain (bars 7-8). Gould's profile provides an appropriate counterpoint in the third dimension, lending depth to the illusion.

[12] Gould plays grace notes and trills metrically, whereas Clynes usually shortens grace notes and plays trills more freely.

References

Clynes, M. (1977). *Sentics: The Touch of the Emotions.* New York: Doubleday. (Reprinted by Prism Press [Bridport, Dorset, UK] in 1989.)

Clynes, M. (1983). Expressive microstructure in music, linked to living qualities. In J. Sundberg (ed.), *Studies of Music Performance* (pp. 76–186). Stockholm: Royal Swedish Academy of Music.

Clynes, M. (1990). Some guidelines for the synthesis and testing of pulse microstructure in relation to musical meaning. *Music Perception,* 7, 403–421.

Clynes, M. (1994). Comments on "Patterns of expressive timing in performances of a Beethoven minuet by nineteen famous pianists" [J. Acoust. Soc. Am. 88, 622-641 (1990)]. *Journal of the Acoustical Society of America,* 96, 1174–1178.

Clynes, M. (1995). Microstructural musical linguistics: Composers' pulses are liked most by the best musicians. *Cognition,* 55, 269–310.

Repp, B. H. (1989). Expressive microstructure in music: A preliminary perceptual assessment of four composers' "pulses." *Music Perception,* 6, 243-274.

Repp, B. H. (1990a). Composers' pulses: Science or art? *Music Perception,* 7, 423-434.

Repp, B. H. (1990b). Further perceptual evaluations of pulse microstructure in computer performances of classical piano music. Music Perception, 8, 1-33.

Repp, B. H. (1990c). Patterns of expressive timing in performances of a Beethoven minuet by nineteen famous pianists. *Journal of the Acoustical Society of America,* 88, 622-641.

Repp, B. H. (1994a). Relational invariance of expressive microstructure across global tempo changes in music performance: An exploratory study. *Psychological Research,* 56, 269-284.

Repp, B. H. (1994b). Response to "Comments on 'Patterns of expressive timing in performances of a Beethoven minuet by nineteen famous pianists'" [J. Acoust. Soc. Am. 96, 1174–1178 (1994)]. *Journal of the Acoustical Society of America,* 96, 1179–1181.

Seashore, C. E. (1936) (ed.). *Objective analysis of musical performance.* Iowa City, IA: The University Press.

Taruskin, R. (1995). *Text and Act.* New York: Oxford University Press.

Gérard Souzay

Modern Music

During the last 50 years, I have witnessed and participated in the transformation of musical recordings from 78s to LPs to CDs. Thanks to the musical and scientific genius of Dr. Manfred Clynes, we are, once again, poised to begin another era of non-live musical performances. Dr. Clynes' work with computer-generated music may change the way that people experience music in their lives.

It is my hope that the work of Dr. Clynes will help the public to appreciate, understand and experience classical music in a new way and enrich the lives of those who would otherwise not have exposure to our great musical heritage.

In today's technological age, I am very glad that we have a marvelous musician and interpreter like Dr. Clynes to represent and help classical music in this fast-changing world.

Happy 70th Birthday, Dr. Clynes—"Long Live Manfred and Long Live Music!"

Part III
The Realm of Sentics

Janice Walker

Sentic Cycles

We like to imagine the impossible. And on the other hand, we love the familiar.

One of the fascinating things about music is its ability to change someone's mood. People like to listen to music because it makes them feel good. For me, Mozart or Mendelssohn, for example, nearly always make me feel joyful and full of energy. Bach gives me a great sense of relaxation and peace. From Beethoven I gain courage and strength, an awareness of the immensity and power of our universe.

Music has power to influence the minds and hearts of human beings. Some performances are so eloquent that they melt the heart of the listener to the extent that all hardness vanishes. We feel safe and free to love in a world of light and harmony.

Musicians and music lovers share a precious world of feeling, which would seem largely inaccessible to other people. We wonder why this is so. It seems miraculous.

But what if it were possible to discover what underlies this mystery? What if it were possible for everyone, not just the music lovers, to experience the pure emotions of music? What if everyone could find refuge in the warmth and love found in a Brahms song, or the tenderness of a Schumann composition, without a note being played? Or experience the energetic strength of Beethoven, really experience the emotion in mind and soul without a note being played? What if there really is powerful MetaMusic which is ours for the taking if only we know how to tap into the source?

With his invention and discovery of Sentic Cycles, Manfred Clynes has unearthed this mystery. He has shown how to achieve the seemingly miraculous. He has show that we are like the man in the old Sufi story who wandered for years in search of treasure, only as an old man to find the treasure in his own back yard. We are all like this wanderer, for we too already possess riches, if we are able and willing to go within. As Shakespeare said, we are "most ignorant of what we are most assured, our glassy essence."

Our challenge is to find the key to unlock the door to our own "within." With this key, the door opens easily enough, even though it may be necessary to cut down the fears and prejudices which often occlude the entrance. Once we place the key in the lock, even internal clamor and outside noises may be stilled. The body itself may become quiet, and an attitude of intense inner listening my be cultivated which in turn reveals...

MetaMusic
for you
and for me
for everyone
the
key

MetaMusic: The Key

Actually, everyone already knows about the key, MetaMusic, but like many obvious things in life, most of us have never really thought about it. For example, the fact that one single caress consistently takes a specific amount of time and flows in a particular direction doesn't usually enter our minds. And what about the fact that a hug from someone you love makes both you and the hugger feel good? Different emotions take different amounts of *time* for their expression. On some level, we all know this. We all know that each emotion needs a certain amount of time for its expression in order to "feel right." For instance, a single expression of anger is quite short, the length of a shout or a kick. (This does not count the period of build up before the expressive "explosion" of anger comes.) We also know from experience that emotion can be very contagious.

When we are feeling tenderness and love for an infant, we typically bring the baby close to our heart and stroke its back gently without even thinking about what we are doing. Unknowingly, we are *using both time and space* for the expression of an emotion. The deeper the love which we feel for the child, the more attention we bestow to the quality of our touch when we stroke the child. Our voice softens, a smile appears, and we have a wonderful glow inside.

The research conducted by Manfred Clynes has clearly shown that each emotion has a spatio-temporal expressive form, distinct for each emotion. This form, which Clynes named *sentic form*, is programmed into our nervous system in a lock-and-key fashion. In other words, when a certain emotion is expressed we are able to recognize it. We can both produce sentic form and readily recognize it. It is the spatio-temporal form which is important. It is really an independent entity which does not mind what kind of output modality is used for its expression. Tone of voice, a look, a touch, a gesture when used for the expression of an emotion have one thing in common: they follow the specific spatio-temporal form of the emotion being expressed. If you had to, or wanted to, it is even possible to express every emotion using only one finger as the means of expression. Indeed, this is the method Clynes used in his research. Ideally, he wanted just a single point but expressive finger pressure was the nearest thing to it.

The MetaMusic Concept

MetaMusic takes place in what Clynes calls *sentic cycles*; "sentic" is derived from the Latin "sentire," to feel. Clynes developed a sequential procedure for expressing emotion, or feeling, in order to help people release tension and achieve emotional balance. This procedure, called Sentic Cycles, is based on Clynes research regarding the patterns of emotional expression (sentic form). Performing Sentic Cycles takes 25 minutes. It gives a person a way to express and experience a cycle of emotions, and has effects partly similar to meditation. It is cathartic.

In the course of a Sentic Cycle session you generate a series of emotions. The emotions are expressed in a specific order: No Emotion, Anger, Hate, Grief, Sex, Love, Joy, and Reverence.

Performing Sentic Cycles

How do you do Sentic Cycles? What is the result of doing them? Do you need special equipment?

Equipment: a straight back chair (no arm rests please), preferably with a small cushion for the lower back; a second straight chair or a coffee table; a finger rest; a cassette player and a Sentic Cycle tape.[1]

Performing Sentic Cycles: Before practicing Sentic Cycles it is well to draw the curtain or otherwise provide for subdued light for the experience. It is important that you will not be disturbed and that you feel secure in the knowledge that you will not be disturbed. Unplug the telephone if that is possible.

Sit comfortably in the straight-backed chair, feet flat on the floor (with or

---

[1] Setnic Cycle kits, including cassette tape and finger rest, are available. See Appendix.

without shoes), cushion at the small of your back. If you are right-handed, place the finger rest to your right, and if you are left-handed place it to your left. The finger rest should be within easy reach so that there is no strain. The middle finger will be used on the finger rest for the expression of each emotion.

Play the Sentic Cycle tape. The tape consists of only the spoken words of each emotion in the order of intended expression, followed by quasi-random clicks. To start out, you will hear the words "No Emotion" followed by a dull thump or click. The thump or click is the signal for you to make a mechanical reaction with the middle finger on the finger rest. The movement is similar to that of hitting a key on a typewriter. (For "No Emotion" you may be feeling emotion, but you do not express it.)

Using the finger to express emotion may seem strange at first, but for most people it soon becomes natural. You only need to search your memory until you find a real event or person that makes you feel the particular emotion stated. Then you use your finger (and arm as well) to express on the finger rest exactly what you feel.

Listen inwardly very carefully to exactly what you feel and then be as precise as possible in its expression. Most people are able to "catch on" to doing sentic cycles within two or three tries. The primary challenges seem to be that in the beginning some people are not clear about the difference between anger and hate. Some people also confuse love and reverence. Typically these quandaries sort themselves out over a few days or weeks of practice. People discover that the emotions are more precise and well defined than the words used to describe them!

On the tape, the quasi random clicks signaling the beginning of each emotion are very important. Their kind of repetition helps to enhance and amplify the quality and intensity of each emotion as it is experienced. (If you were able to predict the exact moment of each click, the effect would be exactly the opposite, a diminishing of emotional intensity, just like the rhythmic three or four pats on the back frequently given in non-verbal cues: "There, there. Everything is going to be all right.") For some emotions, the timing clicks are rather close together. For others, the clicks are spaced far apart.

After two or three minutes of time for "No Emotion," the word "Anger" is spoken. After each click, one discrete expression of anger should be expressed. Again, after two or three minutes, a new word will be spoken.

If the segments were more than two or three minutes long, in most cases the buildup of emotion would cease and the emotion would tend to dissipate itself. A new emotion, however, provides a new impetus and new buildup.

When the Sentic Cycle session is finished, you sit quietly for a few minutes and let the experience sink in. Most people don't feel like talking for a few minutes, allowing time for integration. For maximum benefit from doing Sentic Cycles, it is good to write notes about the cycle, preferably within thirty minutes of doing one (I give some examples of these notes later in this article).

Effects of performing Sentic Cycles: For several hours after a cycle you may feel a sense of being centered, of being able to function in a more relaxed and efficient manner. Colors may appear brighter. You may have more energy.

Principles of Sentic Cycles

Based on his research, Clynes formulated the following biologic principles of sentic (emotion) communication:

Exclusivity Principle. It is only possible to express one sentic (emotion) state at a time. (It can be a mixed emotion, however.) Trying to simultaneously express more than one emotion with different parts of the body will result in blocking.

Equivalence Principle. It is possible to express a sentic state using any one of various output modalities; for example, sound, touch, gesture.

Coherence Principle. Regardless of the output modality the expression of a sentic state is governed by a specific algorithm or brain program—a spatiotemporal form which is called "sentic form." To a given feeling corresponds a given form (which may find many modes of expression). And the more precisely you produce that form the more powerfully it generates the feeling—in yourself, and in the perceiver.

Complementarity Principle. The central nervous system has a biologically coordinated data processing program which can recognize and produce sentic forms. A well produced sentic form can be *recognized* and has the power to generate *in the person who recognizes*, the original sentic state. (We all know this! How often during a sad movie we are found crying right along with the actors!)

How Do Sentic Cycles Relate To Music?

The amazing thing about Sentic Cycles, unbelievable at first blush, is that, like music, they enable you to generate emotions at will, through simple acts of expression. They tap into that place reached by powerful music, but they do this through touch rather than musical notes. Touch requires no special talent and virtually every one can do it. The time course of an expression is similar as in music. That is why it is called Meta music—the time courses that underlie expressive musical phrases—but without the sound.

Examples of Sentic Cycle Notes

As mentioned, it is helpful to write notes after a session. The following notes are from two Sentic Cycle sessions. They were done by a 54-year-old female, Chrissie, and were her first experiences with Sentic Cycles. (Name has been changed to assure privacy.).

Chrissie's First Sentic Cycle Session

Anger. *Prolonged, intense. I had to remind myself of the next click. I could be angry and direct my anger to a specific cause.*

Hate. *Hard to differentiate from anger. I wonder now if my anger in general expresses more hate than I had realized. But my hate is limited to certain people.*

Grief. *I think I block off grief somewhat—a lot. I thought of the sorrow I should have felt under certain circumstances—but it has been covered by other feelings. I'd like to feel grief more. I felt and expressed grief, a prolonged and heavy feeling, but it wasn't nearly enough.*

Love. *Gentle, drawing something of someone towards me; an expression of warmth and pleasure.*

Sex. *More aggressive than receptive, which surprised me. A good feeling.*

Joy. *A sharp feeling, like a pang of beauty, and then lightness, spirits lifted.*

Reverence. *I feel more reverence, wonder, and awe in real life than I did here. I thought of music and people and how I felt about them, but could not fully evoke my daily experiences. This seems strange. But it is a profound emotion not easily evoked at will.*

General comments and experience after doing cycles:

I seemed to prolong all my expressions of emotion. After the tape was finished I felt very relaxed indeed, very heavy, and not wanting to move. . . felt good and healthy.

Chrissie's Second Sentic Cycle Session

Anger: *Tried to be angry without hate and found this hard. Clearly I need to sort these emotions out, my anger isn't pure enough. I begin to feel the difference between anger and hate and that I could be more angry.*

Hate. *I put myself back into my childhood tantrums of hate; I'd like to find out what they are all about. They seem more like frustration though I know I expressed hate at the time – in the tantrum. I also had a separate feeling of hate—cold hate.*

Grief. *I got better into this than I did yesterday, but it was still abstract. I'd like to be more concrete first before I move into the universal form. I let my body droop and my breath stay out—noticed the pause after the outbreak.*

Love. *More easily and satisfyingly expressed than yesterday. I moved my finger more, in a stroking way.*

Sex. *Less aggressive; more felt, both emotionally and in my body.*
Joy. *I found my finger lifted, but not very high. It was a calm joy—light, but not exhilarating.*
Reverence. *I could not feel it on the up breath. I found it very satisfying to let my breath out and then I seemed not to breathe at all, but was lost in wonder.*

General comments and experience after doing cycles:

Perhaps all the emotions vary somewhat in their expression from one time to another, doing sentics.

Perhaps it is important to feel all emotions in a personal way at some stage, as well as universalizing them, so to speak. Does the personal form mean feeling them impurely? Is it the universal (archetypal) form which conveys itself best? Is only the universal form pure?

The following notes were made by Len, a man in his middle thirties, after his first Sentic Cycle experience.

Len's Sentic Cycle Notes

While unaware of the order of the words, the following are my direct impressions and response to my first exposure to Sentic Cycles. Time: 10 p.m. Mood and Tension: normal (for me).

No Emotion. *In the no-thing an orange cloud hung in the center of my vision clinging to the hor-i-zon(e). A misty sun rose, a fine filtered swirl gyrating in fingers of light, soft and bright. It was easy to float in this familiar land where no-thing is and all will become—I really did not want to leave.*

Anger. *Dark wing over the clouds, I resented the intrusion, yet sensed friends in danger. I experienced strength and determination directed against the growing dark shape. I felt my feet were roots and my-Self a barrier. My resentment grew until the wings turned to gold.*

Hate. *Momentarily nothing—I tried to think of all the hate directed against us as Jews, the persecution, the cruelty, century upon century. I tried again, but nothing, then puzzlement and such a strong deep pity. I saw a field of waving green plants, long stemmed with white trumpet-like flowers, they moved slowly and rhythmically, then parted. I seemed to be walking through a passage created as they drew back, I felt overwhelming pity which began to turn to grief just before the word was spoken. I felt like crying.*

Grief. *The plants turned from green to blue, the flowers now bright white and blue tipped. They swirled in a vertical whirlpool, and the trumpet-like flowers although clear to the vision were by experience silent sound, so loud and so strange that it played through my being a song of sirens. I was the center, watcher and watched. Tear drops hung suspended in a web of time.*

Love. *The flowers changed to purple then became lines. The lines stretched and broadened, moved and took shape. Sinai, I had returned. I remembered, I heard a voice, felt a presence, and relived an experience I actually had when visiting Sinai a few years ago. I felt a oneness, a joining, circling love to re-verse in poetry and re-member membership. Love was androgynous, evolving just as the word 'love' implies and does not lie, the last two letters 've' re-verse and added to the beginning of the word, love becomes evolve, a circle, its end its beginning as its beginning its end.*

Sex. *The field of flowers, slim stemmed, returned now green, blue, white and purple, then gathered into a vertical tube like phallic structure, contracting and expanding in sexual rhythm, until the center became smaller and I became intensely aware of a blue-black sky. The structure turned into a nebular shape and burst into uncountable stars.*

Joy. *...I saw H'Kotel (the Western Wall in Yerushalayim), it was Hanukkah and the Hanukkah was lit, the candle flame flickering shadows against the Wall. I could see the outline of peoples heads. The feeling of joy, the flames of the candles rose up within me to a point beyond description. Then I saw the stone Torah Tablets, pure bright white superimposed upon the scene, and the feeling of joy intensified almost too much to be contained physically.*

The scene disappeared and there stood two Shabbat candles, I somehow felt as though I have been given a most wonderful gift. There was pride and responsibility mixed here, yet the joy was more ecstasy which filled the universe of "me." I became and was in ecstatic awe, which united with reverence before the word was spoken.

Reverence. *I thought of Yom Kippur. I was standing before luminous Gates, I could see the Way. A deep feeling of reverence and awe swept over me, and individualism was swept away, "I" became the "Eye," and Ayin, seeing yet unseen. All feelings mingled and became One, I smelt incense, I saw the smoke curling transparent, I felt an acceptance, a Kabbalah.*

Notes. *Afterwards...there was no marked change, maybe a deepening of thought, a feeling like having stopped on a journey by a waterfall, once refreshed it was time to move on, eager to peek around the next corner.*

The following notes were written by Carol, a 38-year-old female, after her thirteenth Sentic Cycles session.

Carol's Sentic Cycle Notes

No Emotion. *Floating needle.*

Anger. *Sharp bursts of explosive energy; little fantasy necessary to bring about feeling.*

Hate. *For the first time noticed a pulling together of abdominal muscles; much easier to express, less fantasy used, more feeling.*

Grief. *Felt logical after Hate, so tired and worn out from hating, can only grieve at total loss. Strong image of Rotterdam's famous war monument "City Without a Heart," caused tears of anguish and grief to flow from a rather deep, normally inaccessible level.*

Love. *Tender caring for first everything in my immediate environment, gradually as a wave spreading out to include more and more people in an atmosphere of tenderness and caring – flowing out from me. But also to me—more a reflection of harmony with a universal state of being-ness. So beautiful and personal at one point, that more tears flowed.*

Sex. *Very, very erotic and nice, nice, nice. All positive, lots of body images, but more a "feeling" of urgency, joy, and pleasure, or cooperation, oneness and direction.*

Joy. *Background music of known composition which at this moment I cannot exactly place, but definitely possessing the nature of Joy. Joy plus nobility and sensitivity of spirit; upright, elegant, refined, harmonious and good—not quite ecstasy, because exquisitely controlled—some gratitude mixed in for the sheer fact of "beingness""awareness."*

Reverence. *From "joy" very easy to get into "reverence"—the nearly ecstatic feeling of harmony (controlled) flowed easily into the "open door" which allowed peace to flow outwards from the depths of my being and also for "light" (energy) to flow from "outwards" to the depths of my being—a two-way flow which increases, amplifies, a central stillness, peace, PRESENCE—total acceptance of everything and everybody and that all is essentially good.*

In doing Sentic Cycles, images are often initially used to evoke and enhance the various emotions. A person thinks of a situation or image, feels an emotion, "listens" inwardly to what he feels, and attempts to express exactly that feeling. If the expression is accurate, the feeling is enhanced, intensified. As the emotion builds up, it sometimes happens that the original fantasy is spontaneously replaced by a new one which resides at a deeper level within the psyche. Sometimes this is a flashback to an old memory. Sometimes it is a new fantasy which plays itself out like a movie of the mind. As the person becomes more experienced with Sentic Cycles, *the emotions can be generated and experienced without specific images.*

The Virtual Body Image

After people do Sentic Cycles for a while, they often notice that for each sentic state there is a biologically programmed virtual body image. People have experienced these again and again while practicing Sentic Cycles. As your body becomes quiet through performing a sentic cycle, it is easy to observe bodily sensations accompanying each sentic state. These sensations are linked with specific motor activity and posture. The mind creates a characteristic sensory projection gestalt.

Many examples which illustrate these projections can be noted in everyday speech. Think of the "lightness" of joy, the "lassitude" of grief, or "waves" of anger. Though we may be unable to pinpoint physiologic correlates to some of these sensations, the words used to describe these states reveal a lot and point to the universality of our responses. The weight of your arm remains the same, whether you are experiencing joy or anger. Yet, when experiencing joy it often *feels* lighter.

Considering virtual body images, we need to differentiate between actual body behavior, which includes body temperature, heart beat, muscle cramping, crying, sighing, spontaneous changes of posture or facial expression, and projected images such as "flow," "lightness," "heaviness," "a sense of Presence," or "a feeling of spaciousness." Often in anger it will feel as if the body is being torn apart. In hatred, there may be abdominal cramping and/or a tendency to snarl. In grief, there is a drooping posture, a sighing, and a sense of heaviness. Love is characterized by a sense of flow. Often a person will find herself smiling very slightly, there is a sense of symmetry. Joy impels one to sit very straight and is associated with a floating feeling and a greater sense of space; tensions in neck and shoulders tend to go away. Reverence has a sense of "Presence," frequently a feeling of absence of boundaries, a physical sense of illumination.

There are also sensations of actual physiologic changes such as abdominal tension, crying, and changes in the sexual organs that occur during Sentic Cycle sessions. Those who have done Sentic Cycles report that virtual body images are quite specific for each emotion and will change slightly for even a minor variation of sentic form. To illustrate this, I present the following observations quoted verbatim from the notes of various persons' Sentic Cycle notes. These have been collected together and categorized under each emotion.

- **Anger**

    "feel like I'm being torn apart, flying in all directions."

    "Suddenly I have an abundance of non-classifiable sensory data, all unique. Help! This is chaos. The shitty little things are flying in all direction through space. Aarrrgghh!"

    "... my breathing has increased and my heart feels constricted." "concentrate on how anger "feels"—the sudden burst of adrenaline, the total readiness for explosive action—Fast heart beat. Faster breathing."

    "the feeling of adrenaline pouring into my blood stream."

"feelings of nausea, headache. Legs kick out a bit with the finger expression of anger ... my breathing is much faster and body temperature feels as if it has risen noticeably."

"noticed quite an increase in breathing rate."

"feel sick and headachy"

"anger rises to my chest, restricting my breathing."

"facial flush."

"in anger and hate I had the sensation of excruciating pain in the nerves of both arms, hands, and shoulders."

"body temperature rose."

- **Hate**

    "feel tightness in stomach, general muscle tension."

    "rather snarly."

    "muscular tension extreme, breathing fast…the tension is so great that I want to scream, but start to cry instead."

    "I feel a huge ear shattering scream beginning deep within me and carrying me out of myself on its energy."

    "mostly pure feeling. Image of trying to move, but this is almost impossible because my body is so HEAVY, so dense. It's like glue is on everything or that instead of having to walk through the invisible air, I have to walk through invisible taffy, or caramel, or bread dough."

    "feeling of getting smaller and denser, blacker and more rigid, very heavy."

    "exhilaration, power. Energy is concentrated, focused, directed…"

    "feeling of tremendous force and speed."

    "dull, deadly weight in my stomach."

    "feel familiar tension, like grinding teeth. Recognize a lot of self-hatred and the physical manifestation of *teeth grinding*."

- **Grief**

    "feeling of falling."

    "time slows way down."

    "feeling of heaviness."

    "I feel a dead spot, like a stone."

    "can't feel grief–there is a wall of invisible glass between the sad things and me."

    "In addition to copious tears and racking sobs, I found myself leaning forward to the extent that my head was nearly between my knees and experienced a rocking motion back and forth."

    "I've cried more this week during sentic Cycles than I have in the past four or five years altogether."

    "dull ache, lethargy."

    "like sighing."

"no imagery at all, but I cried many tears which came from some deep dark spot within me."

- **Love**

  "flowing feeling."
  "my face melted with softness."
  "My body listened quietly to the beautiful flow within me."
  "My quiet breathing echoed my trust."
  "My world seemed a bit wider."
  "a gentle rocking motion."
  "complete change in pattern of breathing for each emotion and fully conscious of what is happening without desire to control in any way."
  "smile on face . . . continuous smile."
  "feel my body relax."
  "a nice flowing feeling from me to me."
  "It feels as if some invisible hand is gently massaging my temples, then behind my eyes and finally the back of my head so that the love can penetrate and be expressed. The fantasy was limited entirely to this physically felt sensation, which was real enough."
  "relaxed...I'm really relaxing into the love feeling."
  "a smile."
  "weightlessness of the body."

- **Sex**

  "got really excited."
  "got too warm."
  "she is guiding me, very gently, telling me to relax, and trust...at this point my sinuses drain."
  "a nice warm glow."
  "I became aware of a mounting excitement in my vagina, along with almost holding my breath. I was not ready for the directive to change emotions, and felt left up in the air."
  "I found my body stiffening into exciting curves and extensions. My neck arched, as did my spine."
  "I felt I had fallen into some archaic body ritual."
  "tension or intensity of feeling especially in area about 1/3 way down from navel to genital area, to 1/3 in from front (i.e. definitely below upper colon area—between colon and bladder)—near top of bladder (precise as that)."
  "My breath was short and sharp."
  "noticeable rise in temperature and congestion of sexual organs. Cycle seemed short."

"noticed a definite physical response in myself."
"got very excited."

- **Joy**

  "energy going in and removing stiffness in my shoulders."
  "I feel the odd sensation of being several miles high."
  "feeling of spaciousness."
  "lovely floating feeling."
  "feel shoulders and upper arms relax. I feel a lot lighter."
  "Something is happening to my temples; some kind of internal movement. Throat also. Feel light. Floating."
  " the feeling was physical, or almost physical and I can describe this feeling the best by comparing it to the sensation right before I have an orgasm and I just want the sensation to go on forever."
  "sensation of traveling, feeling the source of joy coming from the right."
  "My neck stretches and relaxes; all my muscles relax."
  "Physically experienced as a massage beginning in the lower back (wide) extending (narrow) all the way up the spinal column. Produces very pleasant sensation. Later same feeling back of head and temples."

- **Reverence**

  "my space has become infinite."
  "feel safe."
  "great feeling of relaxation and of being myself."
  "Physically I feel much larger than normal and not really in the body at all."
  "the odd sensation of my right arm being on the left hand side and my left arm being on the right hand side."
  "During the last half of Reverence, my left eye, my nose and throat (left side) began to water with the result I had to cough, blow my nose, and wipe my eye."
  "I seemed to hold my breath…an overwhelming expansiveness felled me."
  "My body did not seem greatly relevant."
  "…I had come full cycle and returned home."
  "I was radiant and without boundaries."

Healing Use of Sentic Cycles

That Sentic Cycles lend themselves to healing is not surprising. Ordinary persons leading ordinary lives can find great release through the channels offered by Sentic Cycles. Many people in our society go around feeling emotion which they cannot (or dare not) express, or which they express inappropriately.

A chance to "let it all out" with NO unpleasant consequences is surely very tempting.

The following excerpt from the notes of an experienced Sentic Cycles user shows a way in which Sentic Cycles can be used for self healing.

> *Yesterday evening I was depressed without any reason; the cycle today brought out the cause, very surprising to me in content and direction.*
>
> **Hate.** ...I see myself as a first year Conservatorium student, absolutely terrified and uncertain of my own identity, intimidated by all the new and unknown factors suddenly appearing in my life; a sense of helplessness at my own lack of perspective; panic in not knowing which set of values is correct or workable. Hatred at the injustice. Resentment of a lover who selfishly tried to deprive me of my musical education only to satisfy his own lusts. Furious at all the factors which together nearly destroyed my entire identity during this period.
>
> **Grief.** Great compassion for the very good, gentle, serious, loving and earnest girl, the real person, living on the inside of this chaos and fear, the real me who only acted so unstable and erratic due to a consuming fear and panic—HELP ME, HELP ME., PLEASE, ANYBODY HELP—seeing myself through a time-tunnel—*then is now*—*loving and supporting this lovely person*, myself, giving all the support and encouragement that was then necessary, but is NOW, and feeling at last the intense relief that everything is all right; I'm "at home" seeing myself in the old environment now-then and meeting my teachers then-now with the confidence and trust in myself, the REAL feeling, the strength and beauty, the gentleness of my own self, and NOT being intimidated or squashed out of existence by them, the grown-up sometimes cynical and hardened teachers.
>
> **Love.**—a continuation of the previous, ever more positive and supportive, a flowing of light and goodness into specific scenes of those student days, bringing them into the active present, a feeling of integrating a lost part of my personality, with every "click," every expression a mending of the soul occurred, a healing action, an acceptance of that which had been torn away, stuffed into a dark box of forgetfulness, letting my idealism live again, the lightness and joyousness of youth, the gentleness and tender insights naturally mine, live, but now *protected* from harm and even more precious for having been lost. What is more beautiful than the integration of a fragmented personality?

Notes about this session made on the following day: The insights gained yesterday and the actual "experience" left me somehow exhausted, though strangely satisfied and peaceful. I slept for two hours in the afternoon, and nine hours at night, very much aware that "the physical rearrangement of furniture takes time and energy. It's hard to get used to functioning with equipment which has been 'out of order' for twenty years, but it's wonderful too."

Persons suffering from anxieties, phobias, severe stress, or psychosomatic symptoms may gradually modify attitudes, patterns of behavior, and emotional reactions through the practice of Sentic Cycles. Couples' cycles (discussed later in this article) can be used to rediscover lost emotional togetherness. Sentic Cycles can also be employed as a diagnostic tool. By noting deviations from pure sentic form (allowing of course, for individual variation) it is possible to explore how a person may be blocking the expression of the emotion concerned; the person can then use the Sentic Cycles technique to learn, or relearn, how to express and release emotion in a safe and comfortable way, and perhaps free themselves from living in a largely superficial world devoid of deep, meaningful communication.

The Apollonian and Dionysian Models

As Clynes states in his book *Sentics: The Touch of the Emotions*, there are two fundamental ways in which we experience emotion: the Dionysian way and the Apollonain way.

Dionysian. In everyday life we frequently run into situations which evoke emotion. Most often we are *reacting* to a situation. Your five year old boy comes bounding into the house holding a dandelion and says "Mommy, I love you," as he hands you the flower. Your heart melts and you feel love for the child. Or just at the moment you are late for work, you trip over garbage that the neighbors' dog has strewn all over your yard. Anger rises up and you're thinking "I'll teach that so-and-so a thing or two" as your heart races. Those are the "real situations," the situations in which you are an active participant.

Another whole class of emotional participation is that of "catching" an emotional state from someone else. You are witness to a street fight with much name calling and yelling. You find yourself becoming angry, too. Or a sales clerk is nasty to you and you react with equal nastiness.

Both of the foregoing are in the present state and can only happen in the "now." But most of us probably spend more time in a fantasy world, past or future; in these worlds, we can endlessly create new emotional scenarios for ourselves or can rehash, elaborate, re-experience, or relive past experiences. We can replay the five-year-old bringing us a flower and saying "I love you, Mommy" a thousand times and each time we can be bathed in the warm feeling of love. We can focus on certain aspects of the incident to further amplify the feeling of love—the way the light played on the child's hair, the quality and sincerity of the child's smile, the graciousness of the child's voice. We can even gradually change our memory until the original incident is pale compared to our enhanced version. The opposite is unfortunately also true. We can create a downward spiral for ourselves, getting more and more angry with our poor neighbor—all out of proportion to the event itself.

There is yet a fourth emotional state, still farther removed from "reality." Who has not been moved to tears while watching a good movie in which actors generate various emotional states entirely from fantasy? Sometimes even movies that aren't that well done can get through to us with a little help from our own fantasy.

For many of us, the emotions generated by life's circumstances take us on a roller coaster ride. It's one thing after another. Just when you think you've recovered from the death of a loved one, you lose your job. Fear, panic, and anger take over. Or after working hard for many months, you finally succeed brilliantly at your project and are "over the moon" with elation and joy. And what of the agony and the ecstasy of being in love?

When we experience our emotions as described here, with full blown ego involvement, we are participating in the Dionysian model. Emotions tend to run our lives and, like well trained puppy dogs, we run along as fast as we can.

Of course, people who are living their lives according to the Dionysian model have rich, if sometimes exhausting, emotional lives. If one could only mimic the emotions of others no direct physiological connection, life would be flat.

A flat, mimicked life bereft of deep feeling has little appeal, yet the rollercoaster life of the Dionysian model is simply too exhausting and out of balance. Happily, there is a another ground. One can have deep, rich sentic experiences without drowning in or being slave to these experiences. Clynes calls this the Apollonian model.

Apollonian. Performing Sentic Cycles allows one to experience a more balanced emotional life. Doing this technique provides one the opportunity to express dormant, previously unexpressed emotions, creating catharsis and allowing a new phase to begin. The urgent drive to express emotion is somewhat abated through Sentic Cycles, and you find yourself at a crossroads. You now have the option of embarking on a different mode of experience called the "empathic viewing mode" or the Apollonian point of view. This view corresponds to the meditative state. In the Apollonian model, each sentic state is savored in the same way the various emotions in music can be savored. Even the body responds in a different manner.

The Apollonian mode allows you to retain mental freedom and at the same time savor the quality and purity of each sentic state. This mode illuminates and clarifies the moment. Because you have retained your mental freedom, you can voluntarily and easily switch from the empathic viewing mode of one emotion to the empathic viewing mode of another emotion. The whole spectrum of sentic states lies before you, and like an artist you can pick and choose exactly which sentic state you wish to experience, creating your own "symphonies" of touch.

When you have the ability to switch from one sentic state to another, you can get out of, or avoid entirely, a sentic rut. Sentic control offers a choice. For example, a person who is stressed and difficult to live with might do two Sentic Cycles, the first one a full expression of the Dionysian mode. With the urgent requirements of inner drives having been met with the first session, he/she is then free to embark upon the experience of the Apollonian model. Whereas the former may have been quite draining, the latter will assuredly be calming and revitalizing.

Reactions to other people and outside situations frequently alter after such sessions, often to the amazement of the person who has done the Sentic Cycles. He/she will notice more affirmative action, for example, and less reactionary behavior. Sentic fluidity appears to be an important aspect of mental health.

A significant aspect of the empathic or Apollonian viewing mode is the positive effect it can have on personal relationships. In this mode, one is more easily able to see others in their totality. You can see the "inner self" of the other person. In the Dionysian or sympathetic viewing mode, by contrast, one tends to lose sight of the totality of others, seeing only the anger, the sex, the grief, etc.

The Apollonian perspective precludes being judgmental or tending to offer advice. Originating from a sense of inner quiet, the projection of sentic impressions occurs with full recognition of the potentiality of others. The mental image, or "idiolog," we have of our friends and family, like the dream personalities we so effortlessly create at night, have stability. Viewing others from the Apollonian point of view serves to harmonize our relationships with them. Like a Zen monk we can "walk two inches off the ground and yet experience fully."

World View

One important aspect of the sentic cycle theory is that the various emotions or sentic states represent a series of attitudes. As you express each emotion, you experience the particular world view of that state. Intimate knowledge of these states provides an understanding of aspects of human nature which might otherwise be labeled instinctive or intuitive.

It seems that this world view and honesty are very much intertwined. Each emotion presents its "truth" in different terms. So, accurate expression of sentic form guarantees our sincerity. Commonly, people who speak more than one language notice a link between sentic states and world view. When speaking different languages, a subtle shift in the underlying sentic states also occurs from language to language.

An interesting experiment to do during a Sentic Cycle session is to think about the same event or same persons for the duration of the session. This technique can reveal the world view embodied by every sentic state. Having noticed this phenomenon many times, I share with you a Sentic Cycle done in the imaginary waiting room of an imaginary International Airport. The notes are as follows.

No Emotion. No problem at all, well focused and non-expressive.

Anger. Easy expression of irritability. Was very pleased to immediately get expressed my extremely negative reaction to American tourist lady. The whole scene changed right in front of my eyes and I saw the worst qualities of the people around me, felt highly superior to them, the ass holes. Egotistical as hell.

Hate. Focused on the American tourist lady. She makes me want to throw up. I don't know why, but I'd like to hurt her, strangle her with my bare hands or something. It will be very interesting in America if any more of these strong antipathies occur. This lady is definitely threatening to me. Yuk. Vomit.

Grief. Very easy to tune in on the collective grief feelings of all the people around me. Pure grief expression. I feel one with all these people (who are no longer ass-holes) through our shared experience of grief. Feel more relaxed and loving already.

Love. This feels GOOD. Easy to relax into gentleness, an unassuming expression of being, acceptance of people. Flowing free feeling. No ass-holes anywhere to be seen. I've got this secret now, my private world of love which protects and nourishes me.

Sex. Welcome to the Airport, Fantasy Friend. So you're going to New York with me!! How nice. My discreet and loving Fantasy Friend does not want to create a scandal at the airport so he builds a space just for us—with *walls,* so that the others can't peer in. Actually there are two rooms which alternate back and forth, flash, flash, flash, flash, first the one and then the other. One is a cozy winter room in a cabin with a blazing fire, in a huge fireplace. That's Fantasy Friend. The other room is pastel lavender, green and blue, in the summertime, white marble fireplace, no fire, very luxurious Louis XIV furniture, exquisite taste, That's me! Real sexual feeling, some skin flicks, not much, but intimate, tender, and loving. Exciting and discreet.

Joy. Oh, boy, the whole waiting room is getting bigger. Now I've got this huge amount of space between me and the other people so they're not in my way at all and I'm not in their way either. Just love the sensation. I just sit there watching all those lovely people and feel joy.

Reverence. Gratitude to All-that-is for the personal guidance, the tender consideration and care being shown to each one of us. Gratitude for the power watching over our flight to make it harmonious, joyous, peaceful and safe. Especially feel a real PRESENCE, an intelligence, interested concern, love for each of us down to the tiniest detail.

Visualization As a Means of Expanding Our Awareness

Sometimes while doing a Sentic Cycle, a spontaneous story emerges, as in the following excerpt.

Grief. A very old couple live in a modest cottage on a farm. They have just lost their only child, yet an infant, who was (they had thought) to be the "pearl" of their old age. But suddenly one night, for no apparent reason, the child died. The crib of the infant is now empty, and the old couple sit in the same room with bowed heads—silent, and full of delicate and tender pathos. They have placed one lone rose bud on the place where the child once lay. Neither of them speaks, but they are at one with each other through their loss.

Love. The old couple, now together for more than fifty years, goes about their simple duties. He brings in water and cuts wood for the stove in the kitchen. She is making bread and the smell of two finished loaves fills the room with an aroma of contentment. They are both *caring* as they work, doing each task with an easy precision. He sees her foibles, her weaknesses, her foolishnesses and small stupidities and without thinking further, forgives and accepts these things. She no longer notices his indiscretions and fears, but lovingly supports him, accepts him, and *cares*. They both have an expression of simple dignity, of strength, courage and gladness.

Sex. This loving old couple retires to their old wooden bed (made by him, years ago, of solid oak). Their hands reach for each other with the familiarity that only years can bring. Every inch of each body is known and loved by the other. Their lovemaking is straightforward and tender, the logical and completely natural expression of love grown deep and strong with the passage of the years. Their bodies react to each other as a highly sensitive team, each partner knowing exactly what to do and what, for the maximum pleasure of the other. Their love is tender and exquisitely erotically sensitive.

Joy. The couple walk together on their farm. It is winter and there is snow on the ground. The red of the dog-wood bushes contrasts sharply with the clear blue sky and the white snow. They walk farther to the pond where hay has been put out for the deer. Two does are standing perfectly still near the pond. They are totally alert, ready to spring away at the slightest indication. The couple notice the rabbit tracks in the snow and listen to the rustling wings of a startled pheasant as it makes a quick escape. The pussy-willows in winter are especially beautiful because of their promise. The buds are already formed, ready—just waiting for Nature to give them the proper signals for growth. In all directions, as far as the eye can see, there is peace and harmony—a natural freedom of spirit.

Reverence. I am outdoors in New Mexico, sitting under a pine tree in the wilderness while it rains. I listen to the rain falling on the rocks, on the sagebrush, on the flowers and trees and I am filled with immense peace. I am myself. I am totally "open". That is enough.

Visualization itself can be greatly expanded to include senses other than the visual. The possibilities are endless and chosen to support whatever goal one has in mind. Alternatively, sometimes it is fun just to "play" with the imagination.

Imagine how it feels to stand in a pool of hot mud and squeeze the mud through your toes. Imagine the smell of a steak sizzling on the Barbecue. Imagine the smell of your sexual partner. Imagine the sound of a single violin. Imagine being caught naked (just for one minute!) on the North Pole in Winter.

The following is another example of the use of visualization during Sentic Cycles. These notes are from a Reverence cycle.

Reverence. *The sage brush is wet after a rain. The air is heavy with ozone. I love the smell after a storm and breathe deeply. Something exciting, pure, clean, promising. It's wonderful in fantasy to be able to smell nice smells so sharply and with such delightful accuracy. The dust is settled, wet. I look at the wet dust, then become the wet dust. Hey! It's only an eighth of an inch deep! Then it's dry warm dust I feel, the surface wetness cool, the middle layer of warm-dry and the gradually more compact and cooler earth. I feel the roots of the sage brush in me seeking nourishment far deep down, each root actively moving towards moisture, tiny tentacles manipulating like hands and signaling messages to the main plant. I listen to the sage brush commune with me and with the other sage brush. This scene shifts to a double one. On the left hand side, the sun is brightly and gloriously shining,* *and I am all this, too ... It is not difficult to be both things at once and I delight in the contrast. It feels, in fact, VERY GOOD.*

Next day, further commentary on sentic cycle. Had the definite feeling of wrapping myself with a protective layer which enables me to go safely into the world without fear of damage or of death. Increase of inner freedom of movement.

As you can see from these notes, Sentic Cycle visualizations can be quite powerful and useful for people.

Sentic Cycle for Learning and Achieving Long-Term Goals

The visualization aspect of the Sentic Cycles technique is useful for learning as well as expanding awareness.

In the book "The Inner Game of Tennis" by Timothy W. Gallwey, a remarkable learning technique is presented, one which we probably all used as young children (in learning to walk, for example) but subsequently forgot. The theory behind this technique is that to learn a specific new skill you can literally think yourself to success. Sentic Cycles are particularly well suited for this type of learning.

With Gallwey's technique, you must first find a good model, someone who is thoroughly proficient at his skill. You then watch every motion this person makes and imagine yourself doing the same thing just as beautifully and well. As Gallwey states in his book, this method of learning has been proven effective. It is far more successful that attempting to learn a thing only through verbal or written instructions, for example: "now put your left foot forward two inches, your elbows slightly to the right, knees bent, head turned to the left one-half inch," etc., etc. This latter instructional method produces a great deal of tension and very little else.

If in addition to the strongly held image of yourself performing a particular skill extremely well, you can add a positive emotional component through the use of accurately expressed sentic form, a tremendous driving force may be added to the acquisition of the skill. If you were learning a golf swing and had an emotional undergirding of joy, the result could be pleasantly surprising. The sentic form of love could also be employed for successful results. A well expressed sentic form has a powerful effect upon the mind and body. Why not harness that power? A person skilled at the use of creative visualization will be astonished at what strength an emotional "carrier" can have upon the force of a visualization.

Sentics Used in Training Actors

Though useful for all types of learning, the study of sentics can be of inestimable worth to actors. For example, a whole classroom of students could do

Sentic Cycles together and then discuss what was "discovered" during the experience. Using the typical scenarios created for a drama class, it would be easy to show the class how effective communication can be when there is a one-to-one link with accurate expression of sentic form. The paradox is that in the process of becoming a good actor, the "act" is replaced by a kind of reality. Whether or not a fantasy is being brought to life, the emotion itself is real.

There is probably no other profession for which the intimate understanding of emotion can mean as much to the success or failure of a career. The most famous actors have always been those who can project a sincerity so disarming as to convince the viewer that "this is reality….this is how it really is." The most absurd situations become believable if the spark of emotional communication can be blown into a flame.

An actor, or a school of acting, could well save thousands of hours (to say nothing of dollars) by incorporating the serious study of sentics into the curriculum. Using a combination of guidance and self-discovery, the initial cycles could be done together as a class, followed by group discussion. Students could be required to do three Sentic Cycle sessions each week, keeping a careful journal of their experiences. Both physiological and perceived changes could be discussed by the class. As the students' awareness becomes fine tuned, the characteristics of each emotion could be discussed. Discussions could focus on the role posture, world view, position of the eyes, etc. In the given emotion is there a natural tendency to look up, down, or straight ahead? For muscles to be rigid or soft? Is there any muscular tension? If so, where? Is the head held straight, or to one side? What happens to the breathing?

Once the sentic form of each emotion is well understood by the class, various output modalities could be used, even the voice by itself. Sitting behind a screen, the voice alone could be used to project love, grief, or joy. This could be done by using either vocalized sounds without words, the alphabet, or a neutral sentence. Multilingual classes could have a dialog between two different languages, concentrating on the emotional communication that takes place. Or students could say their lines using only the vowels of the words and no consonants. Students could then study expressive gesture, how to translate one discrete finger pressure pattern into movement, how to modulate the tension found in each gesture for a given emotion. The class could then talk about which options give the greatest communicative power. In this way the students themselves can discover the balance and beauty of the positive emotions, such as the natural symmetry of love. Or they can experience first hand the twisted asymmetry of hate, and the snarl which goes so well with nastiness.

In studying the physiologic characteristics of each emotion, students could do "still life" exercises with their faces in order to express the various emotions. Subtle differences in the musculature around the eyes would become apparent, as would tension of the lips and mouth.

There are many subtle physical signs that communicate emotion. Flaring nostrils, twitching in the corner of the mouth, furrowed brow: these all offer clues to a person's emotional state. The pallor of the skin may also noticeably change in the throes of an emotion. By focusing on every small detail related to sentic form, learning both to initiate and to recognize sentic form will ultimately lead to performance excellence. Such study gives the actor a "suitcase" of available emotional material ready for use at any time. Armed with deep knowledge of timing and intensity, the artist can move easily from one sentic state to another and in so doing touch the minds and hearts of the audience.

Developing Musical Sensitivity Using Sentic Principles

Practicing Sentic Cycles can also help a musician reach an audience, and this is perhaps one of the primary reasons that Manfred Clynes developed this technique. (See related articles on composer's pulse and music in this volume.)

To explore the uses of Sentic Cycles in developing musical sensitivity, I conducted a little experiment. My young music students Anke and Patti were my eager subjects. Anke and Patti, who were about 11 years old at the time, had their violin lesson together. This made it fun and easy to experiment with Sentic Cycles in the context of a learning environment.

For my experiment, Anke, Patti and I began our usual hour-long lesson by discussing the nature of happiness, anger, and sadness. We talked about the things which make us happy, or sad, or angry. Then we talked about how we express these feelings. "Show me how a happy person would walk across the room…a sad person… an angry person…Does a sad person speak with a loud voice or a soft voice?…Show me." We did some play acting as well and invented some situation such as: "Someone has just run over you pet dog. You are across the street and see it happen. What do you do? How do you feel?" or "Another kid at school takes your new bike and deliberately makes a big nasty scratch in the new paint. What do you do? How do you feel?"

Once the children were quite clear about body posture, tone of voice, speed of movement, I said: "Now I want you to make up some music which is all your own. First of all I want you to make up some sad music and play it for me. You can have a few minutes to figure out how to do this." When they were ready and played for me, we went on to experiment with happy music, and then angry music. Finally I asked each girl to play, but to do so without telling which emotion she was playing. Both girls *loved* this game. At the end of the lesson, I asked them to go home and write down an original composition which had the form: Happy – Angry (or Sad) – Happy. They were to bring these compositions to our next lesson and play them for me.

The compositions that Anke and Patti came back with the following week were delightful, and as the children loved these lessons they begged to be allowed to continue in this fashion. It was easy then to begin introducing expressive elements into their playing. Gradually these children began to understand that in the baroque and classical music which they were learning, every note is involved in meaning. They were learning the underlying emotional meaning found in music and they loved every minute of the process. For older students it is very rewarding to also work with the concept of the "composer's pulse" which was discovered by Manfred Clynes many years ago. (For more information on Clynes theory of the composer's pulse, see Denis Vaughan's contribution earlier in this volume. See also related articles.) Even a little understanding of the composer's pulse can quickly yield excellent performance results.

Beyond the Basics

Sentic Cycles have numerous applications, and they don't become boring. One can practice standard Sentic Cycles again and again and again, achieving beneficial results every time. Even so, it is nice to add variation from time to time, and there are some interesting options for those with a strong foundation in the standard technique.

Couples Cycles. For persons who already possess a good working knowledge of standard Sentic Cycles, it can be a unique and rewarding experience to do Sentic Cycles with a partner.

A couples' cycle is intensely personal, much more so than a "single" cycle, simply because of the real physical presence of another person. The other person is a solid, responsive reality rather than a fantasy. In Sentic Cycles for couples, both persons are continuously confronted by the presence of the other.

(To perform a couples' cycle, it is best for the couple to sit cross legged on the ground facing each other. Each person lays his/her left hand, palm up, on his/her own left knee. The fleshy part of the upturned palm is the "finger rest" or expressive arena for the other person. If sitting cross legged on the ground is uncomfortable, as it may well be, then the couple can sit in two straight-backed chairs opposite each other. Some people will feel more comfortable with a pillow to support the small of the back.)

Because of the wide spectrum of the emotions expressed during Sentic Cycles, Clynes has referred to the couples' cycle as being a "mini marriage." The emotional impact of a couples' cycle is considerable. To share sincere communication with another human being in such an intense way is very powerful. In couples' cycles, accurately expressed emotion occurs not once, but many times consecutively, and with a wide spectrum of feeling.

At workshops, I have observed that people sometimes feel so close after a session, even if they began as total strangers, that they are loath to break off the intense feelings of closeness generated during the session. Many couples will spontaneously embrace each other after the last click for Reverence and sit that way for several minutes, savoring the emotional oneness with the other in an atmosphere of love and peace. A whole room full of peaceful and loving human beings, with not one person feeling the need to talk, is indeed a memorable experience.

Advanced Cycles. In addition to Sentic Cycles for couples, there is an advanced version of the regular Sentic Cycles. Clynes developed Advanced Sentic Cycles after some years experience with people doing regular Sentic Cycles. It had become apparent to him that as a person progressed through the various stages of growth, i.e. initially learning to express pure sentic form, then clearing out the backlog of unexpressed emotion, and gradually moving from the Dionysian to the Apollonian mode of expression, there was readiness to progress into a more spiritual realm and to specifically cultivate such qualities as love, reverence and compassion.

In my own attempts to create a more advanced tape using Love, Joy and Reverence, it was my experience that the resultant cycle was somehow "flat" and lacking the powerful afterimage and lucidity of the regular cycle. Clynes' solution to this was characteristically bold in its design and a radical departure from the previous tape. Just as in the initial Sentic Cycle tape, the emphasis is on self discovery. However, for sentic expression one uses full gestures rather than simple finger pressure.

Quoting directly from the instruction manual to the Advanced Sentic Cycles, *"The gestures it uses are self-refining—you will discover that even the slightest variation of the movement pattern will produce a different feeling tone. Pure feeling goes with pure gesture. You will discover what that is."*

There are no finger rests used in the Advanced Cycle. Instead of finger pressure, both arms are used to create gestures. In my experience, it sometimes takes a few sessions for a person to "translate" the sentic form from a pressure pattern into a gesture.

The advanced cycle differs from the standard cycle in that it does not contain Anger, Hate, Sex, or Grief. The only excursion into the "negative" is in the expression of compassion when one descends into the pain of the other, touching the pain for a moment and then returning to a state of love.

The sequence of the Advanced Cycle is as follows:
>
> No Emotion
> Love
> Reverence
> No Emotion
> Bliss
> Reverence
> No Emotion
> Love
> Compassion
> Give Blessing
> Reverence

One could think of the advanced cycle as a compilation of three smaller cycles, each beginning with "No Emotion." The "No Emotion" of Advanced Sentic Cycles is different from that of regular Sentic Cycles. While in the regular cycle there may be an emotion present during this state, it is not expressed. In Advanced Sentic Cycles, however, "No Emotion" signifies an emptiness, a nothing, no thing, the mind is to be emptied.

The advanced cycle comes complete with a video cassette and an instruction booklet called "Doing Advanced Sentic Cycles." The video is at once a help and a hindrance, as pointed out in the instructions. By trying to copy the exact gestures which Clynes uses, it is easy to block the flow and actual experience of the emotion. It also tends to stifle self discovery. But the tape is immensely useful in the beginning to make sure that the user is "in the right ball park." With greater familiarity with the forms, the eyes may be closed (or partially so), enhancing the ability to look deeply inward.

The advanced cycle can be done sitting cross legged on the floor, sitting on an ordinary straight-backed chair, or standing. Each posture indicated has its own set of limitations. Sitting cross legged on the floor presupposes a lean and flexible body capable of sitting for relatively long periods of time without tiring.

Some allowance may be made by the user if s(he) is living at a very high altitude when expressing Reverence. Even at lower altitudes, beginners may want to breathe more frequently than is indicated in the instructions. Also, when standing to do the cycle for No Emotion and for Compassion, the non-active hand and arm may be allowed to hang loosely at the side of the body. (For Give Blessing, however, the non-active hand should have the palm facing upward, elbow bent at a right angle.)

The otherwise perfect symmetry of sentic form in Advanced Sentic Cycles is broken for the expression of both "Compassion" and "Give Blessing." The asymmetry of the Compassion form is distinct, and necessary (i.e. it is not possible to touch the pain without the asymmetry). In Give Blessing, however, there is still a kind of spiritual symmetry because the upturned hand, although inactive, has the palm turned up in a receiving position—in giving we are also receiving.

The advanced cycle can seem considerably longer than the regular cycle, even though it is actually only three or four minutes longer. This may be because the effect of the advanced cycle is more powerful than that of the regular cycle. The after-effect of Advanced Sentic Cycles, which lasts for several hours, is also characterized by an enhanced sense of calm and well being.

It would be wonderful if Clynes would follow Advanced Sentic Cycles with a Sentic Cycle of Sacred Dance. This would obviously involve the whole body and would most likely require considerable physical stamina such as is developed by Tai Chi. An Emotional Sacred Dance could be a wonderful combination of emotional expression, the art of dance, and meditation combined into one cohesive whole.

Summary

Sentic form is an expressive entity which has a specific space/time form for each emotion.

The ability to recognize sentic form, the ability to empathetically feel the same emotion as another, the ability to produce sentic form, embody a biologically based emotional language. Moreover, the degree of one's communicative power depends entirely upon a faithful representation of sentic form. The higher the degree of faithfulness, the greater the power of communication.

To an experienced user, one of the thrills of doing Sentic Cycles is to experience pure emotion without reference to any thing, any one, or any event whether real or imagined—pure un-fantasized emotion, occurring naturally and containing all the bodily reactions inherent in each form.

Performing Sentic Cycles can be healing. Sentic Cycles can also act as an aid to the achievement of long term goals. Given the fact that emotion is a powerful carrier on which our actions ride, it is possible to use directed fantasy during Sentic Cycles sessions to produce powerful and deep-seated "programming" for the successful achievement of our goals.

Couples cycles may be used to refine and enhance communion and communication with a partner or loved one. And, once we've mastered regular Sentic Cycles, Advanced Sentic Cycles can take us to a new level of emotional experience and expression.

E.M. Christine Kris

Manfred Clynes:
A Gift for Our World

It is an honor to write about Manfred Clynes, whom I first met at M.I.T. in the mid nineteen fifties. At the time of our meeting, we were both visiting Dr. Warren S. McCulloch's office at the Research Laboratory of Electronics. Manfred, who had invented the CAT (Computer of Average Transients), was working at Rockland State Hospital's research facility doing surface electrical research and pulse-sensing measurements from the skin through transducers, and recording heart rate and respiration simultaneously. (This research led to his discovery of Cardiopulmonary Unidirectional Rate Sensitivity). Meanwhile, I was working at MIT on Surface Electrical D-C Measurements of Binocular Bi-dimensional scanning eye movements for the Air Force and NASA. I was also studying reciprocal innervation during perception and rating, in combination with recording of heart rate and bihemispheric electroencephalograms, to measure eye-brain interrelationships in changing conditions of vigilance, drowsiness, sleep, arousal, and varied emotional states.

Warren was a catalyst who knew and brought many people together. He mentioned to me that Manfred was doing original work and was a multifaceted "creative genius," and he told us both that we had some life experiences in common. As Manfred and I exchanged both past histories and current research interests, we discovered the truth of Warren's statements. Manfred and I were both from Vienna, Austria where, in 1938, our early education was interrupted by Adolf Hitler's Anschluss, and our respective families left to avoid physical harm, resettling in other countries. Manfred went to Australia, and I landed in England to attend boarding school. We shared the influence of English Moderation, and a tendency towards "Understatement and the Zeal to Complete Tasks We Undertook." We felt an immediate affinity for one another and have been in communication since our first encounter.

Manfred's first interest and public accomplishments were as a very young performing musician who gave piano concerts publicly as a young teenager. After completing high school he studied music in Australia, but was simultaneously drawn to explore technology and the neurosciences. Being a rational and forward thinking person, he became an electronic engineer as well as an accomplished musician. Indeed, throughout his creative life he has used science and engineering in the service of music.

Manfred came from Australia to the United States to conduct research and carry out advanced studies. I came from England after completing my undergraduate degrees in Education and Psychology to study Psychophysiology, Neuropsychology, and Bio-Medical Electronics. In the 1950s, 1960s, and early 1970s, research funds for the development of technological and scientific methods to study Mental Life and related sciences were available to those who proposed a doable project. Manfred's work on Unidirectional Rate Sensitivity (URS) became the topic of a meeting at the New York Academy of Sciences. His work on the transduction of pulses through finger pressure and the invention of the Sentograph[1] to measure pressure and pulsing intervals, led to his invention of sentics (patterns of emotional expression) and what he terms "The Touch of the Emotions." His multi-disciplinary interests made these accomplishments possible. As both a musician and a scientist, the touch of a small round finger pad attached to the surface of a chair for scientific purposes made sense. This notion served to make possible the recording of the force and duration with which finger pressure is transduced in the expression of emotion. The use of a method of associating feelings to this form of touch initiated pressure, in association with elicitation of a named sequence of feelings, led Manfred to develop a system for working through the gamut of lived and relived emotions, a system that he named Sentic Cycles. (Manfred's innovative work in this arena was published in his book *Sentics* in 1977.)

In the 1970s and early 1980s, Manfred started to refine and teach the method of using Sentic Cycles for the relief of pent-up emotions, thereby inventing a new psycho-therapeutic tool. During this time, I was also continuing to refine my work regarding simultaneous measurement of eye movements, brain waves, and heart rate during assessments of learning and practicing basic skills.

---

[1] An instrument that precisely measures, as functions of time, the vertical and horizontal components of the forms of transient pressure on a finger rest.

I had become a licensed Clinical Neuropsychologist, and Director of the Multidisciplinary Institute for Neuropsychological Development (MIND) Inc., a clinical research center for the study, treatment, and habilitation of developmental disabilities and related mentation and learning problems. Manfred repeatedly visited the MIND Center, and offered to work with me to help treat clients. We worked with and treated a young adult client, Mrs. B, using Sentic Cycles to relieve her of her emotional, learning and performance blocks in a computer job.

The young woman was in her late 20's, recently married to a young man near in age who also worked in the same company in a supervisory position. They got along well, until Mrs. B's job security was threatened by a report of slow work, distractibility, and recurring tension headaches. Her condition worsened and she became anxious, emotionally depressed, and less interested in her marital involvement. She became withdrawn, homebound and did not want to come to work. When she was first brought to the MIND Center, she had spent several days in her room, at home, refusing to come out, thereby avoiding going to work.

Personality and Neuropsychological tests were administered, by me, and it was found that she was basically and energetic, motivated achiever who, however, could not accept reprimand or failure. When quite young, as a schoolchild, she had difficulty with learning to read and write, and remained slow at developing these skills efficiently. The use of computers for data entry, at a time when this was still done by card-punching, was sufficiently structured and did not involve reading for information retrieval and handwriting. She did well in her early training, but after a time, could not increase her speed according to the expectations of her supervisors.

On closer examination, it became apparent that she had been left-handed as a child, but had been encouraged to use her right hand to write and to hold her fork while eating. When left on her own, she often switched to her preferred left side, but at her computer job, she had to work on keypunch machines made for right-handed people. She had not become aware of the cause of her rising anger, and disappointment in not being able to compete by doing fast "piece-work" at card punching, and her childhood experiences of failure and reprimand in school were relived during "bad dreams" and even nightmares.

I presented Mrs. B to Manfred Clynes, who introduced her to Sentic Cycles. Manfred encouraged Mrs. B to use her left, dominant hand to perform Sentic Cycles—to express a sequence of named emotions by pressing the sentogram pad with her left middle finger. The sequence of emotions as accessed through Sentic Cycles begins with anger, followed by rage and aggression; sexual arousal feelings followed by love; and finally, reverence for life and all that it contains.

At first, Mrs. B did not know how to associate the past experiences that gave her a poor self-image, and that had blocked her from "feeling good about herself and towards others." However, with some therapeutic, focused guidance based on clinical interviews with her, she was able to begin to associate incidences that made her angry, and conditions that enraged her. She was also able to regain feelings for sexual contact with her husband. After three sessions, she was able to "feel the love" that she had felt for him, and she began to enjoy life again. Although she had kept herself homebound during her anxious "blocked" period, she was, during recovery, willing to go on a "second honeymoon" with her husband.

Before the fourth, controlled Sentic Cycle session, at the MIND Center, Mrs. B was more responsive to the suggestion that she was ready for an exploration of other work and employment possibilities. She smiled at the suggestion and said, "On our trip, we went for walks in the woods and prairies, and I live the flowering branches and the flowers. I want to learn to work in a flower shop, and become a flower arranger."

At this point, Mrs. B's husband reported that she was her cheerful self again, that their relationship had grown and deepened, and that they have both acquired a reverence for all of life, including plants, and all living creatures. They also acquired a pet to care for and enjoy.

During the fifth session of Sentic Cycles at the MIND Center, Mrs. B had difficulty in getting angry and into an emotional rage state. She spent more time on feeling loving and experiencing the reverence she had acquired for plants, animals, and the human condition. Combined eye movement, brain wave, and heart-rate monitoring, which all had shown much tension and difficulty with focusing and resting during her "blocked anxious period," had become calm, regulated, and well controlled. Mrs. B had normalized both physically and emotionally, improved her own outlook on life, and was very grateful for the experience with her Sentic Cycles, which had been initiated by Manfred Clynes and helped to bring her treatment at our center to a successful conclusion.

While Manfred's work has been invaluable in the therapeutic arena, it is not only in this are that he has made outstanding and valuable contributions. Always exploring new ideas and weaving together the worlds of science and art, Manfred took his theory of sentic form beyond the clinical setting. The sentic forms used to characterize individuals' pulse pressure patterns have led to Manfred's analysis and development of synthesizing musical styles of interpretation. Recently, he has become involved in making the "pulse-tone-touch," the hierarchical pulse of many composers available to the public at large by creating software programs that will allow anyone who is interested to interpret and produce the works of the great composers. With these programs, virtually anyone can use a present-day fast PC computer to develop CD disks for their own and other people's enjoyment.

It is amazing and laudable that one man can get so deeply involved in innovative work in electronic engineering; in computer technology; in surface electrophysiology; in the neurosciences, and in the emotional states of mankind, and is able to combine these scientific interests and capacities to innovate in the service and expression of music. Manfred Clynes, the man, and his creations are a blessing.

Walter Horn

My Sentic Cycle Experiences

Though I've not met him personally, Dr. Manfred Clynes has had a profound impact on my life. His invention of Sentic Cycles has, in fact, changed my life dramatically.

Sentic Cycles is a sophisticated technique by which you feel emotions in a specific sequence and express them with specific timing through subtle finger movements or body gestures. I began doing this technique several years ago, and discovered that regularly performing Sentic Cycles has many beneficial effects on a person.

I write here of my own personal experiences with Sentic Cycles. It is, for me, a great honor to be able to share these experiences in celebration of Dr. Clynes. I see Sentic Cycles as a very powerful spiritual tool, especially for our present-day western culture. I think that this technique could transform our society in the same way that it transformed my own life.

My life story is difficult to tell. Our world is full of hate and violence, and my life was no exception. During my childhood I was often confronted with violence. My religion teacher abused me sexually, and other types of violence were an everyday occurrence. Violent behavior seemed "normal" to me. So, I became violent, too.

When I grew older, I had very few friends. Though I did have girl-friends, they would leave me after only a short time. I felt very lonely and unhappy and I recognized that there was something wrong with me. Yet I felt trapped in this unhappiness. My life was flat and boring, like a black-and-white movie without color. Instinctively I knew that I had to change my life. I desperately wanted to do this, but I had no idea of how to go about it.

I began to read a lot of literature about psychotherapy and spirituality. Through self observation, I soon realized that I was completely unable to feel really deep positive emotions, such as love or joy. My mind was always working and overheated by the thousands and thousands of thoughts constantly flowing through it. Most of these thoughts centered on my hurtful past, paralyzing me in the present. I was tremendously nervous and had absolutely no energy. So I decided to try psychoanalysis.

Psychoanalysis was problematic for me on several counts. First, it was very expensive and I had no money. Also, my goal was to quiet my mind and enhance my ability to feel emotions. But psychoanalysis is a thinking process and I already thought too much. Analyzing my past was unhelpful, having no effect on me.

I next tried Transcendental Meditation (TM). However, I had a great resistance to having a "guru," and by doing TM I became even more nervous. So I stopped it after a while, moving on to other personal growth techniques.

I was a typical spiritual seeker, pursuing many paths and trying many things, but stopping them all after a while. Then, a friend who was living in the US gave me the book *Sentics: The Touch of the Emotions* by Dr. Manfred Clynes. This friend didn't have any personal experiences with Sentic Cycles, but gave me the book because he thought I might find it helpful and interesting. And this I certainly did.

While reading Clynes' book I became fascinating by the idea of feeling emotions in a specific time segment and sequence, and expressing them by subtle finger movements. *It seemed possible that one could learn or relearn to feel the full range of human emotion by regularly doing Sentic Cycles.* Perhaps, I thought, this could have a strengthening effect like training a weak muscle. I cannot quite explain the very deep sense of hope that this gave me. I vowed to do Sentic Cycles regularly every day for one year, and at the end of the year analyze and evaluate its effect on me.

Initially, I found it incredibly difficult to get in contact with my emotions during the Sentic Cycles sessions. It was particularly hard for me to access love and reverence, and the stress that I experienced as a result of this difficulty made me even more nervous. So, determined to succeed, I decided to combine the technique with classical music. I always loved this kind of music and understood the ability of classical music to influence the feelings of a person. I made cassette tape recordings of specially chosen music for the emotions of grief, joy, anger, hate, love and so on. For joy, for example, I chose an oboe concerto of Albinoni. For grief I chose the Mozart's *Requiem*. For reverence I chose the slow movement of Beethoven's *Symphony No. 5*. For anger I chose a Wagner opera, and so on. I also changed the music from time to time.

I listened to this classical music and to the clicks on the Sentic Cycles tape at the same time. This was a powerful combination for me, and was particularly helpful in the beginning. Mozart, Bach, Beethoven, Schoenberg, etc. showed me the way to experience deep, intense emotions like I never had before.

My emotions opened up as a result of doing Sentic Cycles. During the phase of grief I cried a lot of tears, and a lot of experiences of the past came into my consciousness. Once I was able to let go my resistance towards grief, I began to enjoy feeling this emotion, and after a while it became both an extremely powerful and pleasurable experience. I learned that grief is not a "negative" emotion. Rather, it is another form of energy. Through doing Sentic Cycles, I got more and more in touch with my emotions. At the same time, I recognized that my mind got quieter and I was able to relax.

I stayed true to my commitment of doing Sentic Cycles every day for a year. When the year was up, I felt much more love and compassion for all people. I asked my friends if they recognized any change in me. All of them told me that I had become much more relaxed and was more warm; my girlfriend was especially happy about this change.

My experimental year was up about three years ago now, and I'm still doing Sentic Cycles regularly. Over time, I have found that doing this technique brings ever-deepening joy and pleasure to my life, and it never becomes boring—every session is different.

Sentic Cycles have become a very important part of my life, and I think I will do them for the rest of my life. They relax my body and quiet my mind. They enhance my awareness and have helped me to relearn what it is to feel and express my emotions. Like a child, I was often overwhelmed by my emotions and could not control them. But through doing Sentic Cycles, I learned to control my emotions and be simultaneously inside and outside of the emotion, observing its expression. I can now control and choose which emotions to express. Instead of being a slave to my past experiences, I am now the creator of my feelings and emotions. *I view Sentic Cycles as a synthesis between western science and eastern wisdom.* The goal of western psychotherapy seems to be to bring the client in contact with his feelings, to help him feel like a child does. The goal of most eastern meditation techniques, on the other hand, is to quiet the mind to enhance awareness, and to stay in the present moment. By practicing Sentic Cycles regularly, these to goals can, I think, be reached simultaneously.

Sentic Cycles have been very powerful for me personally, and I believe that they could also be a powerful healing tool for our world. There is so much hate and violence in our world. Violence is a sign of not being able to control and master emotions, and Sentic Cycles could teach us all to better control our emotions. Indeed, this technique seems to be specially designed for our culture at this time. What Vippassana meditation is for the eastern hemisphere, Sentic Cycles could become for the western hemisphere. Indeed, I hope Sentic Cycles will become as well known as Vippassana meditation and spread all over the world.

I have a beautiful vision of the future. In this vision, children are taught the Sentic Cycles technique in school and practice it together with their friends and families. This would reduce the violence in the world and bring more love, compassion and peace in all our lives.

Doing Sentic Cycles changed my life, and I wish that everybody could benefit from them as much as I have. I hope that this happens and offer many, many thanks and love to Dr. Manfred Clynes for making this possible.

Jaak Panksepp

The Sentic Forms of Manfred Clynes: In Search of the Affective Dynamics of Basic Emotions

How can we measure emotional responses objectively? How might we generate emotions voluntarily? What is an emotion...for real? As research on human emotionality has exploded during the past few decades, legitimized after years of orphan status, questions such as these are tantalizing more and more scholars around the world (see Ekman & Davidson, 1994). A few are seeking to fathom how emotions are created from the neuronal webwork of the brain.

As we look for provocative ideas to guide future inquiries, the thoughts that Manfred Clynes has shared with us across the years come to my mind as readily as any others. Unfortunately, in the frenzy of new empirical findings and conceptual thought on the topic, Manfred's seminal work in this important area of inquiry has received less attention than it should. . . partially because it is so original and unique, partially because some of the ideas remain to be marshaled with the full weight of experimental evidence. Also, the neglect is a result, in part, from his work being so intimately linked to musical issues. Even though music is one of the major ways we can modify our moods and emotions, and even though music theorists have put forward emotional theories as have the social science traditions (e.g., Budd, 1985; Meyers, 1956), the ideas from musically inclined thinkers have typically had little impact on thought in psychological circles.

Manfred's work on emotions emerged in part from his recognition that musicians can express deep feelings through expressive movements. He set out to characterize the dynamics of these movements, and along the way, he generated startling conclusions, some of which, regrettably, have not yet acquired suffiently broad empirical foundations. Partially this is because there has been insufficient replication of his work, largely because of lack of trying. Interested investigators typically do not have the necessary research tools at their fingertips; to empirically pursue emotions from a Clynesian perspective, investigators need one of Manfred's creative devices, a sentograph (a specifically designed touch/pressure sensor), or an equally fine piece of machinery, to initiate any relevant work. Few have sought to build such equipment themselves. Obviously, it is much easier to design and use pencil and paper scales than to construct a good sentograph, and until recently none were commercially available. It is also easier to record on videotape the self-evident facial gestures of individuals exhibiting emotions, along with their vocal utterances, than to measure the pure forms of emotional movements as Manfred set out to do. With the wide availability of polygraphs, it is even easier to measure many of the commotions within the body during emotions than to faithfully record the force of an individual's dynamic emotional movements in simple space-time coordinates. To do that required the Clynesian mind that we celebrate here—that of an engineer, a master musician, a neurophilosopher, blended with the soul of a poet and the spirit of a satiric clown.

Considering his unique dynamic and music-type perspective on emotional matters, it is regrettable that Manfred's contributions have received so little attention. However, the neglect was due in part to the way Manfred chose to frame his ideas. Manfred generated major conclusions, without seeming to fill in some of the empirical details. His emotion work was all too easy to ignore even though it clearly intrigued many. Even as many investigators puzzled over his findings and theoretical claims, Manfred forged ahead, using his new-found knowledge to "teach" computers to generate wonderful music with principles abstracted from his understanding of emotional dynamics (Clynes, 1977, 1982). While many other modern investigators of emotion were entranced by the static features of emotions, Manfred insisted, at the start of his work, that to make major progress we must understand the underlying dynamic forms—the pure and essential patterns in time that characterize emotional communication and expressions. Presumably, such dynamics reflect neuronal characteristics of emotional circuits within the brain which can be expressed in various instinctual and cultural forms, ranging from simple sounds and simple movements to the dancing "sentic" patterns within the complexities of music and other forms of art (Clynes, 1977).

If all this is true, it would be wise for many of us to return to some ideas that Manfred shared at the beginning of the current modern-era emotion research. Of course, the sticking point for many scholars remains encapsulated in that little phrase, "if all this is true." Some of his extensions to other matters, such as the presence of "sentic forms" in some emotionally moving works of art, have all too easily been deemed to be over-generalizations by critics. Thus, even as Manfred was publishing the idealized sentic forms of seven emotions (anger, hate, grief, love, sex, joy, and reverence) and claiming that repeated expressions of these forms were clearly contained in the emotional exercise he called "Sentic Cycles," he did not systematically report on the variability in response patterns that is bound to be evident in a sufficiently large sample of randomly selected subjects.* Until such evidence is provided, some critics will conclude that the dynamic forms of emotions that Manfred revealed through his sentographic analysis, need further empirical foundation. There has been one replication of Manfred's views with respect to the shape of certain emotional movements (Hama & Tsuda, 1990, and also see Lidov's work in this volume), but the overall amount of published experimental evidence remains meager. Likewise, little replicative evidence yet exists for extensions of Clynes' work into the physiological or affective changes that occur when one does Sentic Cycles.

In short, some of the conclusions that Manfred has drawn from his approach (i.e., the product proves the theory), are not welcomed by those who insist that ideas must live and die via "null-hypothesis testing" and "factorial experiments." Thus, while Manfred has provided a powerful and credible solution to one of the great mysteries that permeate our lives—the objective forms for emotional dynamics—many scientists are skeptical. As mentioned, this is not because the skeptics have failed to replicate his findings; *most have simply failed to try.* In this paper, I will share some of the preliminary evidence from our studies at Bowling Green State University (BGSU) that convinces me, with some quibbling about details, that Manfred's conclusions about the expressive dynamics of emotional movements are on the right track. But before I share the results from my own modest studies in the area, I would first share some personal reminiscences about how I became engaged with the splendid fertility of Manfred's mind.

Some Personal Reminiscences

Long before I met Manfred, I had become fascinated by his thoughts. Along with many others, I was especially intrigued by the claim that we could voluntarily evoke specific emotional feelings within ourselves by faithfully expressing the dynamic sentic forms of emotions at a single "point" in space, namely a round plastic finger-rest situated just to one side of your knee, while sitting in

---

*Although Clynes published some data showing individual variation of the forms, the curves obtained for the CAT show average forms, not individual responses. No mathematical technique is available—even today—to provide an index of comparison between two such shapes sensibly suited to the ability of the affective nervous system to differentiate these dynamic forms (Editor's note).

a relaxed upright position. An opportunity to learn the Sentic Cycle technique from Manfred himself materialized in June of 1986, when our paths crossed at the inaugural meeting of the International Society for Research on Emotions (ISRE), held at the William James Lecture Hall of Harvard University. Parenthetically, B.F. Skinner, whose office was a few floors above, did not attend, perhaps because he had already concluded, to his own satisfaction, that "the 'emotions' are excellent examples of the fictional causes to which we commonly attribute behavior" (Skinner, 1953). In any event, it was satisfying to be in the company of those who did not share that pervasive and destructive behavioral prejudice that permeated American psychology throughout much of this century (see Panksepp, 1990).

Manfred presented a superlative workshop summarizing ways to imbue the dry score of music with emotional feelings according to the "pulse structures" of composers and other "microstructural" issues such as predictive amplitude shaping of successive notes. The audience was both entertained and awed. Later, in a private moment, I coaxed Manfred to give me a personal tutorial in the generation of emotions via his Sentic Cycle exercise. The lesson was crisp, clear, and to the point. My first attempt at Sentic Cycles yielded the expected internal feelings. Thus, I decided it was worth the effort to repeat the exercise a sufficient number of times during the ensuing months, and the consistency of my own affective responses convinced me that there was something to Manfred's idea that peripheral dynamics from the "soma" could feed back onto unknown brain systems that governed our emotional feelings. Since I had already undertaken a research program on how brain systems create the basic emotions (Panksepp, 1981a,b, 1982, 1986, 1991, 1993, 1995, 1997), I was attracted to any manipulation in humans that might be able to arouse such feelings (presumably by recruiting the relevant brain systems) in a laboratory setting. Although I was not about to shift my research efforts from the level of neural circuit analysis to more peripheral issues, I became convinced that Manfred's ideas deserved closer experimental scrutiny than they were receiving among those working on the diverse aspects of human emotions. However, I may not have done anything more with the topic, were it not for a propitious event.

Late in 1986, BGSU decided to bring some fresh intellectual blood to campus through a new Distinguished Visiting Professor program. Although many names were bandied about, no one in our department took the initiative to submit a formal proposal, and the Chair descended on my office a few days before the deadline in some despair that our department might not be in the competition. I took the bait, and with some fresh sentic feelings still impressed on my mind, suggested that we invite someone that was sure to have some interdisciplinary impact, for instance, Dr. Manfred Clynes, from the Music Conservatorium of the University of Sydney. The necessary contacts were made, a pact was sealed and our request was funded. Manfred arrived from Australia to spend the Fall 1986 semester with us at BGSU. The rest was fate. My research and thinking became deeply influenced by his sentic views. There is not sufficient space here to describe Manfred's visit, but let me just say that it was a whirlwind—he offered a provocative seminar in our department, was active in the theater and music departments, and shared his artistry with us at an all-Beethoven piano concert for the University Community. Together, we also organized a well-attended and fascinating symposium on "Emotions and Psychopathology," the proceedings of which were published by Plenum (Clynes & Panksepp, 1988).

There are many anecdotes to share from this time, especially ones related to the eager interest Manfred showed in our animal-emotion research we were pursuing at the time (which impressed me fondly, considering how difficult it is to attract my psychologically oriented colleagues to pursue such work). However, the event I would really like to highlight is one that explicitly symbolizes the incredulity that is commonly evoked by Manfred's more creative accomplishments.

Some of my academic colleagues had never heard of Dr. Clynes, and one influential individual in our department (to be left unnamed)

Figure 1: Manfred Clynes (right) and Walter Freeman in Dr. Freeman's Electrophysiology laboratory at the University of California, Berkeley, in the summer of 1994. The original Computer for Averaged Transients is in the lower left of the instrument rack.

became suspicious whether some of the claims on his resume were a bit exaggerated, such as receiving the patent on the first CAT computer (Computer of Averaged Transients)—the technological breakthrough in the early '60s that allowed neurophysiologists to study cerebral evoked potentials efficiently. This cautious colleague insisted that the Chairman verify that claim. With some embarrassment, the Chair phoned Karl Pribram, who proceeded to reminisce, a bit wistfully, about how Manfred had beat him and others out on that achievement (see Pribram, this volume). Because of that regrettable suspicion, I am now especially fond of the photograph depicted in Figure 1 snapped in Walter Freeman's laboratory at Berkeley in the summer of 1994. Walter had just drawn Manfred into the inner sanctum of his lab to show how they were *still using the first generation commercial version of his CAT computer, constructed more than 30 years prior.* Walter emphasized how Manfred's invention was still competing successfully with more recent technologies. Incidentally, it is worth noting that Walter has also recently published a remarkable book on the topic of brain and emotions (Freeman, 1995) which adds new dynamic dimensions to our thinking about emotions.

During Manfred's stay at BGSU, I decided that many of his ideas should be competing on the field of science with more recent ideas. Accordingly, I started to do some systematic evaluation of sentic-cycles and emotions about ten years ago. These experiments were always done *as sidelights* to my main research efforts, and because of other time pressures and the tragedy of my daughter's death early in 1991, they never were properly written-up and submitted for publication. In any event, I had become quite curious to know the extent to which Clynes' claims concerning Sentic Cycles could be supported through an analysis in which I could be confident that no "demand characteristics" or "confounding variables" were operative. In this chapter, I will share two sets of unpublished results from experiments I conducted between 1987 the 1990. First, I wanted to know whether there were characteristic physiological changes in individuals performing Sentic Cycles (Study 1), and then, whether one could demonstrate emotional changes in people doing Sentic Cycles using various psychometric evaluation tools (Study 2). In general, the studies support some of the conclusions advanced by Clynes across the years, but as with any empirical inquiry, there were also some inconsistencies.

Study 1: Physiological Changes During Sentic Exercises

This study was run to evaluate whether visceral changes do emerge during the performance of Sentic Cycles. Breathing rate, heart rate and finger temperature were monitored while young college-age subjects did the standard eight-emotion Sentic Cycle sequence (using the original timing parameters constructed by Manfred, see Clynes 1988). Affect ratings were also taken at the end of each exercise to determine whether certain emotions yielded greater affective changes than others.

Subjects and Apparatus

Twenty subjects were given full instructions in doing Sentic Cycles using the "proper" movement patterns. All subjects had been given at least three opportunities to do the cycles in a group prior to the recording session. Various transducers were used to measure physiological changes. During the test session, respiratory rate was measured by an unobtrusive thermistor gently clipped to one nostril. Heart rate was monitored with a finger-pulse meter that had a tachograph input, and finger temperature was monitored with a small flexible wire thermocouple taped to the left index finger. All sentic expressions were done on a sentograph (body and sentograph in standard position, using the right hand), the outputs of which were connected to physiograph channels for monitoring each movement. A standard Sentic Cycle tape containing the seven emotions, with appropriate timing pulses as described by Clynes (1988), was used. Upon completing the exercise, the subject was asked to rate the intensity of affective experience for each emotion on a scale of 1 to 5, with 1 being no feeling, 3 moderate feeling, and 5 intense feeling.

Results and Discussion

The results for the autonomic measures as a function of the emotions in the cycle are depicted in Figure 2. The number of subjects included in each comparison depended on the quality of recordings. Only a subset could be included in the overall analysis. Heart rate varied among emotions, being highest in hate and anger, and lowest in love and reverence, and intermediate in the others. This yielded a reliable overall F-ratio (F (7,84) = 7.09, p < .0001), with anger and hate being the highest (p's < .01), and with no statistically significant differences among the others. Breathing rate also exhibited differences (F(7,126) = 9.25, p < .0001), with the lowest breathing rates occurring during grief and reverence, which were the only conditions that were reliably different than the others (p's < .05). High and low finger temperature among emotions did not differ (data not shown), even though the difference between high and low temperatures during the discrete emotional segments was highest for anger (1.50°C) with the other average difference scores being no larger than 0.62°C, and the smallest for reverence being 0.13°C.

The affect ratings were similarly intense among the seven emotions ($F(6,96) = 1.59$). Numerically, the highest mean ratings were for anger and love (means of 3.7) and the lowest were for sex and grief (means of 3.2 and 3.1), suggesting that the group as a whole experienced moderate emotional feelings of comparable intensity during each emotion segment. In agreement with findings reported by Manfred (1988), this experiment indicated that one can observe autonomic changes during the moderate emotional states that emerge as a result of doing sentic movements, and the effects are most prominent during anger, grief and love. (See figure 2.)

Study 2: On the Intensity of Affective Changes Induced by Doing Sentic Cycles.

After completing a Sentic Cycle, it may be difficult to accurately describe how one feels, and since Sentic Cycles have been claimed to exert emotionally beneficial effects on individuals (Clynes, 1988), such as alleviating mild depression or anxiety, I sought to evaluate the nature of affective changes using a more traditional psychometric tool than a simple rating scale. An ideal scale should monitor several emotional changes both in terms of "state" as well as "trait" variables. Accordingly, in this study I used Spielberger's State-Trait Personality Inventory (STPI) which monitors both momentary as well as more long-lasting changes in anger, anxiety and curiosity. Also, to evaluate whether the precise mode of doing sentics effected the affective intensity experienced during the exercise, I contrasted two distinct procedures. The first was the classical sentic procedure using a finger-rest (see Clynes 1977, 1988). The second will be called the "free-form" procedure. The students had been exposed to the classical sentic procedure and the free-form procedure on two occasions prior to the start of formal testing.

The STPI was administered as a pretest one week prior to two sentic test sessions. During one pretest session, half the subjects used the traditional procedure with finger rest, and half used the free-form procedure. The procedural approaches were reversed the second time around. All sentic exercises were done in a group session, with lights dimmed, and silence prevailing except for the timing cues provided by the Sentic Cycles tape. Immediately following the session, subjective ratings were requested for the intensity of emotions the subject had felt on a scale from one to five, with five being the highest. Immediately after that rating, all subjects were requested to complete all 60 items on the standard STPI inventory. Following the last test, the subjects were debriefed and given a small questionnaire

132   Part III: The Realm of Sentics

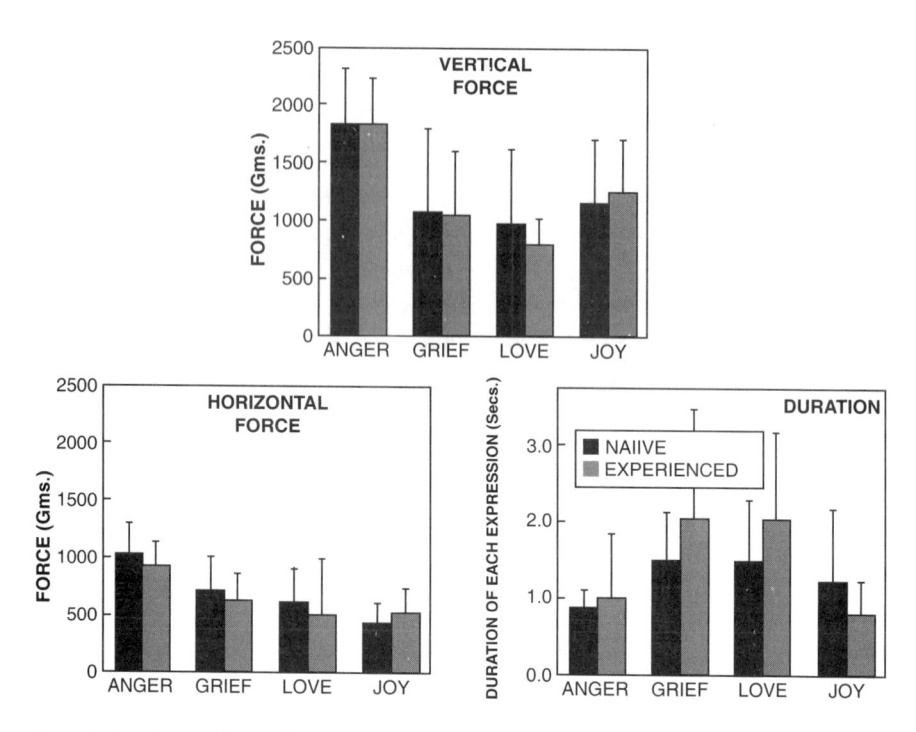

Figure 2a: Maxiumum force and total duration for emotion expressions. While these data do not describe the shapes they generally are in agreement with values expected from Clynes' curves.

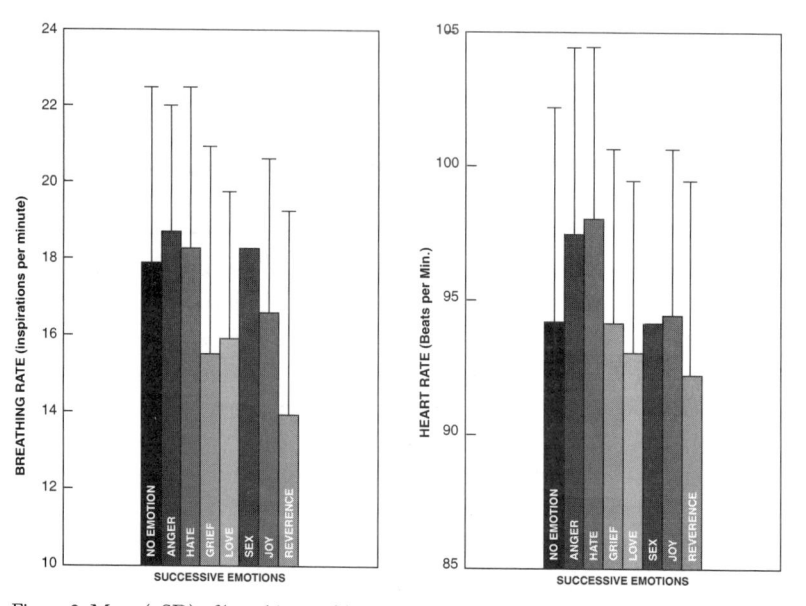

Figure 2. Mean (+SD) of breathing and heart rates during successive segments of the traditional Sentic Cycle exercise.

inquiring about their opinions about Sentic Cycles, including a question as to whether they found the "traditional" or "free form" procedure to be more effective in generating affective feelings.

Results and Discussion

The average state and trait scores for the various test periods are summarized in Figure 3. Following both sentic procedures there were reliable declines in state anxiety, anger and curiosity scores (p's < .05), but the two procedures did not yield differential results. Trait scores generally did not change, except that trait curiosity under the "traditional" procedure was reliably lower, but the slightly smaller decline under the free-form condition was not. (See Figure 3.)

The Likert scale affect ratings for the test periods ranged from 2.0 (for reverence) to 3.0 (for love and joy), with no reliable differences between the traditional and free form procedures. At debriefing, however, 80% of the subjects reported that the free form procedure was generally more conducive to feeling the various emotional states. Indeed, on a 5-point Lickert scale, subjects expressed finding the free-form procedure preferable (mean 2. 1) over the traditional procedure (mean 3.2) (t(9) = 2.3, p < .05). Only one of

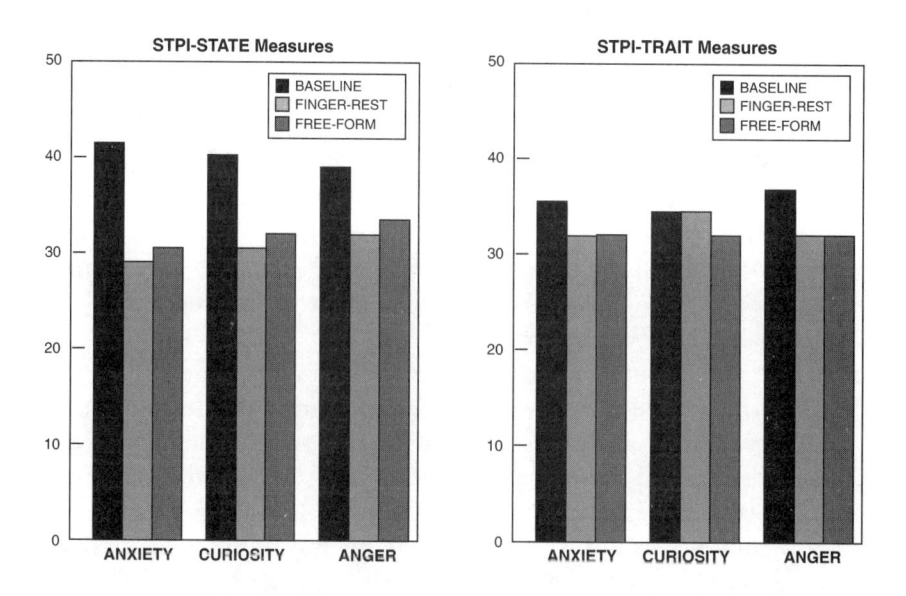

Figure 3. Average ratings of anxiety, curiosity and anger using Spielberger's State-Trait Personality Inventory during a baseline session, and immediately following the conduct of a full Sentic Cycle exercise using either the traditional procedure or the free-form procedure as described in the text.

the subjects preferred the traditional procedure, and one had no preference. A typical comments was: "The free-from method allows me more comfort and individual expression. Having to touch the button took up some of my concentration and did not always feel comfortable." Also, in response to a question of whether they thought they could now generate such feeling totally internally (imagery, etc.), 90% thought the experience with the exercises now allowed them to generate comparable emotional feelings without making any overt movements. Whether one can generate such feelings without external sentic expressions needs to be evaluated empirically.

Comments

These results from the BGSU study partially replicate findings reported by Clynes concerning the physiological and affective changes that result from doing Sentic Cycles. The traditional sentic exercise was found to modify mood states, as well as certain physiological parameters, as predicted by Clynes. The changes were not large, suggesting that sentic exercises do not generate intense emotional resonance in most people, at least when the exercises are done in group sessions as in the experiments described above. It does need to be emphasized that the subjects in these studies were relatively sheltered young of the American middle-class, who have not had broad spectrum emotional experiences from which to draw personal insights (especially for the nature of grief and reverence). Some students thought that these exercises were somewhat silly, while those that seemed to enjoy the exercises also reported experiencing larger internal affective changes.

The traditional procedure for doing Sentic Cycles did not appear to be essential for obtaining some affective changes. The free-form procedure that was contrasted with the traditional procedure was generally found to be preferable by most individuals, though there was no evidence concerning the degree of affective change than the traditional mode of expression.

Parenthetically, about half of the young students reported enjoying this exercise, but the remainder were bored or felt neutral about it. It will be interesting to determine what type of personality characteristic distinguishes the two. It seems is that those who enjoy it, and more commonly report experiencing emotional changes, are generally the "brighter" students in the sense that they are more intellectually engaged in class, receive the higher grades, and impressionistically (i.e., at least to my way of thinking) seem to exhibit higher levels of emotional intelligence and perhaps emotional resonance. Indeed, in the autonomic experiment (Study 1), the students who generated the largest autonomic changes also tended to be those who exhibited sinus arrhythmia (i.e., fluctuation of heart rate with the breathing rate). It will be interesting to determine if that will be a predictor variable for certain relevant personality traits such as those which allow certain individuals to "resonate" more with Sentic Cycles. I would anticipate that individuals who rate high on the dimension of "affective intensity" and social agreeableness will be more likely to experience stronger emotional feelings during Sentic Cycles than those who are low on that dimension.

Although the performance of Sentic Cycles has not been used widely as a mood-inducing procedure, the present results certainly suggest that it may be capable of being deployed for such purposes, and then one might have to exercise a single emotional response during any one session, for completion of a whole cycle generally leads to overall reductions in anger and anxiety as measured with the STPI (Study 2). Other procedures such as the Velten technique, which rely upon imagining oneself in various situations, and alternatives such as musically induced mood induction have been used more extensively (see Pignatiello, Camp & Rasar, 1986). It will be important to experimentally contrast them to see which are most effective in temporarily modifying the moods of individuals.

The idea that there is a characteristic motor dynamic to each emotion is a very appealing one, and it makes sense of the animal behaviors we see around us. The vigorous rough-and-tumble pouncing of playful animals has a movement characteristic similar to that which Clynes describes for joy. Erotic thrusting resembles the movement Manfred has isolated for sex. The sharp and more sustained, powerful pounding movements of anger and hate are characteristic of individuals experiencing those states in both animals and humans. The movement of love resembles that of a good hug, and that of grief the lethargy of despair or perhaps even the plaintiveness of the separation call. The gentle "uplifting" movement of reverence seems to be opposite to that of grief. It is certainly not far-fetched to believe that the overall integrated internal neurodynamics of emotions correspond to characteristic psychodynamics, and vice versa, but it does seem unlikely to me that a simple dynamic movement can induce the most powerful emotional changes.* For those it may be desirable to try to capture the full character of the bodily response that characterizes each emotion.

Of course, Manfred is well aware of such issues, and his choice of a single movement was premised more on measurement concerns: It is mathematically easier to characterize a single discrete movement than a collection of movements. Also, by sitting quietly one is able to sense what is going on

---

*It is not intended, nor desirable, that sentic cycles produce "powerful" emotional chages. (Editor)

in the body, and the repetition of movements allows a feeling to gradually build. Indeed, for the generation of one kind of emotional experience, the hilarity of laughter, Manfred utilized the repetitive motor rhythm of a laughing episode, as in the expression of "silent laughter" (Clynes, 1977). For those who are not familiar with that phenomenon, it is illustrated in Figure 4. Establishing the respiratory (especially expiratory) pattern of laughter, assisted by rhythmic sentic-type repetitive finger movements (on knees or a table at which one is seated), and a rocking of the body to-and-fro, can establish a remarkable feeling of mirth, but one has to willingly allow those gates of the mind/brain to be swung fully open. As might be expected with any such exercises, if one chooses not be a full and open participant, nothing much is likely to happen. Thus, skeptics can probably disprove any of Manfred's assertions to themselves through a perverse act of will, which would only go to show that the cognitive apparatus of certain human brains can prevail over their emotional systems. That, of course, has always been one of the dilemmas for studying human emotional responses in the laboratory—it

Figure 4. Segments from a video-taped demonstration of "silent-laughter" during the Bowling Green State University symposium on "Emotions and Psychopathology" held September 27-29, 1986 (see Clynes & Panksepp, 1988). The behavior sequence cycles through A to C repeatedly at the natural rhythm of laughter with an eventual resolution from C to E.

can only be done ethically and realistically with cooperative subjects. Only when one is an emotionally willing and open participant in these exercises does anything happen.

This brings us to the crux of the whole matter. Among those participants who are willing to be full and open participants in such exercises, are the subjects actually experiencing emotional feelings as they normally occur in nature or are they only imagining such feelings? Although this broaches closely on the solipsistic dilemma which the study of all subjective experience confronts us with (i.e., we will never be able to see directly and objectively the working of other minds), modern brain scanning technologies do allow us a small window into the relevant brain issues. Such techniques do at least give us the possibility of asking the question whether such induced emotions are "real," at least in the sense that they can be objectively measured. Let me provide a small piece of pilot data using such an approach that convinced me that something very important and powerful is happening in my brain when I do Sentic Cycles. Indeed, perhaps this is an appropriate place to end, for it was Manfred's work as much as any other, with his development of the CAT, that allowed us to extract some psychologically meaningful signals from the chaotic EEG waves which inundate the surfaces, as well as the depths, of our brains during each moment of our lives. It is clear than both music (Petsche, et al., 1988) and emotions (Hinrichs & Machleidt, 1992; Vaningan & Panksepp, 1995) can exert powerful effects on EEG activities. The effects of emotions on deeper brain activities have also been visualized (George, et al., 1995).

To determine whether my brain was changing in predictable ways as I was feeling emotional changes while performing Sentic Cycles, I had my EEG measured using a sensitive topographic EEG mapping procedure called Event Related Desynchronization (ERD) analysis (Pfurtscheller, 1991, 1992). This is an averaging procedure for the power-spectrum, quite similar in concept to the time-locked voltage averaging procedure of evoked potentials that was harvested with Manfred's CAT computer. With the Pfurtscheller's ERD approach, one calculates the power-spectrum during a resting reference interval, and computes changes in power as a function of time during subsequent psychological events of interest. This can be computed across many trials, yielding a pattern of relative change in arousal that is occurring on the surface of the brain. Since the alpha range (8-12 Hz) is the "coasting rhythm" of the cortex, it is generally deemed one of the more sensitive frequency ranges of the EEG to do such analyses. Increases in power in the alpha range (namely, event related synchronizations, or ERSs) would reflect decreases in arousal, while reduction in power (namely ERDs) would reflect active processing. To minimize artifacts such as head movements and spurious laterality

138   Part III: The Realm of Sentics

effects, I intentionally kept my head still, and my face and jaw muscles relaxed during the exercise, and employed the bilateral free-form procedure described in Study 2, where I symmetrically and minimally squeezed both thumbs and forefingers together during the various emotions.

Figure 5 summarizes ERD changes in my brain as a function of doing the Sentic Cycle exercise. Clearly, there were different patterns of lateralized cortical arousal in my brain during all of the emotional states I sought to induce. Whether these patterns would replicate from session to session and person to person is presently unknown, and for the time being less important than the fact that the brain changes during sentic exercises, for at least one well-trained person, were measurable and remarkably large. I do not anticipate that the brain changes in others will be very similar to those in my brain, partially because in a second run, only some of the emotions replicated reasonably well. Also, in more recent work analyzing the effects of emotional pieces of music on the brain, we have seen great inter-individual

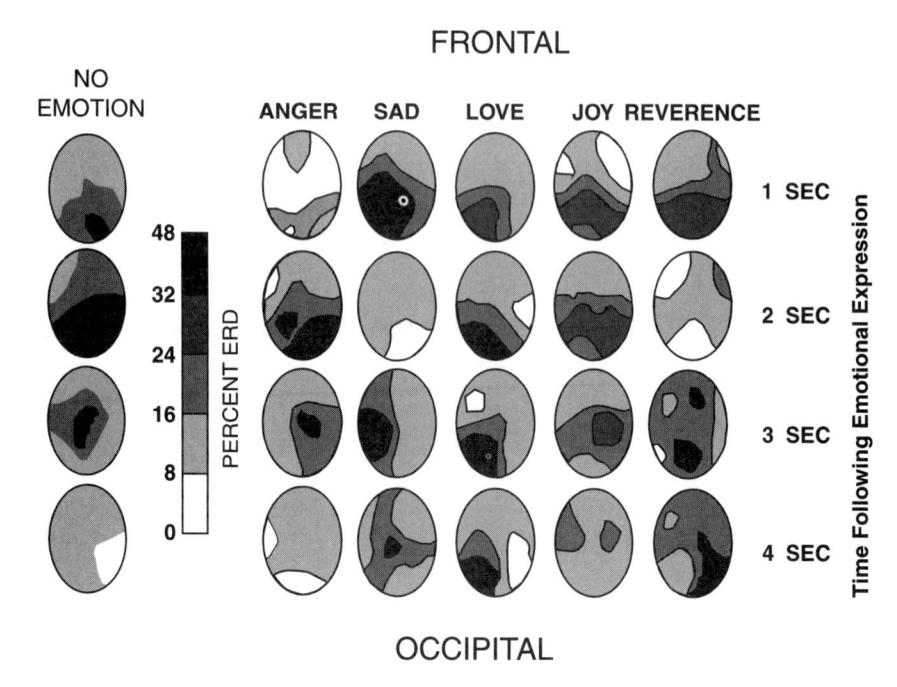

Figure 5. Analysis of event-related desynchronization (ERDs) on J. Panksepp's cranial surface during the performance of a Sentic Cycle session in May of 1988 in Dr. Wolfgang Klimesch's lab at the University of Salzburg. The darker an area, the more evident erousal (i.e., decreased power) within the alpha range. A 29-electrode 10-20 recording montage was used, and in the figure nose/frontal cortex is upward.

variability in the cerebral effects of the same pieces of music on different individuals (Vaningan & Panksepp, 1995). To some extent the emotional changes in the higher areas of the brain may resemble random-access-type memory networks of digital computers than the tightly coded functional circuits that are found in subcortical areas of the brain. Accordingly, across individuals information about similar emotional events may be stored in somewhat different locations depending upon various developmental, personality and situational factors. My emotional habits may be different than the emotional habits of others when it comes to the cortex, even though each of our emotions ultimately relies upon very similar neural functions within the more primitive subcortical areas of the brain where the executive circuits for the basic emotions reside (Panksepp, 1982, 1991, 1997).

I believe that Manfred's work offers a powerful spark that I hope ignites the full flame of human emotion research. And perhaps this should be one of the most important take-away messages of the sentic tales that I have shared in this paper: Although there are essential patterns to our basic emotional processes (in addition to some unique anatomies, physiologies, neurochemistries and dynamics), as those shared processes get elaborated within individual brains and lives, they eventually can generate a variety of manifestations that are more complex than the standard principles from which our basic feelings emerge. Although Manfred's sentic forms may be capturing some shared essence of emotional systems, many types of individual variation could dilute those features in the lives and minds of different people. We have no data on this, but I would anticipate that people with different personalities might exhibit distinct response patterns. I encountered this nemesis recently in an attempt to identify the variables that control the common bodily phenomenon induced by music that we call "chills." It was clear that one of the most robust variables was a personal one—people had "chills" to the music that moved them, namely to the music they had learned to love, and the music selected by others had much less of an effect (Panksepp, 1995). Still, underlying such matters of individual preference and individual variability, there are some general principles. People generally have more "chills" to sad music rather than happy music, and the acoustic structure that may be most effective in provoking the transient feeling is the acoustic dynamic of the separation call (Panksepp, 1995), or some other ancient mode of communication (Wallin, 1991). *Our brains are tuned to certain types of sensory-emotional messages, and that is the profound insight that the Sentic Cycles of Manfred Clynes has encapsulated.*

Manfred's portrayal of the universal, cross-cultural sentic expressions of emotions among humans across the world may reflect a rather idealized signal that is hard to extract from the variable lives of all individuals. This, of course, makes the scientific verification of such underlying processes a difficult one... one that is open to continual refinement... and one that will require the concerted work of many individuals converging from many different perspectives. When we begin to seek such essences from the variable lives of individuals, with all the quirks of personality that characterize members of our species, what type of evidence will be the most compelling for the clarification of general principles?

After all the experiments and statistics are done, perhaps the conclusions we should believe most are those which can demonstrably change the world. Among the many striking intellectual contributions that Manfred has shared across the years, his effort to derive universal principles of musicality from his analysis of emotional dynamics has the potential to influence our culture in positive ways more than any of his contributions. While some of us still ponder whether different emotions can, in fact, be expressed as singular dynamic movements in space, Manfred has proceeded to harness his insights to allow computers to faithfully render the music of the ages (Clynes, 1995). That contribution, more than any other, can help fertilize our withering cultural landscape. To promote such change, the minds of many engineers and artists, as well as scientists, need to work together. It is remarkable when all three can be found in a single brain.

References

Budd, M., *Music and the Emotions*. London, England: Routledge & Kegan, 1985.

Clynes, M., *Sentics: The Touch of Emotions*. New York: Doubleday/Anchor, 1977.

Clynes, M., *Music Mind and Brain, The Neuropsychology of Music*. New York: Plenum Press, 1982.

Clynes, M., "Generalized emotion. How it may be produced, and Sentic Cycle theory." In M.Clynes and J. Panksepp (eds.) *Emotions and Psychopathology*. New York: Plenum Press, 1988, pp. 107-170.

Clynes, M. and Panksepp, J. (eds.), *Emotions and Psychopathology*. New York: Plenum Press, 1988.

Clynes, M., "Microstructural musical linguistics: composers' pulses are liked most by the best musicians." *Cognition*, 1995, vol. 55, pp. 269-310.

Ekman, P. & Davidson, R.J. (eds.), *The Nature of Emotions, Fundamental Questions*. New York: Oxford University Press, 1994.

Freeman, W.J., *Societies of Brains: A Study in the Neuroscience of Love and Hate*. Hillsdale, New Jersey: Lawrence Erlbaum Associates, 1995.

George, M.S., Ketter, T.A., Parekh, P.I., Horwitz, B., Herscovitsch, P., & Post, RM. "Brain activity during transient sadness and happiness in healthy women." *American Journal of Psychiatry*, 1985, vol. 152, pp. 341-351.

Hama, H. and Tsuda, K. "Finger-pressure waveforms measure on Clynes' sentograph distinguished among emotions." *Perceptual and Motor Skill*, 1990, vol. 70, pp. 371-376.

Hinrichs, H. and Machleidt, W. "Basic emotions reflected in EEG-coherences." *International Journal of Psychophysiology*, 1992, vol. 13, pp. 225-232.

Panksepp, J. "Brain opioids: A neurochemical substrate for narcotic and social dependence." In S. Cooper (Ed). *Progress in Theory in Psychopharmacology*. London: Academic Press, 1981, pp. 149-175.

Panksepp, J. "Toward a general psychobiological theory of emotions." *The Behavioral and Brain Sciences*, 1982, vol. 5, pp. 407-468.

Panksepp, J. "The anatomy of emotions." In R. Plutchik (Ed.), *Emotion: Theory, Research and Experience, Vol. III*, "Biological Foundations of Emotions" (pp. 91-124), 1986.

Panksepp, J. "Psychology's search of identity: Can 'mind' and behavior be understood without understanding the brain?" *New Ideas in Psychology*, 1990, vol. 8, pp. 139-149.

Panksepp, J." Affective Neuroscience: A conceptual framework for the neurobiological study of emotions." In K. Strongman (Ed.), *International Reviews of Emotion Research. Vol. 1*. Chichester: Wiley, 1991; pp. 59-99.

Panksepp, J. "Oxytocin effects on emotional processes: Separation distress, social bonding, and relations to psychiatric disorders." *Annals of New York Academy of Sciences*. New York, 1992, vol. 652, p. 243-252.

Panksepp, J. "Neurochemical control of moods and emotions: Amino acids to neuropeptides." In Lewis, M. & Haviland, J. M. (Eds.). *Handbook of Emotions*. New York: Guilford Press, 1993, pp. 87-108.

Panksepp, J. "Affective neuroscience: A paradigm to study the animate circuits for human emotions." In. Kavanugh, Zimmerberg & Fein (Eds.) *Emotions: An Interdisciplinary Approach*. Hillsdale, New Jersey: Lawrence Erlbaum, 1995, pp. 29-60.

Panksepp, J. *Affective Neuroscience, The Foundations of Human and Animal Emotions*. New York: Oxford University Press, 1996.

Panksepp, J., Lensing, P., Klimesch, W., Schimke, H. & Vaningan, M. "Event related desynchonization (ERD) analysis of rhythmic brain functions in normal and autistic people." *Neuroscience Abstracts*, 1993.

Petsche, H., Lindner, K., Rappelsberger, P., and Guber, G. "The BEG: An adequate method to concretize brain processes elicited by music." *Music Perception*, 1988, vol. 6, pp. 133-160.

Pfurtscheller, G. "BEG rhythm-event-related desynchronization and synchronization." In. H. Haken and H.P. Koepchen, *Rhythms in Physiological Systems*. Berlin: Springer-Verlag, 1991; pp. 289-296.

Pfurtscheller, G. "Event-related synchronization (ERS): an electrophysiological correlate of cortical areas at rest." *Electroencephalography and Clinical Neurophysiology*, 1992, vol. 83, pp. 62-69.

Pignatiello, M.F., Camp, C.J. and Rasar, L.A. "Musical mood induction: An alternative to the Velten technique." *Journal of Abnormal Psychology*, 1986, vol. 95, pp. 295-297.

Skinner, B.F. *Science and Human Behavior*. New York: MacMillan, 1953.

Vaningan, M., & Panksepp, J. "Cortical arousal patterns in response to emotional and neutral auditory stimulus." *Abstracts for the Society for Neuroscience*, 1995, vol. 21, p. 951.

Wallin, N. Biomusicology: *Neurophysiological, Neuropsychological, and Evolutionary Perspectives on the Origins and Purposes of Music*. Stuyvesant, NY: Pendragon Press, 1991.

Yehudi Menuhin

Finding Peace

This article first appeared as Lord Menuhin's Foreword to Sentics: The Touch of the Emotions.

Dr. Manfred Clynes' great achievement is to have made emotions and their communication respectable, recognizably ren-dered into graphs, analyzable and measurable. These most intimate, basic and powerful of human drives are no longer imprisoned within the realm of conjecture and blind groping with more or less working hypotheses, but have been released for study, respect and compassion. It is obvious that this signal breakthrough could only have been achieved by a musician: Dr. Clynes is a very distinguished pianist; a scientist who remains a musician at heart. In the same way that painting and drawing furthered our understanding of the human body and of our anatomy, so is music the true and only revelation of emotion, whether as pure music or as the music of language or dance. When, as in Manfred Clynes' case, the music is allied to a penetrating intellect and scientific insight, miracles may happen.

Dr. Clynes' contribution to the interrelationship of emotions, to our crying need for personal expression, and for the cleansing of our minds and souls, illuminates the good sense of our tribal ancestors with their games and gestures and oral traditions, for they knew the supreme importance of sound and contact. Perhaps his gift to humanity will serve to lead us to a more balanced existence, to a coordinated and reciprocal strengthening of mind and heart. Perhaps it will lead to greater harmony and fewer wars. I welcome this sentic science, for the god of love has finally put on the guise of science to lead us into the truly humane—for we, having lost our intuition, and often employing our intellect merely to enhance our brutality, and having lost our faith in feeling and conscience, may rediscover ourselves through the only avenue we acknowledge, that of science.

I pray, however, that just as every thing may be used to both good and evil ends, this new science may be pursued to good, compassionate and wholesome purposes only.

Part IV

Personal Reflections

Tim Smith

Finding the Real Story

"There are two parts to science," Manfred Clynes has said. "There is finding and convincing yourself that something is true, and there is convincing everybody else. It's the second part that's boring."

Boring for Manfred perhaps, but never for those on the receiving end of a Clynes exposition. Manfred is a man of many parts, and the part I like best is the conversationalist—the polymath in whose imagination rigor consorts with fun. I can think of no better illustration than the circumstances in which we met.

I was working for a newspaper, chasing a story that turned out to contain less than met the eye. An editor had discovered that a scientist in California was making music from mouse genes, with supposedly intriguing results: cancer cells were producing dirges, that sort of thing. The scientist spoke no English, so I spent time reading and digesting his papers, consulting the encyclopedia, interviewing musicologists and biologists. After I'd invested enough time to make my editor edgy and impatient, it began to be clear that making music from mouse genes was not much more than a stunt—a matter of assigning tonal values to the paired bases (ACGT) found in DNA and extrapolating tunes from the DNA sequence. The "musicality" derived from a lot of human intervention and the self-similar pattern of DNA.

Anxious to put more meat on the story's bones, I scoured the footnotes of scholarly journals, found Manfred's name, and called him up. He confirmed that mouse-gene music really was mostly a stunt; the trick to it was the self-similar pattern, and such a pattern could just as well be found in stock-market tables, or annual rainfall statistics, as in DNA. It amounted to "flicker noise," no more, no less. My heart fell.

Then Manfred said: "Self-similarity is everywhere. It's like the Law of Like Tits."

Excuse me?

"Clynes' Law of Like Tits. Like tits attract, unlike tits repel."

Come again?

"Didn't you ever notice that on a nude beach, women with similar breasts tend to hang around with each other? And women with non-similar breasts do not. I discovered this years ago on Black's Beach in La Jolla."

At that point, naturally, I abandoned the mouse-gene story and asked Manfred if he could send me some examples of his work. It was the beginning of the most interesting journalistic inquiry I've ever had the pleasure of pursuing, and of a treasured friendship besides.

Hats off to you, Manfred. Also bathing suits.

Janice Walker

Yuendumu

From the years 1979 to 1989, I had the occasional opportunity to assist Manfred Clynes with cross-cultural sentics research. This was exciting and rewarding work. We were able to verify that specific biological forms or patterns resulting from the experience of emotions are the same regardless of culture. Like other biological traits, the form of human emotional expression (sentic form) appears to be genetically programmed. What a wonderful revelation! The implications of this discovery in the fields of psychology and anthropology alone are immense.

Perhaps the most fascinating experiences I had while working with Manfred were our research expeditions to Australia. In 1981, and again in 1989, Manfred and I worked with the Walbiri, an Aboriginal tribe in Yuendumu, Australia. The following article/diary documents our experiences with these exceptional people.

The initial impulse for our work with the Walbiri tribe began innocently enough...

Burnam-Burnam
Tuesday, 18 December 1979 (Written one day after the happening)

We went to lunch, as is our wont, at the Government Centre. Our group was small this time, consisting only of Manfred and myself. The café was busy as usual, full of mostly white government personnel. Yet as I came with my full tray to join Manfred who had already found a table, I noticed a very remarkable man. He was noteworthy first of all for his appearance, which was in stark contrast to the establishment's customary clientele. His skin was quite dark, his gray hair long. He also wore a long, wide beard. I thought that he was from India.

When I reached our table, I was compelled to tell Manfred about seeing this person. Manfred looked in the man's direction and immediately replied, "He's not an Indian: he's an Aboriginal." Manfred then proceeded to suggest that I talk to him. The latter suggestion I dismissed. But Manfred had his own ideas. When I was nearly finished eating, Manfred suddenly got up and left. I assumed that he had gone to fetch a cup of coffee and/or ice cream and was quite astonished when he returned with the Aboriginal gentleman whom he introduced as the "very wonderful man."

The events which transpired within the next few minutes were truly awe inspiring. There was first a period of penetrating eye contact between myself and our new friend. I was being "read" by this man and felt that I could hide nothing from him even if I wanted to. After this initial contact, Manfred and he began to talk.

Our new friend said that he decided at an early age to take the best that white society had to offer him. He spoke of the strength and beauty of Bach, Beethoven, and Mozart and of their universality. He spoke of the joy of hearing Mozart's music and of his deep love for it. He spoke of the unfortunate addiction of many people to alcohol and said that for him Mozart was like alcohol, that he used Mozart for his strength. He spoke of the beauty and joy and love found in Mozart, of the absolute uniqueness of Mozart. Manfred was a picture of transfixed amazement.

Our remarkable friend spoke further of the Great Spirit, of God, and of Beethoven. His poignant question above all others was "Why did not the white man share his best, his wonderful composers, Bach, Mozart, Beethoven? Why instead was the Aboriginal offered his worst: alcohol and disease? Why was the Aboriginal required to sacrifice his own culture and receive nothing in return?" It was a powerful and daunting question. I only wish that we could have recorded this conversation as the power of the moment cannot be adequately portrayed on these pages.

Moved beyond description, Manfred asked the man, "Will you be my friend?" "I am your friend" said the man, whose name was Burnam Burnam. And at Manfred's insistence they clasped hands.

Manfred and Burnam spoke of God, the Great Spirit. They spoke of the cello: Burnam would love to learn to play the cello and feels that it would be an extension of his spirit. They spoke of Casals, the great master. Burnam knew Casals was a great master and seemed not to be surprised that Manfred had studied with him.

At some point in the conversation Burnam mentioned that Bach, Beethoven, and Mozart belong to all people regardless of color, nationality or background. This music transcends all differences. He said that he felt that it was no accident at all that Manfred and he met each other. Burnam recognized Manfred's spirit in a matter of seconds and saw the points of contact between their minds. We then spoke briefly of Dolphins, and of how the Aboriginals spoke to the dolphins telepathically, or through the spirit, and used them to round up fish (at the signal of spears clicking under water the dolphins go and collect the fish). Burnam mentioned a friend in England whom he can contact with his spirit and feel her aura hovering around.

After more conversation, we invited Burnam to go with us to the Conservatorium where Manfred would play for him. He accepted our invitation and the three of us walked together to the Con.

On our walk, Burnam told us that it is very lonely to live in this society in Australia which is without culture. "God created man NOBLE" he said, and is pained by the picture which he sees every day of people on the streets of Sydney who have lost their nobility, who are no longer in touch with their native integrity. At this, Manfred told Burnam of his letter to the director of the Con which suggested an Aboriginal scholarship program. Burnam recognized the purity of Manfred's motives, but questioned the validity of the premise, i.e. European music is better and more desirable than Aboriginal music. (Just for the record, Manfred's idea was that of an exchange of knowledge, but this idea was not adequately expressed to Burnam). Burnam said with great conviction that Aboriginal music has fully the scope, intricacy and communicative potential of Western music, if not more. In view of Burnam's obvious grasp of essentials concerning music, the remark was of great impact.

At the Conservatorium Manfred played the piano for perhaps 40 minutes. Burnam listened thoughtfully; somehow there was a tangible feeling of profundity in the room. When at one point Manfred stopped playing and asked Burnam if he had enough time to spare, Burnam didn't even answer. The silence itself was almost a painful question: "How could you ask such a thing?" Manfred's response was the only one possible; he resumed playing. Afterwards Burnam commented, "I have no doubt at all that what is in your mind as you play Mozart and what is in my mind as I listen, is the same."

We talked some more. Manfred gave Burnam a copy of his book, *Sentics*, and a copy of a recent article in the National Times. In the book Manfred wrote, "To Burnam who is like me, only better." "Look what he wrote!" said Burnam. "How can I accept anything like that?" "Accept it," I said. And with some hesitation, he did. Before leaving the Conservatorium,, Burnam said to Manfred, "Thank you for playing" and this time he grasped Manfred's hand in friendship.

We all walked together to Parliament House where Burnam Burnam has his office. Burnam mentioned that he doesn't like the ridicule he gets because his appearance is different from the norm, ridicule which in fact is coming from "peasants." Burnam's actions also differ from the norm. Burnam does not conform to society, does not like waiting. He acts when the spirit moves him to do so. Perhaps this is why his actions have such great purity. Manfred pointed out to Burnam that he is very beautiful.

Interestingly, Burnam says he feels that he, Manfred, and I will be deeply involved in a project concerning dolphins. This would be very surprising to me, but who am I to doubt his words?

While at Burnam's office, Burnam gave us several posters concerning the Aboriginal and a pamphlet describing his activities. He also said that he would take us to an Aboriginal festival and go with us to Darwin (or wherever) to introduce us and to help us with our research project. This would appear to be a personal gift to us from the Great Giver of all gifts.

In taking leave of each other, the two men embraced like two friends of a lifetime. I, too, hugged Burnam before leaving.

How seldom it is that one has the privilege of encountering a great person of integrity and stature: this was truly an undisguised blessing.[1]

Yuendumu

In 1981 the Music Research Centre (part of the New South Wales State Conservatorium of Music) at Manfred's instigation was granted the right to visit and do research with a group of full blooded Aboriginals known as the Walbiri tribe. Yuendumu is located in central Australia, about 200 kilometers northwest of Alice Springs. The flight over the Australian outback was already spectacular, with its vast stretches of red desert land, and unlike any other landscape. It inspired that typical feeling that Australia often gives to its visitors: the feeling of being on a different planet altogether.

After collecting our bags and equipment at the airport, Manfred and I set about renting a four-wheel drive for the ride to Yuendumu. This accomplished, we set out in the early afternoon on a corrugated dirt track through the desert. The road stretched out endlessly before us. Sometimes we would see herds of brumbies (wild horses) peacefully enjoying the perfect weather, clear blue sky, moderate temperature, and unpolluted atmosphere.

We stopped a few times along the way to rest and were deafened by the profound silence. It is an uncanny feeling to experience, as it were, such complete and utter silence. It causes one to realize just how corrupted our ears really are, how much sound pollution we take for granted, never even considering what stress this places on our bodies, never imagining to what an extent we are becoming desensitized. After a relatively short time it was possible to perceive quite different sounds in the seeming silence, sounds that we are unaccustomed to perceiving—the sound of a twig breaking, the gentle rustle of grass, the sound of an insect walking. For nearly an hour we

---

[1] Burnam Burnam later created an international sensation when, in 1987, on the 200th anniversary of Australia's conquest by Captain Cook, he went to England and, on the White Cliff of Dover, claimed England for all his people.

followed the track of an army of ants, marching single file across the desert floor.

Road signs to encourage us on our way were either singularly lacking, or gave false or misleading information. For instance, we drove quite a distance out of the way because a signpost (insignificant as it was) had been twisted. After all, it seemed, if you don't know where you are, you obviously have no business being there.

The entrance to Yuendumu is announced by a large arc over the main red dirt road, with letters about 12 inches high proclaiming the name of the settlement. We drove around town for a while before we found the "mayor" and/or interpreter of the settlement. This person, Robin, was a handsome full blood Walbiri who spoke English quite well and was the link between our two cultures. Robin was married and had a western style "house" which was given to him by the government. He did not actually live in his house as westerner would, but instead stayed mostly outside or hung around the humpies where most of the people were. Humpies are small tent-like structures made of corrugated iron, cardboard, or anything else offering protection against the elements. The family gathers around the campfire which is usually situated outside of the humpie. Ten-gallon cans are used for boiling water and one water tap serves some 200 people. There are also dogs everywhere in Yuendumu. These dogs have several functions. First, they provide warmth. How cold a particular night was could be indicated by the number of dogs one slept with in order to keep warm. For example, "It was a two dog night," or if it was really cold, "It was a three dog night."

The government, in its attempt to westernize (or stamp out the culture of) the Aboriginal, had made solid structures for the Aboriginal to live in. We dubbed them "bus stops" because they had no doors or windows which could be shut and no running water or electricity. As one would imagine, there were many problems with these structures. One basic problem the government faced in trying to force this housing, and other western values, upon these people was the fact that when a member of a tribe dies the family may not set foot in that place for the next three years. So even if a family liked their government housing, if someone died, they moved out and away. Basically a people unattached to personal possession, the Walbiri had no furniture nor any desire to obtain such. If one person obtained any good thing, the only natural reaction was to share it with everybody else.

The Walbiri shared their wealth with one another, and they openly shared the wealth of their culture with us. Robin, our guide, was particularly cordial, showing us around and bringing us to our quarters, an apartment which was used for Western visitors to the Reserve. The apartment, which had one bedroom, was sparsely furnished with a three-legged (and hence lopsided)sofa, a kitchen table, two chairs, and two filthy mattresses. There was running water and a stove that worked. There was even a shower which had a tiny trickle of highly mineralized water. And there was a covering of red dust on everything. As we were soon to learn, red dust covers everything all the time, everybody, everyday in every way. You get used to it and don't see it after awhile.

On this first evening, Manfred and I decided to settle in. I was asleep within minutes after going to bed, but was soon awakened by a loud yell coming from Manfred. A light was quickly put on and it turned out that a giant cockroach had decided to join Manfred in his sleeping bag. This was no ordinary New York style of cockroach. No, this was a large battleship variety of cockroach completely outfitted to live through atomic warfare, holes in the ozone layer, drought, flood, fire, anything. They were little armored tanks the size of matchboxes, with wings and the reaction time of a Pentium chip. Sickened by this close encounter with the dominant life form of the apartment, Manfred quickly made the decision to 1) sleep with the lights on and 2) hide the salami.

The next morning we had a variety of tasks, one of which was to locate a 35mm projector (I had managed to break ours within the first ten minutes). We also had to buy food and, most importantly, we had to find research subjects. Finding subjects quickly brought us face to face with many Walbiri conventions, particularly the rule that women talk to women and men talk to men. We split up and I went out to find female subjects for our experiments. As an incentive I promised to give participants an orange or a bottle of coke. Happily, the women were mostly very cooperative, yet they were also quite insistent that their orange was really a good one, not too small and with no blemishes.

In addition to finding subjects, I was also given the task of buying supplies at the general store. The store had a very small number of things to buy which can be rather nicely summarized as white sugar, coffee, salami, candy, a bit of meat, a few oranges, and soft drinks. Alcohol was not allowed on the Reserve, and not without reason. Alcohol was the single most disruptive force in Walbiri society. This was primarily the result of the fact that an Aborigine's blood lacks the necessary enzymes to break down the toxicity of the alcohol, resulting in the experience of imbibing pure poison.

During our time with the Walbiri, we came to see that the treatment of the Aboriginal people by the Australian Government is often characterized by a lack of any real understanding or sympathy for the people or for its unique culture. Any attempts at "help" are made with the final goal being to absorb the Aboriginals into a (for them) quite alien culture. Frequently the government makes no attempt to understand the values of the Aboriginal people. This was illustrated in all of their publications as well as their activities. I found the publications produced by the Technical Education Division of the ADULT ABORIGINAL EDUCATION project to be particularly disrespectful. For example, in a booklet designed to teach the Aboriginals how to take care of the western style houses they were being put into, there was no regard at all for Aboriginal custom. The fictional Aboriginal family used to illustrate proper care of the "home" was named Smith, hardly an Aboriginal name! Was this intended to persuade these people not only to take up a whole new way of life, but also to give up their traditional names?

Testing of Subjects

Manfred and I soon discovered that it was not acceptable to work with mixed gender groups. So I worked with the women, and Manfred worked with the men. We also had both a female and a male interpreter. Our first studies involved using emotionally expressive sounds derived from "white urban" emotionally expressive touch. The sounds had been created using only a modulated sine wave. The subjects were to match the sounds with the emotions anger, hate, love, sex, grief, joy and reverence. The global result of this testing showed that the Walbiri recognized the sounds equally well to their white urban counterparts, and were in fact better at identifying love and reverence. Yet while the results of this study were fascinating, the experience of working with the Walbiri was indescribably rich for me.

As Manfred was working with the men, I was sometimes present behind the scenes, often secretly observing what was happening. I remember so well one very old tribal elder who was giving his complete attention to the task at hand. His weather-beaten and leathery face wore an expression of total concentration and focus. He looked out into some eternal space, with his head slightly bent to one side as he pondered the sounds Manfred created. Watching this dignified and proud old man sitting in total concentration and attention was an experience of sheer magic.

Concert

On one morning Manfred organized a concert for the local school. A large room was completely filled with primary aged children. They were all seated on the floor and were relatively quiet; perhaps this was in part because the teachers sat alertly watching the children with a base ball bat in hand, but I think it was also due to a breathless curiosity and anticipation. Manfred sat at the old upright piano, which had been turned so that the children could see. The front of the piano had been removed to improve its sound. And though the smell somewhat dissipated the further away from the piano one got, the stench near the piano was quite overwhelming as somebody sometime had urinated inside of it.

After a short introduction the concert began. These children sat totally enraptured as Manfred played the beautiful slow Aria of the *Goldberg Variations*. Their attention was astonishing to me, used to the common garden variety of over-stimulated urban child. It was like a whole world of magic had opened up to them. When Manfred then played Mozart's "Rondo Alla Turca" the children spontaneously began to laugh, clearly comprehending the intrinsic humor of the music. Uncorrupted by the modern world, these children were able to immediately perceive the message in the music.

In talking to the teachers after the concert, we were saddened to learn that "questions were not encouraged at the school." Rote learning without any creativity allowed was the protocol. Further, in my classroom observations it was painfully obvious that only the few white children were participating in classroom discussions, or answering any of the teacher's questions. There was also the ever present baseball bat strategically placed near the teacher.

Street Life in Yuendumu

Most things mechanical in Yuendumu simply did not work. Yes, they had worked once, but that was long ago. The toilet in the "library" was totally nonfunctional and was full of the torn pages of library books. The windows in the community center were broken. Even though the weather in Yuendumu was always perfect, the red dirt streets housed many little blond children, often with no clothes on, and usually with a runny nose. Many of the smaller children die of respiratory complaints before reaching one year of age. The sanitary conditions of the community definitely left something to be desired. Given that 250 people have to share one tap, and the only available toilets are nonfunctional, it is surprising that the people are not even more sick.

The function of the dogs within the community is twofold. In addition to providing needed warmth in the cold desert night, they help to clean up the camp by eating human feces. The birds in turn clean up what the dogs leave behind. Although alcohol was strictly forbidden at the reserve, the effect of alcohol was still clearly seen when we went to Alice Springs.

Part IV: Personal Reflections

Alice Springs

The bars in Alice Springs all have signs saying "No Admittance Without Shoes and Tie." The significance of this rule did not immediately dawn on me until I realized that the native population has neither. It was a way of keeping non-whites out without "being racist." But the presence of Aboriginal culture made its way into town anyway. In town you could buy long strings of red-brown beans strung together in long loops, still smelling very strongly of the campfires around which they were made—and you could buy alcohol.

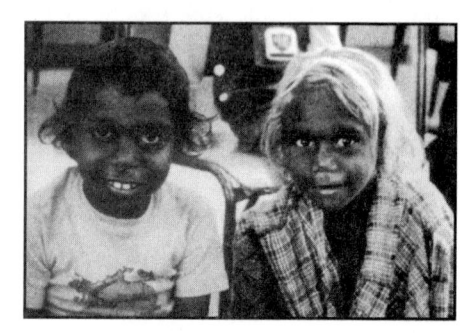

Corroboree

In the evening one night we went to a corroboree. This was like a church service done with native music. There were quite a few people using rhythm sticks made from native wood. The sticks, one each held loosely in the hands, make a resonant sound when clacked together that is similar to a wood block. The rhythmic beating of these sticks along with the sounds of the didgeridoo punctuated the desert night. There were also the sounds of the men's voices speaking in native tongue, but I could not understand what they were saying. The women did not speak at all, at least not out loud. In actual fact, they were speaking constantly, having developed a sophisticated *sign language*. They were singing to each other with such alacrity that I could well imagine that I was in an institution for the deaf. I watched this scene utterly fascinated as suddenly laughter would ring out from one of the women, a reaction to a signed message.

Nova

In 1988, Manfred and I returned to Yuendumu to do a program for *Nova*. Our old interpreter Robin was initially nowhere to be found. Finally, after a lot of trouble and bother we did find him. He had changed a great deal, had become an alcoholic, and was a mere shadow of the vital young man of a few years before. We greatly saddened by this. There were other desultory changes in the settlement as well. During a couple of hours when I was not needed, I took a walk through the settlement and was horrified to see bits of rubbish everywhere: wrappings from packages of potato chips, candy wrappers, soft drink cans. They had been abandoned just where they were used. Traditionally, there were no non-biodegradable materials associated with eating. Thus, there was no concept of trash collection and removal among the tribe.

Most of the western style houses provided by the government were in great disrepair. In one house we visited, the walls were full of obscene writing, windows were broken, doors were pulled off their hinges, all the rooms were dirty. The feeling of the place was very negative, hopeless. The wind continued to blow the fine red dust everywhere as it had done for thousands of years, unmindful of the changes.

The most positive note on this last visit to Yuendumu was watching a native artist at work. I think they called the man Nelson, but I could be mistaken. He sat squatted on the ground, with a large rectangular board in front of him, a small can full of paint, and a handful of matches. In one hand he held a match stick which he dipped into the can of paint. Carefully, he made endless rows of little dots, gradually creating an elaborate scene from the Dream Time. Later this same rectangular board would probably hang in one of the world's great museums.

What would never be able to hang in the museum would be the story and the life behind the painting, the significance and deep symbolism of a way of life that, despite thousands and thousands of years of existence, was suffering from the slow anguish of total extinction.

Alf Gabrielsson

Manfred Clynes Encounters and Reflections

I have discussed and referred to Manfred Clynes' ideas and research in various publications (e.g., Gabrielsson, 1986; 1993; 1995; in press). Now, facing his 70th birthday, I would rather dwell on some personal recollections of my meetings with him, which also inevitably lead to some reflections on what he has come to mean.

Manfred Clynes became a person for me—I may have met his name earlier—during the Tenth International Congress on Acoustics, held in Sydney, Australia, July 1980. I was there together with Swedish colleagues to present our work on perceived sound quality of sound-reproducing systems. However, as my main interest was in the psychology of music, I was eager to see if there was anything on this matter in the session on music and musical instruments. I browsed through the abstracts. Most papers seemed to be hard-stuff acoustics, interesting but not what I was looking for. Suddenly, after nineteen abstracts, there appeared four abstracts in a row with the same senior author—Manfred Clynes from the New South Wales State Conservatorium of Music, Music Research Center, Sentic Laboratories. The titles of the papers evoked my curiosity: "Transforming emotionally expressive touch to similarly expressive sound," "Recognition of emotionally expressive sounds derived from emotionally expressive touch," "Recognition by Aborigines of expressive sounds derived from expressive touch of urban subjects," and "Sound pattern and movement: Introduction to a neurophysiologically based theory of musical rhythm." As I was doing research on rhythm and expression in music, I decided to attend.

This was my introduction to sentics and the use of the sentograph, things that for most acousticians present seemed very strange. After the four presentations I approached Manfred, told him who I was and what I was doing, and asked for further material. He kindly invited me to visit his laboratory, and I went there together with Johan Sundberg, professor of music acoustics at the Royal Institute of Technology in Stockholm. I still have some photos from this encounter showing Manfred playing the grand piano and demonstrating the proper position and way of handling the sentograph. He expressed his interest in our rhythm research in Uppsala and we agreed to continue our contact.

In fact, Manfred Clynes and I met again within a month. But this time we met in a quite different environment, the wonderful monastery in Austrian Ossiach, where we attended a workshop on the "Physical and Neuropsychological Foundations of Music" organized by Juan Roederer. I remember that Manfred's presentation of his ideas concerning composers' "inner pulse" evoked a lot of excitement in the audience—a blend of curiosity and skepticism. I also remember—with special pleasure—that he complemented me for my performance, on the grand piano, of "An der schönen, blauen Donau," the famous Strauss waltz. I played it in order to demonstrate some results from our Uppsala rhythm research, since the rhythm of the Viennese waltz was a favorite example used by my teacher and research colleague, Ingmar Bengtsson, professor in musicology at Uppsala University. Before our departure, Manfred gave me a copy of his book "Sentics: The Touch of the Emotions"—now a rarity—with a pleasant dedication referring to our two meetings in Sydney and Ossiach as "a bimodal distribution of pleasure in knowing you."

Back home in Uppsala, I told Ingmar Bengtsson about Manfred and his inner pulse concept. Ingmar immediately became interested as he was familiar with similar thoughts in old German writings, especially in Gustav Becking's work "Der musikalische Rhythmus als Erkenntnisquelle" (1928). Becking described "Taktfiguren" for different composers, suggesting different down-beats for, say, Mozart or Beethoven in a way that seemed similar to representations of the inner pulse given by expert musicians using the sentograph (Clynes, 1977; 1983; see also Gabrielsson, 1986).

We invited Clynes to visit Sweden. In a seminar on music performance in 1982 in Stockholm, Manfred demonstrated computer-generated examples of Mozart, Beethoven and Schubert pieces performed according to his realization of their respective inner pulse. "Incorrect" examples were given as well; for instance, a performance of a Schubert piece using the Mozart pulse (Clynes, 1983). Beside this, he presented a multitude of examples showing how musical expressiveness may be affected by tone amplitude envelopes, by subtle deviations from the temporal values prescribed in the score, and by still other factors. The audience's response was mixed. Some were fascinated, others just puzzled, and still others completely reluctant. To many people adhering to the cognitive mainstream in music psychology and music theory, Manfred's ideas appeared strange, unscientific or just crazy. But to us, his proposals suggested some possible ways of coming to grips with elusive phenomena in the experience of rhythm and music.

Thus, at Uppsala we began considering the sentograph as a means of capturing motional-emotional components of musical rhythm which I had studied in my dissertation (Gabrielsson, 1973). We had already obtained a technical description of the sentograph from Manfred, and our skilled engineers in the Department of Psychology constructed a new sentograph in time for Manfred's visit in 1982. In continued work, they improved the sentograph to allow independent recording of finger pressure in all three dimensions (Manfred used two dimensions), and this construction soon captured the attention of other researchers and was applied to another application described later.

In 1985 Manfred again visited Uppsala, this time invited by me to present his research in a symposium on "Action and Perception in Rhythm and Music" (Gabrielsson, 1987). His contribution (Clynes, 1987) comprised further specifications of the composers' pulse (Beethoven, Mozart, Haydn, Schubert, Schumann, Mendelssohn) in pulse matrices, providing values for relative durations and amplitudes at various levels of a hierarchical pulse structure. Clynes further described a principle for predictive amplitude shaping, which governs the amplitude envelope of each tone dependent on its position in the melodic context.

What I perhaps remember best from this visit, however, are two unforeseeable events. The first one happened during Manfred's invited lecture. He presented several computer-generated examples, especially an impressive version of Beethoven's *Hammerklavier Sonata, Op. 106*. He wanted to set the sound level and tone controls himself and I let him do so—but perhaps I should not have. Suddenly, the amplifier broke down and could not be brought to life again. I tried to jokingly apologize for the failure, suggesting that this music was emotionally too much for the amplifier. We had to postpone the demonstration until a later occasion when another amplifier was available.

Another invited lecture was given by Paul Fraisse from Sorbonne University in Paris, the grand old man in psychological rhythm research. I arranged a meeting between Fraisse and Clynes in our laboratory with a view to have Manfred demonstrate the sentograph to Fraisse. Mari Riess Jones, professor of psychology at Ohio State University in Columbus, happened to be present and afterwards vividly described it as a clash between two paradigms. For Paul Fraisse, the sentograph was a new acquaintance, but he rapidly put it into his own frame of reference concluding that it was in principle nothing else than another device like, for instance, a telegraph key, for studying how people tapped various rhythms. Of course, Fraisse had used tapping equipment for decades in his excellent studies of temporal structuring in rhythm performance. However, the idea that the sentograph may be used to express emotional characters (Clynes, 1977), or composers' inner pulse, or the pulse of ethnic and rock music (Clynes & Walker, 1982) etc., seemed strange to him, even though he witnessed Manfred's sensitive and artistic handling of the sentograph. (I never asked Manfred, but I take for granted that his experience as a pianist must have influenced the construction of the sentograph with its dependence on sensitive finger touch.)[1]

Another memory crops up as well. I try to have visitors in my home take a walk in the forest surrounding our home outside Uppsala and then also use the equipment for gymnastic exercises placed along the path in the forest. I have photos of many music researchers over the world climbing up ladders, lifting weights, doing stretching exercises, and so on—Manfred, too. A lot of my own ideas usually come during walking or jogging in the forest. Manfred seemed to have similar experience, because he wanted to have a walk for himself in the forest to contemplate and think of some problems. He went away on a sunny morning in July only to return almost immediately complaining of flies and insects attacking him while he was sitting down expecting great ideas. Small creatures and great ideas did not go together.

In 1987 I first met Bruno Repp during a conference on acoustics in the United States. He talked about Manfred Clynes as an extraordinary person and wanted to hear my opinions about him. With Manfred he shared a European background and a sincere interest in and knowledge of classical music. He was soon to start empirical tests of listeners' apprehension of composers' inner pulse. These investigations have led to a long-standing discussion which I have reviewed elsewhere (Gabrielsson, in press). Thanks to Repp, some of Manfred Clynes' ideas have come to be better known and more studied than would otherwise have been the case.

As mentioned earlier, the sentograph seemed to provide a means for studying the motional and emotional characters of musical rhythms, which usually are studied "only" with regard to their structural properties. Using the sentograph to accompany the pulse in various pieces of music, I was surprised to discover, in the polygraph output of my finger pressures, several

---
[1] Note from Manfred Clynes: Not so, it was the idea of approximating a point, with which to express!

phenomena of which I had not been aware. In a special study we used the sentograph with eight-year-old children to study their sense of rhythm. We instructed them to "press the button in a way that fits the music." The music consisted of seven short excerpts including examples of pop and rock'n'roll, a children's song, a march, a "hambo" (a Swedish dance), and music by Bach and Vivaldi. The children's behavior was recorded on video. Both the sentograph recording and the video recording showed considerable inter-individual variation in the children's rhythmic behavior. For instance, one boy accompanied the hambo in a springy fashion on the sentograph but also used his other hand and his feet to mark the pulse, his head to follow the measures, and the upper part of his body to accompany the phrases. His whole body was involved. In contrast, one of the girls passively pressed the sentograph button in a monotone manner and showed no bodily involvement, irrespective of what music we played.

We presently use the sentograph in studies on emotional expression in musical performance. The purpose is to see what means musicians use to express various emotional characters using various instruments. They are asked to play short pieces of music to express happiness, sadness, anger, fear, tenderness, solemnity, and "no expression." That is, each piece should be played with a different character, a task that the musicians take a great interest in and think much about.

In one experiment (Gabrielsson & Lindström, in press), we asked four keyboard players to play "Oh, my darling Clementine" and "Happy birthday to you" on a synthesizer and then on a sentograph (without auditory feedback). The tempo of the sentograph performances was generally slower than in the synthesizer performances (cf. Clynes & Walker, 1982, who reported that musicians thinking music "perform" it slower than when they actually play it on an instrument). Allowing for the tempo difference, the timing and dynamics were similar in both kinds of performances, showing that the performers had a clear mental representation of how they wanted the piece to be in order to convey the different emotional expressions. However, the amplitude envelopes of the synthesizer tones were the same throughout the piece, fixed as they were in the instrument itself, whereas the sentograph recordings showed amplitude envelopes that varied in correspondence with the intended emotional expression.

When I first introduced the sentograph to my friend, composer Tamas Ungvary, another creative mind, he immediately began thinking about creating music using the sentograph. A composer of electro-acoustic music, he and his coworkers soon developed advanced facilities for having the sentograph govern various sound-generating devices, including sampled sounds. They use the improved three-dimensional sentograph constructed in Uppsala. The pressures exerted on the button are used to control various parameters; for instance, vertical pressure may be used to control loudness, and pressures in the remaining two dimensions may govern pitch and tempo. Other variables may be manipulated as well by supplementary devices. It feels fantastic to be able to create music by just using one's finger on a button without having to bother about all technicalities connected with usual instruments—a direct expression of inner thoughts and feelings comparable only to the immediate expression by one's own voice. In fact, Tamas Ungvary, also professor at the Vienna Academy of Music and Dramatic Arts, and his coworkers now often use the sentograph for live performance on stage, also demonstrated on radio and television. An example of their composition "Sentograffito" (Ungvary & Lundén, 1994) appears on a CD in the proceedings of a conference in Stockholm.

Manfred Clynes is, in my eyes, an inventor and a curious traveler into many domains of human knowledge. Only a small part of his activities has been exemplified in this contribution. Hopefully other authors in this volume will highlight his achievements in other respects. Manfred has evoked—and will probably continue to evoke—a spectrum of responses ranging all the way from fascination to disbelief. I have certainly been deeply affected by his thinking, bridging as it does between pure intuition and scientific rigor, by his creative pick-up of ideas from different fields, his engineering abilities, and his use of computer technology to study the most subtle shades of music. Sometimes he goes astray, perhaps, but that belongs to the privileges of inventive minds. But that may be the price one has to pay in order to get that new and often unexpected knowledge that some humans seem more likely to generate than others. A leading researcher in the psychology of emotion once said to me when we were discussing Manfred's contribution in a conference: "He is a genius, you know. And they go their own ways."

Dear Manfred, keep going!

References

Becking, G. (1928). Der musikalische Rhythmus als Erkenntnisquelle. Augsburg: Benno Filser.

Clynes, M. (1977). Sentics: The touch of emotions. New York: Anchor Press/Doubleday.

Clynes, M. (1983). Expressive microstructure in music. In J. Sundberg (Ed.), Studies of music performance (pp.76-181). Stockholm: Publications issued by the Royal Swedish Academy of Music, No. 39.

Clynes, M. (1987). What can a musician learn about music performance from newly discovered microstructure principles (PM and PAS)? In A. Gabrielsson (Ed.), Action and perception in rhythm and music (pp. 201-233). Stockholm: Publications issued by the Royal Swedish Academy of Music, No. 55.

Clynes, M., & Walker, J. (1982). Neurobiologic functions of rhythm, time, and pulse in music. In M. Clynes (Ed.), Music, mind, and brain. The neuropsychology of music (pp. 171-216). New York: Plenum Press.

Gabrielsson, A. (1973). Studies in rhythm. Acta Universitatis Upsaliensis: Abstracts of Uppsala Dissertations in Social Sciences, 7.

Gabrielsson, A. (1986). Rhythm in music. In J. R. Evans & M. Clynes (Eds.), Rhythm in psychological, linguistic and musical processes (pp. 131-167). Springfield, Illinois: Charles C. Thomas.

Gabrielsson, A. (1987) (Ed.), Action and perception in rhythm and music. Stockholm: Publications issued by the Royal Swedish Academy of Music, No. 55.

Gabrielsson, A. (1993). The complexities of rhythm. In T. J. Tighe, & W. J. Dowling (Eds.), Psychology and music. The understanding of melody and rhythm (pp. 93-120). Hillsdale: Erlbaum.

Gabrielsson, A. (1995). Expressive intention and performance. In R. Steinberg (Ed.), Music and the mind machine. Psychophysiology and psychopathology of the sense of music (pp. 35-47). Heidelberg: Springer Verlag.

Gabrielsson, A. (in press). Music performance. In D. Deutsch (Ed.), The psychology of music (2nd ed.). New York: Academic Press.

Gabrielsson, A., & Lindström, E. (in press). Emotional expression in synthesizer and sentograph performance. Psychomusicology.

Ungvary, T., & Lundén, P. (1994). Sentograffito. In A. Friberg, J. Iwarsson, E. Jansson, & J. Sundberg (Eds.), SMAC 93. Proceedings of the Stockholm Music Acoustics Conference July 28 - August 1, 1993 (p. 598). Stockholm: Publications issued by the Royal Swedish Academy of Music, No. 79.

Part V

Animal Poems by Manfred Clynes
(1990–1997)

Winsects

The red ants have come to visit

as they do every year,

in June

they know what they are doing

they come and go by the clock

and disappear again as if they were never here

—they say they come to find water,

and yet they shun the pool

we cannot know what they know so well

togetherness, they come in all different sizes

and are brothers. When one of them is hurt or dies

others come by—are they comforting each other? we don't know

but see a fleeting meeting

a slow surround, a gap in what they know they are doing.

there are hundreds, perhaps thousands in my house now

beautiful red ants

I used to chase them out, even gently,

gently for me, but ferociously for them, sweep them out through the door

hoping they would not be hurt

But it was hopeless, they would come back next day, as if the broom was

only a fantasy, a dream perhaps—if they dream,

as they probably do

And next day I would sweep them out again, to no avail.

I lost my cool, and started killing them one year,
and even that made no difference. They loved to congregate in certain spots
sometimes chained to one another, it seemed, in large groups
but when the appointed time came like fairies and elves, they left, and
left no trace.
And would come back again next year only, in June, after cold winters
and long times I was alone here without ants.

This year, I welcomed them, they don't bite
I don't chase them out, don't kill them.
When they fall into the sweet-potato can, they
drown. There is nothing I can do about that. If one or two fall into the
pool, they last for a long time before they drown, unlike many others
and often I can save them in time, as I see them
battle in the water.
But I know that soon they will be gone, all of them.
Already I miss them.
They are so beautiful
and so perfect
they have no questions, only answers.

How did they get that way?

Spy-der

The Life and Likes of Spy-der, Spy-der:
Genes for liking, and liking for genes.

I don't like the spider in my house
But it prefers my house to the outside
There are but few insects inside
Yet it waits patiently, in its web. And spies.

Waiting and waiting, for a moment that
seems never to occur. To us.
Is it asleep? No, it darts forth the rare moment
a hapless prey is caught, totally alert.
But not for days on end.
It has sacrificed the fun of exploration
to achieving patience.
Sometimes two spiders share a common territory,
a common web. And mate.
Later the little spiders are carried
on their back, until they grow enough to make their own web.

Never do they get caught in their own marvellous structure.
Not even the little ones. They are not afraid of it.
It is home.
Of thousand spiders not a single one is caught.
More perfect than required
for survival of the fittest, for evolution.

What does the spider think and feel?
Combining patience so with aggression, hunger,
Sex, and maternal care?
And when it spins that web and recycles it
what enjoyment is it?
The sense of power, does it feel it? from a fiber stronger than
almost any we can get molecules to make,
And so so sticky?

The spider feeds on insects that have six legs, and
spiders having eight legs are not insects, we say.

I don't like a spider. And it bothers me not to know why.
I marvel at it and its web, but to like its form and behavior
is hard.
Yet I don't really want to kill it:
I feel its right to live, to live the way a spider lives.
But how does nature train it to like what it has to do?
Perhaps evolution makes choices that
who likes what he has to do most survives:
A new paradigm for science to try.
But where are the genes for liking, for liking to wait?
We dont like waiting for them to be found.
And we dont like spiders.

Bee Saved

This sunny morning
playing in the warm pool
suddenly, I see a bee
struggling for its life

thrashing the surface water.

Warmly aglow, I look to find a way
to bring it to the shore—
hoping
it would not drown

before I thought of a way.
And then, I saw a single floating leaf:
I brought this leaf
to where the bee was thrashing wildly-

The bee climbed on the leaf
and in amoment,
—flew away.

    And never knew
      a thought had saved it.

Impending Revision of the Legal System

It is early,

Soon animals will speak

All it takes is for us to implant

Speech genes into some of them

And then they will speak

English

        And immediately they will

have human rights (and use computers).

Turkeys in the Raw

The central issue of our time is:

to breed turkeys, or not

Because we like to eat them

(And care little for what follows from that appetite) :

Healthy for us,

It improves our quality of life,

as we put it

But what does it do

for the turkeys? Their quality of life is

    not on the table.

They are.

Let's talk turkey!

Is it better for turkeys to live for a while,

    under those grim conditions

        than not at all ?

That is the central issue of our time.

Word Wrongs I.
Itness
The A word, and the other F word.

We speak: that gives us the right

to call all those who do not Animals.

A right that is wrong:

Unspeakables are animals—

Equal in the fuzzy sight of our language.

How blinded we are by that word:

We are not animals it says, and lies.

All animals are animals it says, and lies the more

 Our glassy essence of which we are most assured

Is that essence ours alone? Not yet have we seen seen through

prejudice that calls a child a Fetus before he or she is born:

an *"it"*

Taking away its itness, that would re-mind us.

So it is with Animals.

They all are *its.*

Our racist language so decrees.

Word Wrongs II
Brutality? An (unbeastly)
"strange dog."

Post coitam omni animale triste, we say
wistfully—
suddenly we can share with them:
good
to be called an animal.

More often
we use that word
to indicate:
insensitivity, cruelty, and violence-
the word maligning the beast,
as beastly,

and yet, that strange dog came, unasked,
and licked me, licked my face
when I suddenly cried a little, on hearing
Rabin's
violent death.

Licked me, licked my face
When I cried.

Special Spots: Animals are Created

All Animals are Created Equal

needed: a book of Job for animals.

I

The spotted owl thinks
Why have my spots saved me
When millions of animals die every day
Killed by the masters.

Why does it matter that I have spots?

The spotted owl feels guilty
Like some survivors of the holocaust.

II

Animal Constitution.
All animals are created equal
But by whom?
All animals are created equal
given the right to pursue
their needs
their happiness is not to be questioned
All animals are created equal
so it says, from ancient days on
they have their inalienable rights
they have the right of life

of liberty

they have it written in the constitution

they have it written in their constitution.

All animals are created equal

If indeed they are created at all

And if they are not created, they have

earned their life as have we:

And if we are not created

Indeed we are not created equal.

Even if it says so in the constitution.

The constitution we wrote,

without a thought to animals.

III

All species are crated equal.

Goethe thought God's Love is present when other birds feed
the fledgling cuckoo on the fly*, the cuckoo who has just learned to fly
No more in the nest. whence he threw out his non-brothers to a grim death
But we think they are cuckoo to do so.

He thought that God's Love is present everywhere
when he was eighty (though not when he wrote the earlier Faust).
Surprising, for a naturalist who discovered evolution eighty years before
Darwin.

But if Love belongs to God, why so often does he keep it to himself, it is asked.

When others could use it.

It seems unfair that he should love the spotted owl above so many animals.

Survival of species is put above survival of the individual.
That's what the Nazis did, in their way,
and picked the species they liked above all others.
But we like all species equally. And more among equals, if they are rare.
All species are crated equal, we say, though its not in the constitution.
Its in our interest. A pity to lose even one species. We love them all.
God help us.

* Conversations with Eckerman, 1830

Equation of Life.

Mathematicians have forgotten to figure out
an equation: how many animals' lives equal one human life?
In it they need to take into account the quality of life,
of the animals and of the humans,
the proportion of their lives
they have been allowed to live:
the mathematics are not that hard, truly—they win Nobels for equations of economics,
they should find it not too hard,
if they remember to try.

I hope they will soon. This is to remind them.
How many animals are equal to one abortion?
That depends on the animal.
How many humans are equal
to a million animals dying early in their life,
to be eaten, or for experiments?
Per kilogram, that depends on the animal.
Big animals have more kilograms per life.

Lets make a hypothesis.

(Leave out the suffering,
> as a first approximation. That needs to be integrated
> over time. Everybody has to suffer (sometime),
> so to equalize suffering among the many
> as far as is possible
> is a different problem.
> To be tackled, maybe, after the first problem has been solved.)

Here we are concerned merely with the possibilty of life,
as it is subtracted from one who lives.

Shall we propose a prize for the solution?
A steak dinner maybe at the Two Seasons, or a filet mignon?
Perhaps one every week for a year, to the winner?

Mathematics is an honorable profession, not concerned with prizes. Why not let it be concerned with life, the best prize of all ?

Here is the hypothesis.
Let us assume that one (human) life equals
x lives of animal y living z years,
under equivalent conditions. Then let us see where that takes us.

Harris Ranch
Class picture of 1996: 80,000 Sad, Depressed Cattle

I see them still:

80,000 Cattle stand, isolated
on brown, flat earth
Head bowed — they shuffle a bit, slowly,
just a bit, that shows they are still alive—
not sculpted figures like the chinese soldiers
in the ancient mass grave.

For three months

for three months they stand like this
depressed, isolated, not interacting at all,
before they are led to slaughter

Can you imagine
how 80,000 depressed animals look?
No? Nor could I, until I saw them
I had to stop the car, and look.
I had not seen anything like this—
outside concentration camps.

80,000 forlorn,

forlorn animals, not 100, not 500,

the color of the soil on which they rigidly stand,

an ocean of brown big animals, all depressed,

as far as eyes could sweep,

One has not seen depression, until one sees this,

No, one has not felt depression til

faced to face

80,000, 80,000 depressed animals.

Standing, standing, so many, they define depression — and that nobody cares.
        Nobody cares
            Nobody cares
              Is nobody

                    calling a doctor?

Stars

A nocturnal walk along a country road
with Crinkles, shaggy dog.

Peacefully, with measured joy
We walk along the lone path

He on the leash,
I holding it in hand

Curiously,
It is me
Who has to piss
First
Crinkles watches,
Unconcerned.

A little later
He pisses too.

We walk on, aware
Of sounds, of shadows
In the night
Distant and close.

He more than I.

Above us
A wide flimmering carpet
The iridescent starry sky
Strewn in random radiant play
Yet each in its right place.

"Look at the stars, Crinkles,"
I say
As I raise my head
"Look at the stars!"

But he does not respond
And looks straight ahead
"Look at the stars, Crinkles"
I say again,
And point his head up.

But he does not seem to notice
Not aware
Of the wonder,
The promise, the security

I try to teach him :
"Look, Crinkles"
Over and over again

I don't know what he sees
When he looks there.

As yet
His brain
Does not see the stars.

Modern Zoo

Here the animals have regained
Some of their dignity
No longer in cages, their fenced
Preserves, green and wooded
Give them a modicum of freedom,
And protection from one another.
They don't watch the people
Who watch them.

But I watched people
Watching the animals:
Relieved
Temporarily
Of their own cages
They bounded!
The zoo was music played
For them by the universe.

Yet animals need no music
To have their dignity.

And even through the music of the zoo
Humans did not regain their lost dignity
As did those beautiful animals
Living in the modern zoo.

And I, writing this poem

Am filled with gratitude and sorrow

Gratitude for seeing out of my own cage

And sorrow for those shut in

Appendix A:
Published Works of Manfred Clynes

122. *Interpretation of Music for the 21st Century.* Cambridge, MA: MIT Press. In preparation.
121. *SuperConductor, the Global Music Interpretation and Performance Program.* In press.
120. "Microstructural musical linguistics: composers' pulses are liked most by the best musicians." *Cognition* 55 pp. 269-310, 1995
119. Comments on "Patterns of expressive timing in performances of a Beethoven minuet." *Journal of the Acoustic Society of America*, V. 96 (2), 1174-1178, 1994.
118. Entities and brain organization: Logogenesis of meaningful time-forms. In K. H. Pribram ed. Origins: brain and self organization, Proceedings of the Second Appalachian Conference on Behavioral Neurodynamics, pp. 604-632, 1994. Hillsdale, NJ: Erlbaum Press
117. Program of the Annual Meeting of American Association for the Advancement of Science, (AAAS,) Symposium on Music, Boston, February pp. 58-59, 1993
116. Time-forms, nature's generators and communicators of emotion, Proc. *IEEE Intl. Workshop on Robot and Human Communication* Tokyo Sept. 1992, pp. 18-31, 1992
115. Some guidelines for the synthesis and testing of pulse microstructure in relation to musical meaning. *Music Perception*, 1990, Vol. 7, 4, 403-422
114. Clynes, M., Jurisevic, S., and Rynn, M. Inherent cognitive substrates of emotion: Love is blocked by lying, but not anger. *Perceptual and Motor Skills*, 70, 195-206, 1990.
113. Mind-Body Windows and Music in: "Musik und Koerper", ed. W. Puetz, *Musikpaedagogische Forschung*, Vol. 11, pp. 19-42, 1990. Essen: Verlag Die Blaue Eule.
112. Sources of Musical Meaning: Test of Composer's Pulses. Proceedings of the First International Conference on Music Perception and Cognition, Kyoto, Japan, pp 275-281, 1989
111. Time, Timeconsciousness and Music, Proceedings of the First International Conference on Music Perception and Cognition, Kyoto, Japan 1989, pp 124-130
110. Guidelines to Sentographic Methodology and Experimentation *Perceptual and Motor Skills*, 1989,
109. Evaluation of Sentic Theory nullified by misunderstood theory and inferior sound: a reply to Nettelbeck et al., *Australian Journal of Psychology*, 41,no.3, pp327-337, 1989.
108. Methodology in sentographic measurement of motor expression of emotion: two-dimensional freedom of gesture is essential. *Peceptual and Motor Skills*, 68 ,779-783, 1989.
107. Generalised emotion, its production, and sentic cycle therapy, in *Emotions and Psychopathology*, M.Clynes and J. Panksepp, eds., pp. 107-170, Plenum Press, New York, 1988.
106. Clynes, M., and Panksepp, J. eds. *Emotions and Psychopathology*, Plenum Press, New York, 1988.
105. Panksepp J., Crepeau, L., Clynes, M. Effects of CRF on Separation Distress and Juvenile Play, Neuroscience and Society Abstract, 1987.
104. Thompson, W., and Clynes, M. Expressing the composer in musical performance, presented at the Australian Psychological Society Annual Conf. 1988.
103. What a musician can learn form newly discovered principles of musical thought, PM and PAM., in: *Action and Perception in Rhythm and Music*, A. Gabrielsson ed., Publication of The Royal Swedish Academy of Music, No. 55, Stockholm, pp. 201-233, 1987.
102. When Time is Music, in Rhythm in Psychological, Linguistic and *Musical Processes,* Evans and M. Clynes (eds.), C.C. Thomas, Chicago, pp. 169-224, 1986.

101. Evans, J., Charles.C. and Clynes, M. *Rhythm in Psychological, Linguistic and Musical Processes.* Thomas, Chicago, pps. 291, 1986.
100. Clynes, M., and Walker, J. "Music as Time's Measure", *Music Perception*, Vol. 4, No. 1, 85-120., 1986.
99. Musical Thought and Action, Third International Conference on Event Perception and Action, June 24-30, 1985, Uppsala, Sweden.
98. On Music and Healing, Proceedings of the II. International Symposium on Music in Medicine, 1984. Ludenscheid, in: Music and Medicine, ed. R. Spintke and R. Droh, Springer Verlag, Berlin, Heidelberg, New York pp. 13-31, 1987.
97. Secrets of Life in Music, in *Analytica, Festschrift for Bengtsson*, Royal Swedish Academy of Music, Publication No.47, Stockholm, pp. 3-15, 1985
96. (I) Solving the equation of life in Music: Musical Score + Microstructure = Living music, (II) A Composing program incorporating Microstructure, 8th International Computer Music Conference, Paris, September 1984, Abstracts.
95. Music Beyond the Score, presented at Symposium on Music, Reason and Emotion, held in Ghent, Belgium, 1983. Somatics V, No. 1, pp. 4-14, and Communication and Cognition, Vol. 19, No.2 pp. 169-194, 1986.
94. The hidden code of musicality : A real time solution, Proceedings of the 7th International Computer Music Conference, Rochester, N.Y., October 1983.
93. Expressive Microstructure in Music, linked to Living Qualities in Studies of Music Performance, J. Sundberg (ed.), Royal Swedish Academy of Music, Publication No. 39, pp 76-181. Stockholm.
92. Music, Mind and Brain, (ed.): *The Neuropsychology of Music*, Plenum Press, New York, 1982. pp. 430.
91. Clynes M., and Nettheim, N. The Living Quality of Music: neurobiologic basis of communicating feeling, in *Music, Mind, and Brain: The Neuropsychology of Music*, M. Clynes (ed.), pp 47-82, Plenum Press, New York, 1982.
90. Clynes. M., and Walker, J. "Neurobiologic functions of rhythm, time and pulse in music", in *Music, Mind, and Brain: The Neuropsychology of Music* M. Clynes (ed.), pp. 171-216, Plenum Press, New York, 1982.
89. Clynes, M., Nettheim, N., McMahon, B. Musical thought discloses a highly stable psychobiologic clock, 12th Annual Meeting, Society for Neuroscience, Nov. 1982. Abstract.
88. Specific human emotions are psychobiologic entities: Psychobiologic coherence between emotion and its dynamic expression, Commentary, *Behavioral and Brain Sciences*, 1982. No. 3. pp 424-425.
87. Clynes, M., Walker J., Touch and sound have a common brain program for the production and and recognition of emotion expression, 11th Annual Meeting, Society Nettheim, N.for Neuroscience, Nov, 1981. Abstract.
86. The communication of emotion: theory of sentics, in *Emotion: Theory, Research and Experience, Vol. 1: Theories of Emotion*, R. Plutchik, H. Kellerman (eds.), pp 271-300, Academic Press, New York, 1980.
85. Clynes, M., and Dobkin, M. Generation of emotionally expressive sounds from the dynamic forms of expressive finger pressure. How is expressive touch transformed to expressive sound? *Journal of the Acoustical Society of America*, Abstract, Vol 67, 1980.
84. Transforming emotionally expressive touch to similarly expressive sound, 10th International Congress on Acoustics, Sydney, July, 1980. Abstract.
83. Recognition of emotionally expressive sounds derived from emotionally expressive touch, 10th International Congress on Acoustics, Sydney, July, 1980. Abstract.
82. Clynes, M., Walker, J. Recognition by Aboriginals of expressive sounds derived from expressive touch of urban subjects, 10th International Congress on Acoustics, Sydney, July, 1980. Abstract.

81. Clynes, M. and Walker, J. Sound pattern and movement: introduction to a neurophysiologically based theory of musical rhythm, 10th International Congress on Acoustics, Sydney July, 1980. Abstract.
80. The source of laughter and essentic form: Is evolution dis-covery?, *Somatics*, Vol. 2, No. 3; 3-9, 1979.
79. The source of laughter and essentic form: Is evolution dis-covery?, *Humanitas*, Vol. XV; 29-45, Duquesne University Press, Pittsburgh, 1979.
78. Sentics: communication and generation of emotion through dynamic expression, in *Nonverbal Communication*, S. Weitz (Ed.), 386-397, New York, Oxford University Press, 1979.
77. Article on Sentics, Handbook of Psychotherapies, *Psychology Today*, 1978.
76. The joy (grief, love, hate, anger, sex and reverence) of music: Interview in *Human Behaviour*, Vol. 6, No. 4: 25-30. Los Angeles, April, 1977.
75. Space-time form printing by the human central nervous system, Society for Neuroscience, Los Angeles, 1977, Abstract.
74. Sentics: *The Touch of Emotions*, 250 pp, Doubleday/Anchor, New York, 1977.
73. Communication and generation of emotion through essentic form, in *Parameters of Emotion*, L. Levi, ed, Raven Press, New York, pp. 561-601, 1975.
72. Speaker recognition by the central nervous system, Society for Neuroscience, Abstract, New Orleans, November, 1975.
71. The biological basis for sharing emotion, *Psychology Today*, July, 1974, pp 51-55.
70. A new laughter homologue: predicted by sentic theory, The Society for Neuroscience National Meeting, Abstract, October, 1974.
69. Sentics: biocybernetics of emotion communication, Annals of the New York Academy of Science, Vol. 220, Art, 3: 55-131, 1973.
68. Sentography: dynamic forms of communication of emotion and qualities, *Computers in Biology & Medicine*, Vol, 3: 119-130, 1973.
67. Essentic form: E-actons as programmed communication space-time forms in the nervous system, IFAC Symposium on Dynamics & Control in Physiological Systems, Rochester. N.Y. in: *Regulation and Control in Physiologic Systems*, ed. A. S. Iberall and A. C. Guyton, pp. 604-607, 1973.
66. Sentography: dynamic measure of personal relationship profile, Proceedings of 25th ACEMB Conference, October 1972.
65. Biocybernetics of emotion communication: sentics Panel Annual Meeting of the American Psychiatric Association, Dallas, Texas, May, 1972.
64. Introduction to sentics: exact science of emotion communication. Proceedings, 5th World Congress of Psychiatry, Mexico, November, 1971.
63. Dynamics of emotion communication in the present moment. Proceedings, 9th International Conference of Medical Electronics and Biological Engineering. Melbourne, August 1971.
62. The function of rein control and unidirectional rate sensitivity in living systems. Proceedings of the Symposium on Nonlinear Estimation Theory. San Diego, Calif. September 1971.
61. Sentics: precision of direct emotion communication. Pres. at Symposium entitled Sentics, Brain Function and Sources of Human Values, American Association for the Advancement of Science, Vol. 174, p. 726. November, 1971.
60. Sentics, brain function and sources of human values AAAS Symposium. Science. vol, 174, p. 726. November, 1971.
59. Biocybernetics of space-time forms in the genesis and communications of emotion. 55pps. AAAS Symposium Biocybernetics of the Dynamic Communication of Emotion. Chicago, 1970. See also Science, Vol. 170, pp. 764-765, 1970.

58. Sentics. Dynamic profiles of qualities and the nonverbal communicative environment. Fed. Proc. 29: E50. March-April, 1971.
57. Dynamic differentiation between animate and inanimate sound in brain processing. Proceedings of 24th Annual Conference on Engineering in Medicine and Biology. 1971.
56. Towards a theory of man. *Human Context* 3: no. 1, 1-75 March 1971
55. Towards a theory of man. *Human Context* 2: 367-449 December, 1970.
54. Biocybernetics of the dynamic communication of emotions and qualities. *Science*, 170: 764-765. November 13, 1970.
53. Sentics. The quantitative profiles of qualities and some human system applications. 54th Annual Meeting of the Federation of American Societies for Experimental Biology. April, 1970. Abstract
52. Toward a view of man, in *Biomedical Engineering Systems*. Eds, M. Clynes and J.H. Milsum, McGraw-Hill New York pp. 272-358. 1970
51. Toward a theory of man. Precision of essentic form in living communication, in *Information Processing in the Nervous-System*. Eds. K.N. Leibovic and J.C. Eccles,. Springer-Verlag, New York. pp. 177-206, 1969.
50. Dynamics of vertex evoked potentials: the R-M brain function. In *Average Evoked Potentials*, Publication of NASA. Ed. E. Donchin. pp. 177-206, 1969.
49. Discussions. In *Average Evoked Potentials*, NASA. Ed. E. Donchin pp. 86, 135-139, 337-339, 234-235, 326-327, 1969.
48. Clynes, M., and Milsum, J.H., eds. *Biomedical Engineering Systems*. New York, McGraw-Hill, 665 pps 1970.
47. On being in order. Symposium on Computers and Religion. Proceedings of the 15th Summer Conference of the Institute on Religion in an Age of Science. Star Island, New Hampshire 1968. Zygon, vol. 5. No.1, pps. 63-84, 1970.
46. Rein control, or unidirectional rate sensitivity a fundamental dynamic and organizing function in biology. Annals of N.Y. Acad. of Sciences, vol. 156. art. 2, pp. 627-968, 1969.
45 Essentic form—aspects of control, function and measurement Proceedings of the 21st annual Conference of Engineering in Medicine and Biology. Houston, Texas. November, 1968.
44. After-image motion and the eye's kinesthetic sense. Proceedings of the 21st Annual Conference on Engineering in Medicine and Biology. Houston, Texas. November 1968.
43. Kohn, M. and Clynes, M. Color responses of the pupil and brain on a monchromat. Proceedings of the 21st Annual Conference of Engineering in Medicine and Biology. Houston, Texas. November, 1968.
42. Kohn, M., and Clynes, M. Paradoxical pupil contraction to removal of colored light. Proceedings of the 21st Annual Conference on Engineering in Medicine and Biology. Houston Texas. November, 1968.
41. Biocybernetic principles of dynamic asymmetry: unidirectional rate sensitivity and rein control (or: How to create opposites from a single measure). Proceedings of the International Biocybernetic Symposium. Leipzig, Germany. September 1967. In *Biokybernetik*. Drischel and Teidt, Eds. pp. 29-29. Leipzig, Germany.
40. Cybernetic implications of rein control in perceptual and conceptual organization. In Rein Control, or Unidirectional Rate Sensitivity, A fundamental Dynamic and Organizing Function in Biology. Ed. M. Clynes. Annals of the N.Y. Academy of Sciences. Vol. 156, art. 2, 629-671. April 21, 1969.
39. Kohn, M., and Clynes, M. Colour dynamics of the pupil. Symposium on Rein Control, or Unidirectional Rate Sensitivity, a Fundamental Dynamic and Organizing Function in Biology. Annals of the N.Y. Acad. of Sciences, vol. 156, art. 2, pp. 931-950. April 21, 1969.

38. Conference on the Future of the Brain Sciences. N.Y. Academy of Medicine. New York., N.Y. May 2–4 1968. Discussion. Little Brown.
37. Kohn, M., Litchfield, D., and Clynes, M. Storage of averaged responses on magnetic tape. Medical Research Engineering 8, 29-31, March–April, 1969.
36. Clynes, M. and Kohn, M., Recognition of visual stimuli from the electric responses of the brain. Proceedings of the 3rd International Psychiatric Congress. Madrid, Spain. September 1966. In (Eds, Kline, N.S.. and Laska, E.) *Computers and Electronic Devices in Psychiatry.* pp. 206–237.
35. Clynes, M,. Kohn, M., and Gradijan, J. Computer recognition of the brain's physiologic language. IEEE International Convention Record part 9, pp. 125-142. March 21, 1967.
34. Clynes, M., and Kohn, M. Spatial Visual evoked potentials as physiologic language elements for color and field structures. The International Conference on Evoked Potentials. Siena, Italy, July, 1966. Electroenceph. Clin. Neurophysio. suppl. 26, pp. 82-96. 1967.
33. Clynes, M., and Kohn, M. Nonlinear detection processes in brain function. Proceedings of the 19th Annual Conference on Engineering in Medicine and Biology. November 16, p. 170, 1966
32. On the regulatory function of unidirectional rate sensitivity in the cardiovascular system. Proceedings of the 18th Annual Conference on Engineering in Medicine and Biology Philadelphia. Pa. November 10-12, . p. 112, 1965.
31. The electrical chromaticity waves in the brain, color vision and their relation to the basic biologic function of unidirectional rate sensitivity. Proceedings of the XXIII International Congress of Physiological Sciences. Tokyo, Japan, September 1-9, p. 369, 1965.
30. Brain space analysis of evoked potential components applies to chromaticity waves. Digest of the 6th International Conference on Medical Electronics and Biological Engineering Tokyo, Japan. August 22-27, pp. 460-461, 1965.
29. Clynes, M., Kohn, M., and Litchfield, D. Chromaticity waves of evoked human brain potentials in normal and color blind vision. Proceedings of the 49th Annual Meeting of the Federation of American Societies for Experimental Biology. Atlantic City. N.J. April 9-14, Vol, 24, no. 2, p. 274, 1965
28. Clynes, M., and Kohn, M. Specific responses of the brain to color stimuli. Proceedings of the 17th Annual Conference on Engineering in Medicine and Biology. Cleveland, Ohio. November 16-18, 1964. pp. 22-23.
27. Clynes, M., Kohn, M., and Lifshitz, K. Dynamics and spatial behaviour of light evoked potentials, their modification under hypnosis, and on line correlation in relation to rhythmic components, Annals of the N.Y. Acad. of Science, vol. 112, art. 1, pp, 468-509. May 8 1964.
26. Electronic and computer-assisted studies of biomedical problems Contributor. Eds. Schmitt, Otto H., and Caceres, Cesar A. New York: Charles C. Thomas Publishing Co., 1964.
25. Bio-telemetry. Contributor. Symposium. March 28-31, 1962 Ed. Slater, Lloyd, New York: Pergamon Press, 1964.
24. Clynes M., and Kohn, M. The Information code of light intensity evoked brain potentials and unidirectional rate sensitivity; "on" and "off" responses constitute separate dynamic channels and also follow separate paths in the brain. Proceedings of the 16th Annual Conference on Engineering in *Medicine and Biology.* Baltimore, Md. November 18-20, . pp. 22-23, 1963.
23. Use of computers for physiological discovery and for diagnosis by dynamic simulation. *Circulation Research,* vol. XI, No. 3, part 2, pp. 515-528. September, 1962.
22. The nonlinear biological dynamics of unidirectional rate sensitivity, illustrated by analog computer analysis, pupillary reflex to light and sound, and heart rate behavior. Annals, of the N.Y. Acad of Sciences. Vol. 98. art. 4, pp. 806-845. October 30, 1962.
21. CAT (Computer of average translents). Instruments and Control Systems, vol. 35, no. 8, pp, 87-91. August 1962.

20. Clynes, M., and Kohn, M. Portable 4 channel on-line digital average response computer. CAT II, Digest of the 4th International Conference on Medical Electronics. New York. N.Y. July 16-21, 1961.

19. Clynes, M., Blair, J., Stearns, H., Landis, C., Kline, N.S. and Litchfield, D. Continuous servo control system for the study and improvement of homeostatic blood sugar level control. Digest of the 4th International Conference on Medical Electronics. New York, N.Y. July 16-21, 1961.

18. Unidirectional rate sensitivity: a biocybernetic law of reflex and humoral systems as physiologic channels of control and communication. Annals of the N.Y. Acad. of Sciences vol. 92, art. 3, pp. 946-969. July 28, 1961. Presented at the Pavlovian Conference on Higher Activity. October 13-15, 1960. and Proceedings of the San Diego Biomedical Engineering Symposium, Session IV B April 20-21 1961.

17. Kline, N.S. and Clynes, M. Psychophysiological aspects of space flight. In (Ed. Flaherty, B.E.) *Drugs, Space and Cybernetrics: Evolution to Cyborgs.* New York: Columbia University Press, 1961. pp. 355-371.

16. Respiratory sinus arrhythmia: laws derived from computer simulation. *Journal of Applied Physiology*, vol. 15, no. 5, pp. 863-874. September, 1960.

15. Clynes, M., and Kline, N.S. Cyborgs and space. In *Astronautics*, pp. 26-27, 74-75. American Rocket Society Inc, New York, N.Y. September 1960.

14. Computer study of the dynamic interrelations of functionally separate and Kohn, M. neurological control systems. Proceedings of the 3rd international Conference on Medical Electronics. Institution of Electrical Engineers. London, Eng. Part II, pp 184-186. July 22, 1960.

13. Computer dynamic analysis of the pupil light reflex: a unidirectional rate-sensitive sensor. Proceedings of the 3rd International Conference on Medical Electronics. Institute of Electrical Engineers. London, Eng. Part III, pp. 356-358. June 24 1960.

12. The use of the Mnemotron for biological data storage reproduction, and Kohn, M. for an average transient computer. Proceedings of the 4th Annual Meeting of the Biophysical Society. Philadelphia, Pa. p 23. February 24-26, 1960.

11. Respiratory control of heart rate: Laws derived from analog computer simulation. I.R.E. Transactions on Medical Electronics, vol ME-7 pp 2-14, January 1960. And I.R.E. National Convention Record. March, 1959.

10. Computer analysis of reflex control and organization: respiratory sinus arrhythmia. Science vol 131, no 3396, pp 300 - 302. January 29, 1960.

9. Respiratory heart rate control. Some nonlinear control techniques, novel to control engineers, employed by a biological control system. Automatic and Remote Control pp 362-369. London: Butterworths Scientific Publications. Proceedings of the 1st International Congress of the International Federation of Automatic Control. Moscow, U.S.S.R. 1960.

8. Circulatory system: mathematical law of the respiratory heart. *Physics, Vol. 3, pp. 184-193*. Chicago: Year Book Publishing, Inc. 1960.

7. Biology: applications of control system theory. (Ed. Glasser, Otto). *Medical Physics*, vol, 3, pp. 72-80 Chicago: Year Book Publishers 1960.

6. Reflex control of heart rate through respiration: laws derived from analog computer simulation. Circulation Research, vol. XX no 4 p 679. Proceedings of the 32nd Scientific Sessions of the American Heart Association. Philadelphia, PA October 23-25 1959.

5. Recent progress in neurophysiologic and cardiovascular studies through computer simulation: the control of heart rate in man. Proceedings of the 2nd International Conference on Medical Electronics. Paris, France, June 24-27, 1959. *Medical Electronics*, pp. 437-444. London Iliffe & Sons, Ltd. 1960.

4. Clynes, M., Walker J.,and Kohn, M., Recording biological date on tape: A simple method using two transistors. Proceedings of the 2nd International Conference on Medical Electronics. Paris, France. June 24-27 1959. *Medical Electronics,* pp 497-499. London Eng: Iliffe & Sons, Ltd. 1960

3. Clynes, M., Kohn, M., Atkin, A. Analog computer heart rate simulation dynamic analysis of the effect of respiration on heart rate in the resting state: a neurophysiological reflex study. Proceedings of the 11th Annual Conference on Electrical Techniques in Medicine and Biology. Minneapolis, Minn. November 19-21, 1958.

2. Clynes, M., and Cranswick, E.H. Dynamic analysis: an analog computer study of thyroid function. Proceedings of the Psychopharmacology Symposium of the 2nd International Congress of Psychiatry, Zurich, Switzerland, September 2-4, 1957. (Ed. Kline, N.S.) *Psychopharmacology Frontiers,* pp. 515-533. Boston, Mass: Little, Brown and Co., 1959.

1. Simple analytic method for linear feedback system dynamics. Proceedings of the American Institute for Electrical Engineers Chicago, IL October 2-7, Part 2, pp. 377-383, 1955.

0. The Piano and the Art of Touch. *Australian Musical News and Digest,* pp. 27-28, Jan. 2, 1951.

00. The Piano and How to Practise. *Australian Musical News and Digest,* pp. 29-34, Nov. 1, 1950.

Appendix B:
Sources of Manfred Clynes' Works

Music CDs:

J.S. Bach	6 Brandenburg Concertos (2 CDs)	23.50

Historic first recording interpreted and performed with SuperConductor contains:

J.S. Bach:	Double Violin Concerto (slow movt)	
	Brandenburg Concerto No. 5	
Mozart:	The Marriage of Figaro - Overture	
Beethoven:	Violin Concerto Op. 61 (complete)	
	String Quartet, Op.131 (5th movement)	
	1 CD	$12.50

Live concert performance recordings featuring Manfred Clynes as pianist – digitally remastered

J.S. Bach:	Goldberg Variations – piano (2 CDs)	$23.50
Beethoven:	Diabelli Variations, Op. 120 piano (1 CD)	$12.50

Software:

SuperConductor Pro $ 395.00
Desktop Music Interpretation and Performance Software for composers and amateurs. Also includes 240 masterworks, 40 hours of music

SuperConductor Deluxe $ 159.00
Same as the above, but without the ability to enter your own sound samples

Wow! Bach $ 39.95
All the Brandenburg Concertos plus their scores, includes also the 2 Audio CDs of the Brandenburg Concertos, with many interactive and fun features.

Books:

Sentics, The Touch of Emotion $ 17.50
*Paperback of the now classic work of 1977.
Published originally by Doubleday Anchor*

Emotions and Psychopathology, ed. M. Clynes and J. Panksepp
Plenum Press, N.Y. 1989.
Please order direct from publisher.

Music Interpretation for the 21st Century
MIT Press, in preparation
The secular and sacred of music newly and meaningfully enabled in people and computers

Sentic Cycles:

Sentic Cylce Kit $49.50
For doing sentic cycles at home to improve emotional balance and well being. It can be used for decades, or longer. Learn to do it in 30 minutes.

The above listed items are available from:

MMB Music, Inc.
Contemporary Arts Building
3526 Washington Ave.
Saint Louis, MO 63103-1019
800 543-3771 (USA)
www.mmbmusic.com

MicroSound International
19181 Mesquite Court
Sonoma, CA 95476
800 999-8344
www.superconductor.com
www.microsoundmusic.com

Index

A

American Association for the Advancement in Science 60
American Sentic Association 72
Animal poems 168–187
Apollonian and Dionysian models, sentic cycles and 102–104
Appalachian Conference on Behavioral Neurodynamics 43–44
Apreene 50–55
Artificial intelligence 31
Australia
   research expeditions to 148
   Yuendumu 148–158

B

Bach's *Goldberg Variations* 34, 50, 71–83, 156
Baker Award 39
Baker, Kenneth 15
Bateson, Gregory 18
Becking, Gustav 62, 160
Beecham, Sir Thomas 59, 60
Bengtsson, Ingmar 160
Bernal, J. D. 47
Biggins, Lindsay 56
Biocybernetics 40
Biomedical Engineering Systems 40
Bogue Electric 38–39
Bowling Green State University, studies at 126, 127, 129–137
Brain wave activity 27–28

C

Cardiopulmonary Unidirectional Rate Sensitivity 115
Casals, Pablo 36, 54, 57, 59, 149
Chills 139
Clynes' SuperConductor software 30–31, 36, 37
Cole, Maggie 72
Composer's pulse theory 63, 68–69
Computer music 23–26
Computer of Average Transients
   (CAT) 13, 14, 17, 18, 27, 40, 42, 115, 129, 137

Computer software music programs 19, 23, 29–31, 36–37
Computers 52–55
Couples cycles 111–112
Cranswick, Ted 39
Crowder, Robert 70
Cybernetics 39, 46
Cyborg 39, 46–49, 52
    Cyborg Anthropology 49

D

Distortions 3
"Dynamic analysis: an analogue computer study of thyroid function" 39

E

Early scientific years 38–41
EEGs (recorded brain waves) 12–13
    EEG potentials 40
Einstein, Albert 31, 35
Electrical wave activity in living organisms 27–28
Elixir Effect 21
Emotions 5–11, 51–55, 102–104, 128
Empathy 6, 7–9, 10–11
Essentic form 6, 52
Event Related Desynchronization (ERD) analysis 137–138
Event Related Potentials (ERPs) 13

F

Fraisse, Paul 161
Freeman, Walter 128
Freud, Sigmund 53

G

Genius, phenomenon of 16–18
Gilbert, Kenneth 72
Goldberg Variations 34, 50, 71–83, 156
Gould, Glenn 72, 81–84

H

Haraway, Donna 46
Heart rate (the HR reflex) 39
Heinze, Bernard 57

Hoagland, Hudson 13
Hofstadter, Douglas R. 17
Homeostasis 20, 21
Human emotions, study of 5–11, 51–55, 102–104, 128
Human pupillary reflex to light, study of 39

I

Inner Game of Tennis, The by Timothy W. Gallwey, ... 108

J

James, William 18
Jewish Gymnasium 38
Jones, Mari Riess 161
Juilliard School of Music 34, 57

K

Kline, Nathan 27, 39, 41, 48–49
Kuhn, Thomas 34
Kuth, Ernst 62

L

Lambert, Raymond 56
Landowska, Wanda 72
Legge, Walter 59
Leonhardt, Gustav 72
Logogenesis 42–45

M

M.I.T. 115
Macrostructure and microstructure of music 29–30, 62–69
Malls, Leonard 42
McCulloch, Walter S. 115
McCullough, Warren 14
Melbourne
   musical influences in 56–57
   Symphony Orchestra 57
   University of 56–57
Menuhin, Yehudi 3–4, 141–142
Milsum, J. H. 40
Mnemetron Company 40
Moral imagination 7–11

Multidisciplinary Institute for
    Neuro-psychological Development (MIND) Inc. 117–119
Music 6, 43, 64, 92
    Clynes as pianist 44–45, 70–84
    Clynes' musicality 56–61
    computer generated 23–26
    essentic forms of 6
    how do sentic cycles relate to? 92
    macrostructure and microstructure of 29–30, 62–69
    MetaMusic 90
    Musical sensitivity using sentic principals, developing 110–111
    Musical structure and microstructure 62–69

N

Narratives and moral imagination 7–11
New South Wales State Conservatorium of Music 70, 159
New York Academy of Sciences 40
Nickson, A. E. H. 56

O

Objectivity 10

P

Pathbreakers 34
Pauling, Linus 18
Personal reflections 145–165
Phrases 44
"Physical & Neuropsychological Foundations of Music" workshop 160
Pribram, Karl 12, 129
Princeton University 35
Psychoanalysis 121
Pulse-tone-touch 119
Pupilary Paradox 17

R

Repp, Bruno 162
Rites of passage 8–9
Rockland
    Research Center 40–41
    State Hospital 27–46
Roederer, Juan 160
Rosen, Charles 72, 77–80

S

Sensory communication 6
Senthics 5–11
Sentics 5, 18, 21, 28, 36, 40, 41, 48, 92, 100, 104–105
   American Sentic Association 72
   MetaMusic concept 90
   Sentic cycles 28, 51, 54, 88–114, 116–119, 120–124
      advanced 112–113
      and visualization 106–108
      Apollonian and Dionysian
      models and 102–104
      for learning and achieving long-term goals 108
      healing use of 100–102
      notes 92–96
      personal experiences with 120–123
      world view of 104–105
   Sentic form 51–52, 89, 125
   Sentic states 40
   used in training actors 108–109
   Sentics: The Touch of the Emotions 19, 116, 121, 160
Sentograph 29, 116, 124, 161
Serafine, Mary Lou 70
Serkin, Rudolph 36
Shagass, Charles 12
Shepherd, Roy 56
Silent laughter 136
Skinner, B. F. 127
Spatio-temporal form 89–90
State-Trait Personality Index (STPI) 131–133, 135
   Free-form procedure 131
   Velten technique 135
Subjectivity 10
Sundberg, Johan 160
SuperConductor software 30–31, 36–37
Sweden 160

T

Taruskin, Richard 83
Time forms, concept of 43–44
Tones and phonemes 44
Touch-sensitive pad 36

Transcendental Meditation (TM) 121
Tukey, John 14
Tureck, Rosalyn 72

U

Ultra–sound diagnostic instruments 28
Ungvary, Tamas 163
Unidirectional Rate Sensitivity (URS) 14, 17, 39, 116
"Unidirectional Rate Sensitivity as a Biologic Function" (monograph) ... 40

V

Velden technique 135
Virtual body image 96–100
Visualization, sentic cycles and 106–108

W

Walbiri tribe 148–158
Walter, Bruno 59
Walter, Grey 41
Webster, Beveridge 65
Wiener, Norbert 46
Woodward, Don 13
World, the Flesh, and the Devil, The 47

Y

Yuendumu 148–158

Z

Zhu, Xiao-Mei 72, 74–77